NorthStar 4

Reading and Writing

THIRD EDITION

AUTHORS
Andrew K. English
Laura Monahon English

SERIES EDITORS
Frances Boyd
Carol Numrich

PEARSON
Longman

Dedication

To all our NorthStar readers worldwide whose enthusiasm has made this third edition possible. And of course, to Sam.

NorthStar: Reading and Writing Level 4, Third Edition

Copyright © 2009, 2004, 1998 by Pearson Education, Inc.
All rights reserved.

Pearson Education, 10 Bank Street, White Plains, NY 10606

Contributor credit: Margot Gramer and Helen S. Solórzano contributed material to FOCUS ON
WRITING in *NorthStar: Reading and Writing Level 4, Third Edition.*

Staff credits: The people who made up the *NorthStar: Reading and Writing Level 4, Third Edition*
team, representing editorial, production, design, and manufacturing, are Andrea Bryant, Aerin Csigay,
Dave Dickey, Ann France, Melissa Leyva, Sherry Preiss, Robert Ruvo, Debbie Sistino, Kelly Tavares, and
Paula Van Ells.

Cover art: Silvia Rojas/Getty Images
Text composition: ElectraGraphics, Inc.
Text font: 11.5/13 Minion
Credits: See page 269.

Library of Congress Cataloging-in-Publication Data

Northstar. Reading and writing. — 3rd ed.
    4 v. ; cm.
   Rev. ed. of: Northstar / Natasha Haugnes, Beth Maher, 2nd. ed. 2004.
   The third edition of the Northstar series has been expanded to 4
separate volumes. Each level is in a separate volume with different
contributing authors.
   Includes bibliographical references.
   Contents: Level 2 : Basic Low Intermediate / Beth Maher, Natasha
Haugnes — Level 3 : Intermediate / Carolyn Dupaquier Sardinas, Laurie
Barton — Level 4 : High Intermediate / Andrew English, Laura Monahon
English — Level 5 : Advanced / Robert F. Cohen, Judy L. Miller.
    ISBN-13: 978-0-13-240991-9 (pbk. : student text bk. level 2 : alk. paper)
    ISBN-10: 0-13-240991-7 (pbk. : student text bk. level 2 : alk. paper)
    ISBN-13: 978-0-13-613368-1 (pbk. : student text bk. level 3 : alk. paper)
    ISBN-10: 0-13-613368-1 (pbk. : student text bk. level 3 : alk. paper)
   [etc.]
  1. English language—Textbooks for foreign speakers. 2. Reading
comprehension—Problems, exercises, etc. 3. Report writing—Problems,
exercises, etc. I. Haugnes, Natasha, 1965– Northstar. II. Title:
Reading and writing.
 PE1128.N675 2008
 428.2'4—dc22
                            2008024492

ISBN 10: 0-13-613318-5
ISBN 13: 978-0-13-613318-6

Printed in the United States of America
 10—V011—13 12 11

CONTENTS

WELCOME TO **NORTHSTAR**
THIRD EDITION

NorthStar, now in its third edition, motivates students to succeed in their **academic** as well as **personal** language goals.

For each of the five levels, the two strands—*Reading and Writing* and *Listening and Speaking*—provide a fully integrated approach for students and teachers.

WHAT IS SPECIAL ABOUT THE THIRD EDITION?

NEW THEMES

New themes and **updated content**—presented in a **variety of genres**, including literature and lectures, and in **authentic reading and listening selections**—challenge students intellectually.

ACADEMIC SKILLS

More purposeful **integration of critical thinking** and an enhanced focus on **academic skills** such as inferencing, synthesizing, note taking, and test taking help students develop strategies for **success** in the **classroom** and on **standardized tests**. A **culminating productive task** galvanizes content, language, and **critical thinking skills**.

➢ In the *Reading and Writing* strand, a new, **fully integrated writing section** leads students through the **writing process** with engaging writing assignments focusing on various rhetorical modes.

➢ In the *Listening and Speaking* strand, a **structured approach** gives students opportunities for **more extended and creative oral practice**, for example, presentations, simulations, debates, case studies, and public service announcements.

NEW DESIGN

Full **color pages** with more **photos**, **illustrations**, **and graphic organizers** foster student engagement and make the content and activities come alive.

MyNorthStarLab

MyNorthStarLab, an easy-to-use **online learning and assessment program**, offers:

➢ Unlimited access to reading and listening selections and DVD segments.

➢ Focused test preparation to help students succeed on international exams such as TOEFL® and IELTS®. Pre- and post-unit assessments improve results by providing individualized instruction, instant feedback, and personalized study plans.

➢ Original activities that support and extend the *NorthStar* program. These include pronunciation practice using voice recording tools, and activities to build note taking skills and academic vocabulary.

➢ Tools that save time. These include a flexible gradebook and authoring features that give teachers control of content and help them track student progress.

THE NORTHSTAR APPROACH

The *NorthStar* series is based on **current research in language acquisition** and on the **experiences of teachers and curriculum designers**. Five principles guide the *NorthStar* approach.

PRINCIPLES

1 The more profoundly students are stimulated intellectually and emotionally, the more language they will use and retain.

The thematic organization of *NorthStar* promotes intellectual and emotional stimulation. The 50 sophisticated themes in *NorthStar* present intriguing topics such as recycled fashion, restorative justice, personal carbon footprints, and microfinance. The authentic content engages students, links them to language use outside of the classroom, and encourages personal expression and critical thinking.

2 Students can learn both the form and content of the language.

Grammar, vocabulary, and culture are inextricably woven into the units, providing students with systematic and multiple exposures to language forms in a variety of contexts. As the theme is developed, students can express complex thoughts using a higher level of language.

3 Successful students are active learners.

Tasks are designed to be creative, active, and varied. Topics are interesting and up-to-date. Together these tasks and topics (1) allow teachers to bring the outside world into the classroom and (2) motivate students to apply their classroom learning in the outside world.

4 Students need feedback.

This feedback comes naturally when students work together practicing language and participating in open-ended opinion and inference tasks. Whole class activities invite teachers' feedback on the spot or via audio/video recordings or notes. The innovative new MyNorthStarLab gives students immediate feedback as they complete computer-graded language activities online; it also gives students the opportunity to submit writing or speaking assignments electronically to their instructor for feedback later.

5 The quality of relationships in the language classroom is important because students are asked to express themselves on issues and ideas.

The information and activities in *NorthStar* promote genuine interaction, acceptance of differences, and authentic communication. By building skills and exploring ideas, the exercises help students participate in discussions and write essays of an increasingly complex and sophisticated nature.

THE NORTHSTAR UNIT

① FOCUS ON THE TOPIC

This section introduces students to the unifying theme of the reading selections.

> **PREDICT** and **SHARE INFORMATION** foster interest in the unit topic and help students develop a personal connection to it.
>
> **BACKGROUND AND VOCABULARY** activities provide students with tools for understanding the first reading selection. Later in the unit, students review this vocabulary and learn related idioms, collocations, and word forms. This helps them explore content and expand their written and spoken language.

UNIT 9 — The Grass Is Always Greener...

Jamaica Kincaid
Born: Antigua,[1] 1949
Occupation: Writer
Immigrated to the U.S. in 1966

Arnold Schwarzenegger
Born: Graz, Austria, 1947
Occupation: Actor/
Governor of California
Immigrated to the U.S. in 1968

Gloria Estefan
Born: Havana, Cuba, 1957
Occupation: Singer
Immigrated to the U.S. in 1959

① FOCUS ON THE TOPIC

A PREDICT

Look at the photographs and the unit title. Then discuss the questions with a partner.

1. What do the people have in common?
2. How do you think their life would have been different if they had not immigrated?
3. The unit title is part of a famous saying, "The grass is always greener on the other side of the fence.[2]" Do you think the saying is about other things besides grass and fences? What do you think the unit will be about?

[1] **Antigua:** an island in the Caribbean
[2] **fence:** a structure made of wood, metal, etc. that surrounds a piece of land

201

B SHARE INFORMATION

Throughout history, people have sought immortality. People today are living longer than at any time in history; however, we are still a long way from reaching immortality.

Work with a partner or in a small group and discuss the questions.

1. If scientists could create a pill that would allow you to live twice as long while staying healthy, would you take it?
2. How would life be different if you lived longer? How would it be better? How would it be worse? Think about how such issues as relationships, marriage, family structure, and career might be affected.

C BACKGROUND AND VOCABULARY

Reading One is a story about Marilisa and her husband, Leo. Read the letter Marilisa wrote to a friend about Leo. Choose the definition that best defines the boldfaced word.

1. a. mean
   b. energetic
   c. lazy
2. a. on time
   b. well dressed
   c. considerately
3. a. understandably
   b. incredibly
   c. to some extent
4. a. difficult
   b. fascinating
   c. different
5. a. slightly
   b. always
   c. completely
6. a. complicated
   b. impressive
   c. terrible
7. a. doing things slowly after thinking about them
   b. doing things because somebody told you to
   c. doing things quickly without thinking
8. a. annoying
   b. friendly
   c. interesting

Dear Susannah,

I know you are worried about my marrying Leo, but please realize he has many good qualities. For example, he is quite **(1) vigorous**. Despite his age, he still exercises for hours and then works in the garden. In addition, he is very thoughtful. Unlike some of my friends, he always arrives **(2) punctually**. If he says he will meet me at 10 o'clock, he will be there exactly at 10.

He is also **(3) immeasurably** wise. He has so much knowledge and experience and is interested in so many **(4) disparate** subjects such as Greek history, diamond mining, dinosaurs, and alternative medicine. Even though they are not related, he enjoys them all. I find this quality **(5) utterly** fascinating. I am totally amazed by his vast knowledge. Leo really has had an **(6) awesome** life when you think about everything he has done. It is so exciting living with someone who has had so many incredible experiences.

However, I'm not claiming Leo is perfect. For one thing, he can be very **(7) impetuous**. Just last week, he bought a new car. He didn't even think about the fact that we needed that money to pay our credit card bills!

Furthermore, at times, he can be **(8) insufferable**. I was trying to watch television last night and he was constantly interrupting me to ask questions. Couldn't he understand that I was trying to concentrate on the show? His family is another problem. Take his ex-wife, Katrin, for example. I don't understand why he ever married her. Leo, of course, is very nice and friendly to everyone.

92 UNIT 5

② FOCUS ON READING

This section focuses on understanding two contrasting reading selections.

> **READING ONE** is a literary selection, academic article, news piece, blog, or other genre that addresses the unit topic. In levels 1 to 3, readings are based on authentic materials. In levels 4 and 5, all the readings are authentic.
>
> **READ FOR MAIN IDEAS** and **READ FOR DETAILS** are comprehension activities that lead students to an understanding and appreciation of the first selection.

---

② FOCUS ON READING

A READING ONE: The Education of Frank McCourt

Read the first two paragraphs of The Education of Frank McCourt. Work with a partner to answer the questions. Then read the rest of the article.

1. Where is Frank McCourt now?
2. What do you think he means by "They gave me so much more than I gave them?"
3. What do you think happened to Frank between 1949 and 1997?

THE EDUCATION OF FRANK McCOURT

By Barbara Sande Dimmitt
(from *Reader's Digest*)

1 Frank McCourt sat on a stage in New York City's Lincoln Center, his white hair glistening under the lights overhead. He was still boyish of expression at 66, and smile lines radiated from hazel eyes bright with inquisitiveness. Soon he would be addressing the 1997 graduating class of Stuyvesant High School, where he had taught English for 18 years.

2 He let his mind wander as he gazed out at the great hall. *I've learned so much from kids like these,* he thought. *They gave me much more than I gave them.*

3 "Yo, Teach!" a voice boomed. Frank McCourt scanned the adolescents in his classroom. It was the fall of 1970 and his first week of teaching at Seward Park High School, which sat in the midst of **dilapidated** tenement buildings on Manhattan's Lower East Side. McCourt located the speaker and nodded. "You talk funny," the student said, "Where ya from?"

4 "Ireland," McCourt replied. With more than ten years of teaching experience under his belt, this kind of interrogation[1] no longer surprised him. But one question in particular still made him squirm[2] "Where'd you go to high school?" someone else asked.

5 If I tell them the truth, they'll feel superior to me, McCourt thought. They'll throw it in my face. Most of all, he feared an accusation he'd heard before—from himself: You come from nothing, so you are nothing.

6 But McCourt's heart whispered another possibility: Maybe these kids are **yearning for** a way of figuring out this new teacher. Am I willing to risk being humiliated in the classroom to find out?

[1] **interrogation:** intense questioning
[2] **squirm:** feel embarrassed or ashamed

28 UNIT 2

▌ READ FOR MAIN IDEAS

Reading One has four main ideas. What does the reading say about each idea? Circle the sentence that best summarizes the idea.

1. Reporting of facts
   a. Journalists sometimes use their own judgment and leave out certain facts when reporting a story.
   b. Journalists usually report all the facts that they know about a story.

2. Reporting about famous people
   a. In the old days, certain facts about famous people were held back from the public. This is not always true today.
   b. In the old days, certain facts about famous people were held back from the public. This is still the case today.

3. Choosing to report all stories
   a. The decision to report or not report a story is based only on the reporter's judgment.
   b. The decision to report or not report a story is influenced by many factors. The reporter's judgment is just one of these factors.

4. Respecting the right to privacy
   a. All people agree that the public has a right to know about a famous person's life.
   b. Some people believe that you lose the right to privacy when you are famous. Others disagree.

▌ READ FOR DETAILS

Complete the chart with examples or details the author uses to support each main idea.

MAIN IDEA	EXAMPLE OR DETAIL THAT SUPPORTS THE MAIN IDEA
1. Reporting of facts	*retired minister*
2. Reporting about famous people	
3. Choosing to report all stories	
4. Respecting the right to privacy	

6 UNIT 1

Following this comprehension section, the **MAKE INFERENCES** activity prompts students to "read between the lines," move beyond the literal meaning, exercise critical thinking skills, and understand the text on a more academic level. Students follow up with pair or group work to discuss topics in the **EXPRESS OPINIONS** section.

READING TWO offers another perspective on the topic and usually belongs to another genre. Again, in levels 1 to 3, the readings are based on authentic materials, and in levels 4 and 5, they are authentic. This second reading is followed by an activity that challenges students to question ideas they formed about the first reading, and to use appropriate language skills to analyze and explain their ideas.

INTEGRATE READINGS ONE AND TWO presents culminating activities. Students are challenged to take what they have learned, organize the information, and synthesize it in a meaningful way. Students practice skills that are essential for success in authentic academic settings and on standardized tests.

B READING TWO: The Miracle

Diane Schuur is an accomplished jazz musician who is blind. She compares her struggles and triumphs with those of Helen Keller, the famous writer and political activist who was not only blind, but deaf as well.

1 *Discuss the questions with a partner. Then read the article by Diane Schuur.*

  1. What do you think the title, "She [Helen Keller] altered our perception of the disabled and remapped the boundaries of sight and sense" means?

  2. How do you think Diane Schuur "remapped" her boundaries?

THE MIRACLE:
She altered our perception of the disabled and remapped the boundaries of sight and sense.

By Diane Schuur (from *Time*)

1   Helen Keller was less than two years old when she came down with a fever. It struck dramatically and left her unconscious. The fever went just as suddenly. But she was blinded, and very soon after, deaf. As she grew up, she managed to learn to do tiny errands, but she also realized that she was missing something. "Sometimes," she later wrote, "I stood between two persons who were conversing and touched their lips. I could not understand, and was vexed. I moved my lips and gesticulated[1] frantically without result. This made me so angry at times that I kicked and screamed until I was exhausted." She was a wild child.

Diane Schuur

2   I can understand her rage. I was born two months prematurely and was placed in an incubator. The practice at the time was to pump a large amount of oxygen into the incubator, something doctors have since learned to be extremely cautious about. But as a result, I lost my sight. I was sent to a state school for the blind, but I flunked first grade because Braille[2] just didn't make any sense to me. Words were a weird concept. I remember being hit and slapped. And you act all that in. All rage is anger that is acted in, bottled in for so long that it just pops out. Helen had it harder. She was both blind and deaf. But, oh, the transformation that came over her when she discovered that words were related to things! It's like the lyrics of that song: "On a clear day, rise and look around you, and you'll see who you are."

3   I can say the word see. I can speak the language of the sighted. That's part of the first great achievement of Helen Keller. She proved how language could liberate the blind and the

[1] **gesticulated:** motioned
[2] **Braille:** a form of printing with raised round marks that blind people can read by touching

---

• "You must understand that even more than sighted people, we need to be touched. When you look at a person, eye to eye, I imagine it's like touching them. We don't have that convenience. But when I perform, I get that experience from a crowd."

_____

_____

_____

C INTEGRATE READINGS ONE AND TWO

◀ **STEP 1: Organize**

Both Frank McCourt and Diane Schuur faced many obstacles and challenges in their lives. These same challenges also helped them to discover and develop their talent and become successful. Complete the chart comparing Frank McCourt and Diane Schuur.

	READING ONE **Frank McCourt**	**READING TWO** **Diane Schuur**
1. Obstacles they faced		
2. Person or people who influenced and inspired them		
3. Personal values, traits, or characteristics that helped them face their obstacles		
4. Talent or gift that resulted from the challenges they faced		

◀ **STEP 2: Synthesize**

On a separate piece of paper, write a short paragraph comparing the lives of Frank McCourt and Diane Schuur using the information from Step 1. Describe their obstacles and triumphs.

③ FOCUS ON WRITING

This section emphasizes development of productive skills for writing. It includes sections on vocabulary, grammar, and the writing process.

> The **VOCABULARY** section leads students from reviewing the unit vocabulary, to practicing and expanding their use of it, and then working with it—using it creatively in both this section and in the final writing task.
>
> Students learn useful structures for writing in the **GRAMMAR** section, which offers a concise presentation and targeted practice. Vocabulary items are recycled here, providing multiple exposures leading to mastery. For additional practice with the grammar presented, students and teachers can consult the GRAMMAR BOOK REFERENCES at the end of the book for corresponding material in the *Focus on Grammar* and Azar series.

---

③ FOCUS ON WRITING

Ⓐ VOCABULARY

◀ REVIEW

The chain diagram shows the three stages of overcoming obstacles: facing an obstacle, dealing with an obstacle, and overcoming an obstacle. Write the words from the box in the correct circle. Some of the words may be put in more than one circle. Discuss your answers with a partner.

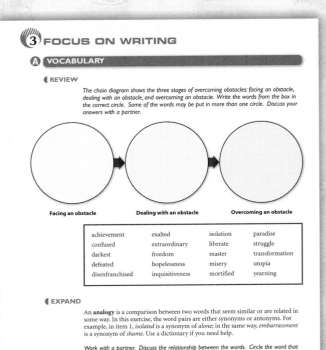

Facing an obstacle　　**Dealing with an obstacle**　　**Overcoming an obstacle**

achievement	exalted	isolation	paradise
confused	extraordinary	liberate	struggle
darkest	freedom	master	transformation
defeated	hopelessness	misery	utopia
disenfranchised	inquisitiveness	mortified	yearning

◀ EXPAND

An **analogy** is a comparison between two words that seem similar or are related in some way. In this exercise, the word pairs are either synonyms or antonyms. For example, in item 1, *isolated* is a synonym of *alone*; in the same way, *embarrassment* is a synonym of *shame*. Use a dictionary if you need help.

Work with a partner. Discuss the relationship between the words. Circle the word that best completes each analogy. Then circle synonym or antonym for each set of words.

1. isolated : alone = embarrassment : _____ 　(synonym)　 antonym
   a. struggle　　b. sadness　　ⓒ. shame

Ⓑ GRAMMAR: Contrasting the Simple Past, Present Perfect, and Present Perfect Continuous

1 *Examine the sentences and answer the questions with a partner.*

a. Marilisa and Leo **went** to Nairobi and Venice on their honeymoon three years ago.

b. Leo **has been** an architect, an archeologist, a space-habitats developer, a professional gambler, an astronomer, and a number of other disparate and dazzling things.

c. People **have been searching** for the "fountain of youth" since the beginning of recorded history.

1. In sentence *a*, is Leo and Marilisa's honeymoon over? How do you know?
2. In sentence *b*, is Leo still an architect, an archeologist . . . ? How do you know?
3. In sentence *c*, are people still searching for the fountain of youth? How do you know? When did people start searching?
4. What verb tenses are used in sentences *a*, *b*, and *c*?

CONTRASTING THE SIMPLE PAST, PRESENT PERFECT, AND PRESENT PERFECT CONTINUOUS	
The Simple Past	
1. Use the simple past for things that happened in the past and were completed.	Leo **watched** the movie. (Leo is no longer watching the movie. He finished watching the movie.)
2. Use past time expressions such as: *last, ago, in, on, at, yesterday, when . . .* to indicate that an action or event was completed at a definite time in the past.	Leo **watched** the movie **yesterday**. (Leo is no longer watching the movie. He finished watching the movie yesterday.)
The Present Perfect	
3. Use the present perfect for completed actions that happened at an indefinite time in the past.	Marilisa **has eaten** breakfast. (She has finished her breakfast, but we don't know exactly when she ate it, or it is not important.)
4. You can also use the present perfect for repeated actions that were completed in the past, but that may happen again in the future.	Leo **has visited** Paris six times. (Those six visits are finished. However, he may visit Paris again in the future.)

(continued on next page)

The **WRITING** section of each unit leads students through the writing process and presents a challenging and imaginative writing task that directs students to integrate the content, vocabulary, and grammar from the unit.

- Students practice a short **pre-writing strategy**, such as freewriting, clustering, brainstorming, interviewing, listing, making a chart or diagram, categorizing, or classifying.

- Then students organize their ideas and write, using a **specific structural or rhetorical pattern** that fits the subject at hand.

- Students then learn **revising techniques** within a sentence-level or paragraph-level activity to help them move towards **coherence and unity** in their writing.

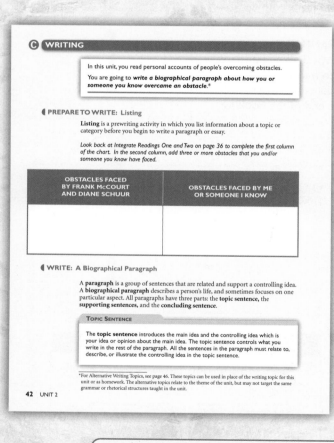

C   WRITING

In this unit, you read personal accounts of people's overcoming obstacles.

You are going to **write a biographical paragraph about how you or someone you know overcame an obstacle.***

PREPARE TO WRITE: Listing

Listing is a prewriting activity in which you list information about a topic or category before you begin to write a paragraph or essay.

Look back at Integrate Readings One and Two on page 36 to complete the first column of the chart. In the second column, add three or more obstacles that you and/or someone you know have faced.

OBSTACLES FACED BY FRANK McCOURT AND DIANE SCHUUR	OBSTACLES FACED BY ME OR SOMEONE I KNOW

WRITE: A Biographical Paragraph

A **paragraph** is a group of sentences that are related and support a controlling idea. A **biographical paragraph** describes a person's life, and sometimes focuses on one particular aspect. All paragraphs have three parts: the **topic sentence**, the **supporting sentences**, and the **concluding sentence**.

TOPIC SENTENCE

The **topic sentence** introduces the main idea and the controlling idea which is your idea or opinion about the main idea. The topic sentence controls what you write in the rest of the paragraph. All the sentences in the paragraph must relate to, describe, or illustrate the controlling idea in the topic sentence.

*For Alternative Writing Topics, see page 46. These topics can be used in place of the writing topic for this unit or as homework. The alternative topics relate to the theme of the unit, but may not target the same grammar or rhetorical structures taught in the unit.

42   UNIT 2

5. Read paragraph 8. Write a one-sentence summary of the main idea.

6. Read paragraphs 9 and 10. Write a one-sentence summary of the main idea.

3 Now write your first draft of your summary of Reading Two. Use the information from Prepare to Write and Write to plan your summary. Make sure you state the thesis and eliminate any unimportant details. Be sure to use grammar and vocabulary from the unit.

REVISE: Paraphrasing

Summary writing often requires the writer to restate an author's ideas. It is very important to restate an author's ideas in your own words while keeping true to the author's ideas. This is called **paraphrasing**. (*Note:* When you choose to use author's direct words, you must use quotation marks.)

AUTHOR'S OWN WORDS	PARAPHRASED TEXT
"The things that are important to animals can be different than those that matter to humans. When studying animals, we must test them in situations that have meaning for their lives, not ours, and not just look to see how much they **resemble** us."	Hinshaw concludes that testing an animal's intelligence is very difficult and we should not apply our own human beliefs about what intelligence is to them. Specifically, animals must be tested against measures that are important and useful to them, not to the human world.
When using a direct quote, use these punctuation rules:	When paraphrasing or quoting, use a variety of reporting verbs to introduce an author's ideas:
1. Lift the quote directly as is from the text. Do not change the capitalization or punctuation.	says notes tells mentions acknowledges thinks
2. Place a comma before the quote: Hinshaw does however acknowledge that, "Animals that are easy to train may also be highly intelligent."	concedes writes states believes explains concludes
3. Place the final punctuation mark at the end of the sentence before the final quotation mark: Hinshaw does however acknowledge that, "Animals that are easy to train may also be highly intelligent."	

When paraphrasing, first think of the main idea or what the author is trying to tell you. Think of ways to say the same thing using your own words. Do not just replace words in a sentence with synonyms.

Original   **Paraphrase**

Many animals have extreme perception.   ~~Many animals have excellent awareness.~~

88   UNIT 4

In the final phase of the writing process, students **edit** their work with the help of a **checklist** that focuses on mechanics, completeness, enhancing style, and incorporating the vocabulary and grammar from the unit.

ALTERNATIVE WRITING TOPICS are provided at the end of the unit. They can be used as *alternatives* to the final writing task, or as *additional* assignments. RESEARCH TOPICS tied to the theme of the unit are organized in a special section at the back of the book..

COMPONENTS

TEACHER'S MANUAL WITH ACHIEVEMENT TESTS

Each level and strand of *NorthStar* has an accompanying Teacher's Manual with step-by-step **teaching suggestions**, including unique guidance for using *NorthStar* in secondary classes. The manuals include time guidelines, expansion activities, and techniques and instructions for using MyNorthStarLab. Also included are reproducible unit-by-unit achievement **tests** of **receptive** and **productive** skills, **answer keys** to both the student book and tests, and a unit-by-unit **vocabulary** list.

EXAMVIEW

NorthStar ExamView is a stand-alone CD-ROM that allows teachers to **create and customize** their own *NorthStar* tests.

DVD

The *NorthStar* DVD has **engaging**, **authentic video clips**, including animation, documentaries, interviews, and biographies, that correspond to the themes in *NorthStar*. Each theme contains a three- to five-minute segment that can be used with either the *Reading and Writing* strand or the *Listening and Speaking* strand. The video clips can also be viewed in MyNorthStarLab.

COMPANION WEBSITE

The companion website, www.longman.com/northstar, includes resources for teachers, such as the **scope and sequence**, **correlations** to other Longman products and to state standards, and **podcasts** from the *NorthStar* authors and series editors.

MyNorthStarLab

PEARSON LONGMAN mynorthstarlab™ | AVAILABLE WITH the new edition of *NORTHSTAR*

NorthStar is now available with **MyNorthStarLab**—an easy-to-use **online** program **for students and teachers** that saves time and improves results.

> **STUDENTS** receive **personalized instruction** and **practice** in all four skills. Audio, video, and test preparation are all in **one** place—available **anywhere, anytime**.

> **TEACHERS** can take advantage of many resources including online **assessments**, a flexible **gradebook**, and **tools for monitoring student progress**.

CHECK IT OUT! GO TO www.mynorthstarlab.com FOR A PREVIEW!

TURN THE PAGE TO SEE KEY FEATURES OF **MyNorthStarLab**.

MYNORTHSTARLAB

MyNorthStarLab supports students with **individualized instruction**, **feedback**, and **extra help**. A wide array of resources, including a flexible **gradebook**, helps teachers manage student progress.

The MyNorthStarLab **WELCOME** page **organizes assignments and grades**, and **facilitates communication** between students and teachers.

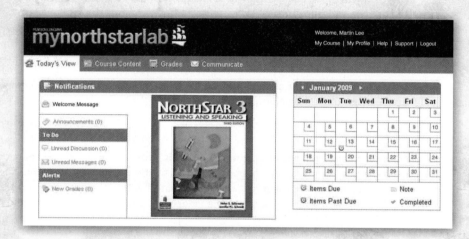

For each unit, MyNorthStarLab provides a **READINESS CHECK**.

➤ Activities **assess** student knowledge **before** beginning the unit and **follow up** with individualized instruction.

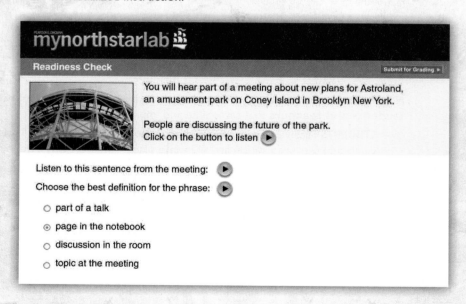

Student book material and **new** practice activities are available to students online.

➤ Students benefit from virtually unlimited **practice anywhere, anytime**.

Interaction with **Internet** and **video** materials will:

➤ Expand students' knowledge of the topic.

➤ Help students practice new vocabulary and grammar.

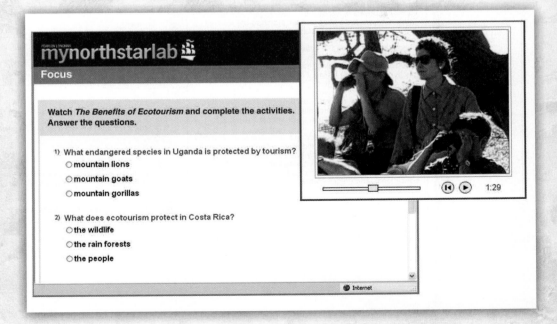

INTEGRATED SKILL ACTIVITIES in MyNorthStarLab challenge students to bring together the **language skills** and **critical thinking skills** that they have practiced throughout the unit.

Integrated Task - Read, Listen, Write   Submit for Grading ▶

THE ADVENTURE OF A LIFETIME

We at the Antarctic Travel Society <u>encourage</u> you to consider an excited guided tour of Antarctica for your next vacation.

The Antarctic Travel society carefully plans and operates tours of the Antarctic by ship. There are three trips per day leaving from <u>ports</u> in South America and Australia. Each ship carries only about 100 passengers at a time. Tours run from November through March to the ice-free areas along the coast of Antarctica.

In addition to touring the coast, our ships stop for on-land visits, which generally last for about three hours. Activities include guided sightseeing, mountain climbing, camping, <u>kayaking</u>, and <u>scuba diving</u>. For a longer stay, camping trips can also be arranged.

Our tours will give you an opportunity to experience the richness of Antarctica, including its wildlife, history, active research stations, and, most of all, its natural beauty.

Tours are <u>supervised</u> by the ship's staff. The staff generally includes <u>experts</u> in animal and sea life and other Antarctica specialists. There is generally one staff member for every 10 to 20 passengers. Theses trained and responsible individuals will help to make your visit to Antarctica safe, educational, and <u>unforgettable</u>.

READ, LISTEN AND WRITE ABOUT TOURISM IN ANTARCTICA
Read.
Read the text. Then answer the question.

According to the text, how can tourism benefit the Antartic?

▶ **Listen.**
Click on the Play button and listen to the passage.
Use the outline to take notes as you listen.

Main idea:

Seven things that scientists study:

The effects of tourism:

Write.
Write about the potential and risks in Antarctica.
Follow the steps to prepare.

Step 1
• Review the text and your outline from the listening task.
• Write notes about the benefits and risks of tourism.

Step 2
Write for 20 minutes. Leave 5 minutes to edit your work.

The MyNorthStarLab **ASSESSMENT** tools allow instructors to customize and deliver achievement tests online.

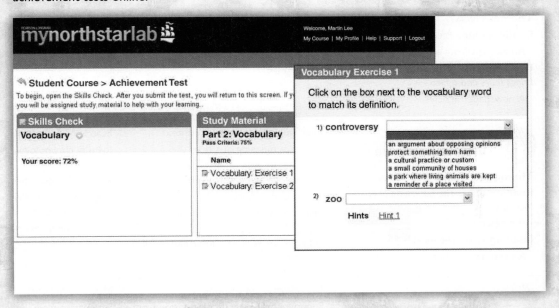

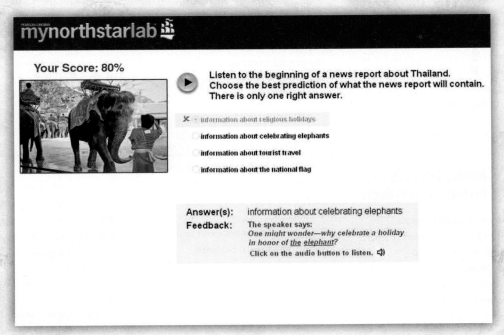

SCOPE AND SEQUENCE

UNIT	CRITICAL THINKING	READING
1 Untruth and Consequences **Theme:** Media **Reading One:** *Peeping Tom Journalism* An excerpt from a book **Reading Two:** *Focus on Bomb Suspect Brings Tears and a Plea* A newspaper article	Interpret a photograph Recognize how details support main ideas Use examples to support answers Classify information Draw conclusions Hypothesize another's point of view	Interpret quotations Make predictions Categorize main ideas Scan for supporting details Make inferences about author's viewpoint Form and express opinions based on a text
2 Dreams Never Die **Theme:** Overcoming obstacles **Reading One:** *The Education of Frank McCourt* A magazine article **Reading Two:** *The Miracle* A personal account	Infer word meaning from context Interpret meaning of a text Evaluate the role of obstacles and character in personal success Interpret quotations Differentiate between main ideas and details Support answers with information from a text	Scan for information Identify chronology in a text by using a timeline Find correlations between two texts Organize and synthesize information in different texts Form and express opinions based on a text
3 Dying for Their Beliefs **Theme:** Medicine **Reading One:** *Dying for Their Beliefs: Christian Scientist Parents on Trial in Girl's Death* A newspaper report **Reading Two:** *Norman Cousins's Laugh Therapy* An expository account	Draw logical conclusions Support answers with information from a text Research medical treatments Categorize information Re-evaluate assumptions Analyze the development of an argument	Make predictions Summarize main ideas Identify details Relate texts to personal values and experiences Identify philosophical rationale for a text Paraphrase Make inferences Use a Venn diagram as a note-taking device
4 Animal Intelligence: Instinct or Intellect? **Theme:** Animal intelligence **Reading One:** *How Smart Is Smart?* An excerpt from a book **Reading Two:** *Extreme Perception and Animal Intelligence* An excerpt from a book	Infer word meaning from context Interpret meaning of a text Recognize how details support main ideas Find correlations between two texts Interpret animals' behavior	Make predictions Identify main ideas Scan for supporting details Make inferences Identify chronology in a text Form and express opinions based on a text Organize and synthesize information in different texts Use a sequence organizer as a note-taking device

WRITING	VOCABULARY	GRAMMAR
Develop topic sentences Paraphrase Write a letter to a newspaper editor Write an opinion paragraph Compose topic sentences Brainstorm ideas using a web organizer Use time transitions	Categorize vocabulary words Use context clues to find meaning Use idiomatic expressions	Passive and active voice
Write a compare and contrast paragraph Use a list as a pre-writing device Write supporting sentences using transitional expressions Write concluding sentences Recognize sentences that do not support main ideas Summarize research in a report	Find and use synonyms Categorize vocabulary words Use context clues to find meaning Use idiomatic expressions	Gerunds and infinitives
Write an opinion essay Use tree-mapping as a pre-writing device Write hooks Develop an opinion in outline form Support an opinion with evidence Develop a classroom survey	Find analogies Compare and contrast word meanings	Past unreal conditionals
Write a summarizing essay Use wh- questions to summarize Paraphrase	Find and use synonyms Identify word roots Use context clues to find meaning	Identifying adjective clauses

SCOPE AND SEQUENCE

UNIT	CRITICAL THINKING	READING
5 **Longevity: Too Much of a Good Thing?** **Theme:** Longevity **Reading One:** *Death Do Us Part* An excerpt from a short story **Reading Two:** *Toward Immortality: The Social Burden of Longer Lives* An online article	Interpret a cartoon Compare observations on living longer lives Infer word meaning from context Extract logical arguments from a text Establish cause and effect relationships Evaluate advantages and disadvantages of living longer	Make predictions Compare characters' views to real world views Scan for details Make inferences based on a text Form and express opinions based on a text Identify cause and effect in a text Identify connecting themes between texts Draw a cause and effect diagram
6 **Give and Learn** **Theme:** Philanthropy **Reading One:** *Justin Lebo* An excerpt from a book **Reading Two:** *Some Take the Time Gladly* A newspaper op-ed column *Mandatory Volunteering for High School Diploma Not a Good Idea* A newspaper op-ed column	Re-evaluate personal attitudes and values Infer information not explicit in a text Identify an author's opinions Identify motivations of characters Hypothesize another's point of view Relate specific examples to broad themes Analyze concessive language	Make predictions Paraphrase main ideas Scan for supporting details Identify contrasting arguments in a text Make inferences Expres opinions Complete a chart as a note-taking device
7 **Homing in on Education** **Theme:** Education **Reading One:** *The Satisfied Learner: How Families Homeschool Their Teens* A magazine article **Reading Two:** *The Fun They Had* An excerpt from a science-fiction novel	Re-evaluate personal assumptions Evaluate and classify information Compare and contrast models of education Infer information not explicit in a text Relate specific situations to broad themes Hypothesize another's point of view	Predict content Read and interpret bar graphs Paraphrase main ideas in a reading Scan for details Compare the content of two texts Use a chart as a note-taking device View ideas from differing perspectives Express opinions

WRITING	VOCABULARY	GRAMMAR
Develop descriptive writing skills Write a descriptive essay Write cause and effect sentences Use figurative language Use an idea web as a pre-writing device Summarize research in a report	Categorize vocabulary Use context clues to find meaning Learn adjective suffixes	Contrasting the simple past, present perfect, and present perfect continuous
Use commas, semicolons, colons, and dashes Write a persuasive essay Use concession clauses Use T-charts as a pre-writing device Practice writing introductions and conclusions	Find and use synonyms Recognize word forms Use context clues to find meaning	Concessions
Write a classification essay Use parallel sentence structure Classify information as a pre-writing device	Find and use synonyms Use context clues to find meaning Identify word forms	Direct and indirect speech

SCOPE AND SEQUENCE

UNIT	CRITICAL THINKING	READING

8 Eat to Live or Live to Eat?
 	
Theme: Food
Reading One: *The Chinese Kitchen*
  A cook's narrative
Reading Two: *"Slow Food" Movement Aims at Restoring the Joy of Eating*
  A newspaper report
	Re-evaluate personal attitudes and values
	Compare and contrast information
	Infer meaning not explicit in a text
	Identify different perspectives within one text
	Support opinions with information from a text
	Analyze techniques in narrative voice
	Identify connecting themes between texts
		Make predictions
		Restate main ideas
		Scan for specific details in a text
		Relate the text to personal culinary experiences
		Express opinions
		Organize and synthesize information in different texts
		Use a chart to compare and contrast beliefs

9 The Grass Is Always Greener . . .
 	
Theme: Immigration
Reading One: *Poor Visitor*
  An excerpt from a novel
Reading Two: *Nostalgia*
  A poem
	Classify observations and life experiences
	Identify similarities in three different life histories
	Interpret imagery in a text
	Compare and contrast imagery in a text
	Hypothesize another's point of view
	Support answers with information from a text
		Make predictions
		Scan for information
		Identify main ideas
		Relate text to personal experiences
		Make inferences
		Interpret a poem
		Organize and synthesize information in different texts
		Express opinions
		Complete a chart

10 Take It or Leave It
 	
Theme: Technology
Reading One: *Inside the House*
  An excerpt from a book
Reading Two: *Thoreau's Home*
  An excerpt from a book
	Interpret a cartoon
	Compare and contrast concepts of technology
	Evaluate personal standards in technology
	Infer word meaning from context
	Hypothesize another's point of view
	Classify information
	Support answers with examples from a text
	Recognize organization of a text
		Make predictions
		Summarize main ideas
		Locate examples and details in a text
		Make inferences
		Express opinions
		Organize and synthesize information in different texts
		Relate a text to personal values

WRITING	VOCABULARY	GRAMMAR
Write a narrative essay Evaluate a classmate's narrative using a rubric Practice parallel structures and sentence variation Take notes to organize information Write sentences with varying sentence lengths Use chronological sequencing showing how events relate to each other in time	Use context clues to find meaning Find and use synonyms	Phrasal verbs
Write a comparison and contrast essay Use transitional expressions and subordinating conjunctions to combine sentences Write comparison and contrast statements Organize ideas in different frameworks Make a comparison and contrast chart	Find multiple definitions of words Use context clues to find meaning Understand and use analogies	Past perfect
Write a cause and effect essay Take notes in outline form Develop an essay from an outline Use signal words Brainstorm ideas using a graphic organizer Write and respond to interview questions Use a flow chart as a pre-writing device	Find and use synonyms Use context clues to find meaning Recognize word forms	Future progressive

ACKNOWLEDGMENTS

We would like to once again express our gratitude and thanks to the entire *NorthStar* team of authors, editors, and assistants. Special thanks go to Carol Numrich and Frances Boyd for their vision, ideas, and guidance. We are, as always, honored to be on their team. Thanks also to Andrea Bryant for her unending support and attention to detail. To everyone else at Pearson, many thanks for all of your hard work in bringing this third edition to fruition.

Reviewers

For the comments and insights they graciously offered to help shape the direction of the Third Edition of *NorthStar*, the publisher would like to thank the following reviewers and institutions.

Gail August, Hostos Community College; **Anne Bachmann**, Clackamas Community College; **Aegina Barnes**, York College, CUNY; **Dr. Sabri Bebawi**, San Jose Community College; **Kristina Beckman**, John Jay College; **Jeff Bellucci**, Kaplan Boston; **Nathan Blesse**, Human International Academy; **Alan Brandman**, Queens College; **Laila Cadavona-Dellapasqua**, Kaplan; **Amy Cain**, Kaplan; **Nigel Caplan**, Michigan State University; **Alzira Carvalho**, Human International Academy, San Diego; **Chao-Hsun (Richard) Cheng**, Wenzao Ursuline College of Languages; **Mu-hua (Yolanda) Chi**, Wenzao Ursuline College of Languages; **Liane Cismowski**, Olympic High School; **Shauna Croft**, MESLS; **Misty Crooks**, Kaplan; **Amanda De Loera**, Kaplan English Programs; **Jennifer Dobbins**, New England School of English; **Luis Dominguez**, Angloamericano; **Luydmila Drgaushanskaya**, ASA College; **Dilip Dutt**, Roxbury Community College; **Christie Evenson**, Chung Dahm Institute; **Patricia Frenz-Belkin**, Hostos Community College, CUNY; **Christiane Galvani**, Texas Southern University; **Joanna Ghosh**, University of Pennsylvania; **Cristina Gomes**, Kaplan Test Prep; **Kristen Grinager**, Lincoln High School; **Janet Harclerode**, Santa Monica College; **Carrell Harden**, HCCS, Gulfton Campus; **Connie Harney**, Antelope Valley College; **Ann Hilborn**, ESL Consultant in Houston; **Barbara Hockman**, City College of San Francisco; **Margaret Hodgson**, NorQuest College; **Paul Hong**, Chung Dahm Institute; **Wonki Hong**, Chung Dahm Institute; **John House**, Iowa State University; **Polly Howlett**, Saint Michael's College; **Arthur Hui**, Fullerton College; **Nina Ito**, CSU, Long Beach; **Scott Jenison**, Antelope Valley College; **Hyunsook Jeong**, Keimyung University; **Mandy Kama**, Georgetown University; **Dale Kim**, Chung Dahm Institute; **Taeyoung Kim**, Keimyung University; **Woo-hyung Kim**, Keimyung University; **Young Kim**, Chung Dahm Institute; **Yu-kyung Kim**, Sunchon National University; **John Kostovich**, Miami Dade College; **Albert Kowun**, Fairfax, VA; **David Krise**, Michigan State University; **Cheri (Young Hee) Lee**, ReadingTownUSA English Language Institute; **Eun-Kyung Lee**, Chung Dahm Institute; **Sang Hyock Lee**, Keimyung University; **Debra Levitt**, SMC; **Karen Lewis**, Somerville, MA; **Chia-Hui Liu**, Wenzao Ursuline College of Languages; **Gennell Lockwood**, Seattle, WA; **Javier Lopez Anguiano**, Colegio Anglo Mexicano de Coyoacan; **Mary March**, Shoreline Community College; **Susan Matson**, ELS Language Centers; **Ralph McClain**, Embassy CES Boston; **Veronica McCormack**, Roxbury Community College; **Jennifer McCoy**, Kaplan; **Joseph McHugh**, Kaplan; **Cynthia McKeag Tsukamoto**, Oakton Community College; **Paola Medina**, Texas Southern University; **Christine Kyung-ah Moon**, Seoul, Korea; **Margaret Moore**, North Seattle Community College; **Michelle Moore**, Madison English as a Second Language School; **David Motta**, Miami University; **Suzanne Munro**, Clackamas Community College; **Elena Nehrbecki**, Hudson County CC; **Kim Newcomer**, University of Washington; **Melody Nightingale**, Santa Monica College; **Patrick Northover**, Kaplan Test and Prep; **Sarah Oettle**, Kaplan, Sacramento; **Shirley Ono**, Oakton Community College; **Maria Estela Ortiz Torres**, C. Anglo Mexicano de Coyoac'an; **Suzanne Overstreet**, West Valley College; **Linda Ozarow**, West Orange High School; **Ileana Porges-West**, Miami Dade College, Hialeah Campus; **Megan Power**, ILCSA; **Alison Robertson**, Cypress College; **Ma. Del Carmen Romero**, Universidad del Valle de Mexico; **Nina Rosen**, Santa Rosa Junior College; **Daniellah Salario**, Kaplan; **Joel Samuels**, Kaplan New York City; **Babi Sarapata**, Columbia University ALP; **Donna Schaeffer**, University of Washington; **Lynn Schneider**, City College of San Francisco; **Errol Selkirk**, New School University; **Amity Shook**, Chung Dahm Institute; **Lynn Stafford-Yilmaz**, Bellevue Community College; **Lynne Ruelaine Stokes**, Michigan State University; **Henna Suh**, Chung Dahm Institute; **Sheri Summers**, Kaplan Test Prep; **Martha Sutter**, Kent State University; **Becky Tarver Chase**, MESLS; **Lisa Waite-Trago**, Michigan State University; **Carol Troy**, Da-Yeh University; **Luci Tyrell**, Embassy CES Fort Lauderdale; **Yong-Hee Uhm**, Myongii University; **Debra Un**, New York University; **José Vazquez**, The University of Texas Pan American; **Hollyahna Vettori**, Santa Rosa Junior College; **Susan Vik**, Boston University; **Sandy Wagner**, Fort Lauderdale High School; **Joanne Wan**, ASC English; **Pat Wiggins**, Clackamas Community College; **Heather Williams**, University of Pennsylvania; **Carol Wilson-Duffy**, Michigan State University; **Kailin Yang**, Kaohsing Medical University; **Ellen Yaniv**, Boston University; **Samantha Young**, Kaplan Boston; **Yu-san Yu**, National Sun Yat-sen University; **Ann Zaaijer**, West Orange High School

Untruth and Consequences

①FOCUS ON THE TOPIC

A PREDICT

Look at the photograph of Princess Diana and the unit title. Then discuss the questions with a partner.

1. What is happening? What do you think the photographers are thinking? Why are they taking Princess Diana's picture? What do you think she is thinking?

2. Where do most people learn about news? What news source do you most frequently use—newspapers, magazines, television, radio, the Internet? Why? Do you think your source is reliable? Why or why not?

3. What do you think "untruth and consequences" means? What do you think the unit will be about?

1

Work in a small group. Circle the best interpretations for quotations 1 and 2. Then write your own interpretation of quotations 3 and 4. Discuss your answers. Do you agree with any of the quotations? Why or why not?

1. "When a dog bites a man, that is not news; but when a man bites a dog, that is news."   —Leo Rosten, Polish-American political scientist and author

   a. News is only about exciting or unusual events.
   b. News is only interesting when someone gets hurt.

2. "A dog fight in Brooklyn (New York) is bigger than a revolution in China."
   —*Brooklyn Eagle* (newspaper)

   a. News about the United States is always more newsworthy[1] than international news.
   b. People are more interested in local news than international news even when the international news is more newsworthy.

3. "Good news isn't news. Bad news is news."
   —Henry Luce, founder of *Time* (magazine)

   This means: _____

   _____

   _____

4. "The media's the most powerful entity[2] on earth. They have the power to make the innocent guilty and to make the guilty innocent, and that's power, because they control the minds of the masses[3]."
   —Graham Greene, English writer

   This means: _____

   _____

   _____

1 *Read the passage on the next page about the news. Try to understand the boldfaced words from the context.*

---

[1] **newsworthy**: interesting or important enough to be reported in the news

[2] **entity**: thing

[3] **masses**: ordinary people in society, as distinct from political leaders, aristocracy, or educated people

News is everywhere and serves many different functions. The news gives instant coverage of important events. News also provides facts and information. On the other hand, news is sometimes manipulated[1] by the government as a way to control a population. In addition, in many countries, news is business—a way to make money by selling advertising and/or newspapers and magazines. However you define news, it is all around us. You can't escape it. Every day we are bombarded by information from newspapers, magazines, television, radio, and the Internet.

However, just because something is presented as "news" does not always mean that it is unquestionably true. Although the news *seems* to be based on facts, these facts are interpreted and reported the way the media *chooses* to report them. In other words, news is provided to us from the **perspective** of the media source. Therefore, it may not always be **legitimate**. For example, every day reporters **allege** stories to be true and present them as fact. In reality, they are no more than **speculation** or theories formed by reporters. Furthermore, many journalists and reporters sensationalize or dramatize a news event in order to make a story more interesting. Unfortunately, sensationalism often stretches the truth and omits **relevant** or important facts. In addition, sensationalism can also cause **anguish**, especially to those people mentioned in the stories.

Why does the media twist the truth? Media outlets **justify** their decisions by saying they can only sell high-interest news. **Suppose** news were presented as only hard and dry facts; would you continue to listen to or watch the news or buy the paper or magazine? Would it keep your interest?

As consumers of news we must learn to think critically about the news and the media, and make our own **judgment** as to what the truth is. Therefore, because of the ways news is used and manipulated, it should always be put under close **scrutiny.**

2 *Find the boldfaced words in the reading passage above. Circle the best synonym or definition for the word.*

1. **perspective** =	picture	or	point of view
2. **legitimate** =	valid	or	legal
3. **allege** =	claim	or	deny
4. **speculation** =	fact	or	assumptions
5. **relevant** =	interesting	or	related
6. **anguish** =	suffering	or	confusion
7. **justify** =	allow	or	explain
8. **suppose** =	imagine	or	guess
9. **judgment** =	trial	or	decision
10. **scrutiny** =	examination	or	imagination

[1] **manipulated**: presented in a way that is false but beneficial to the person presenting it

Read the first three paragraphs of Peeping Tom Journalism. *Work with a partner to answer the questions in paragraph 3. Then read the rest of the article.*

PEEPING TOM[1] JOURNALISM

BY NANCY DAY

(from *Sensational TV—Trash or Journalism*)

1   Reporters constantly struggle with what and how much to tell. Sometimes the facts are clear. Other times, journalists must rely on their own **judgment**.

2   A retired minister[2] in a small town does not return from a fishing trip. Police find his car parked about halfway to the lake. It is locked and undamaged. In it they find a half-eaten ham sandwich, fishing tackle, a gun with one shell fired, and a copy of *Penthouse* (a magazine that contains pictures of naked women). The minister is missing. You're the reporter and your story is due.

3   What do you report? **Suppose** the minister just went for a walk? Do you risk embarrassment and mention the magazine? Is the gun important? Should you propose any theories about what might have happened?

4   The reporter who actually faced these decisions decided to mention the gun, the

sandwich, the fishing tackle, and the condition of the car, but not the magazine or any **speculation**. The minister's body was later found. He had been killed by a hitch-hiker, who had left the magazine in the minister's car.

5   In the old days, reporters knew politicians (including presidents) who slept around, movie stars who were gay, and public figures who used drugs or abused alcohol. They just kept it to themselves. Now, at least in part because the public seems to have an endless hunger for it, reporters sometimes cover these aspects of celebrities' lives more than any other.

6   Some of the interest can be **justified** on the basis that character affects how people perform their jobs. But what if the information isn't **relevant**? For example, does the public need to know that a senator is gay?

---

[1] **Peeping Tom:** someone who secretly watches other people
[2] **minister:** a religious leader in some Christian churches

When a famous person dies, does the public have a right to all the details? Should the public know which public figures are unfaithful to their spouses? Are these things we need to know or just things we want to know?

7   When Gennifer Flowers **alleged** a twelve-year affair with President Bill Clinton, she first sold the story to the tabloid[3] *Star*. CNN reported the story and so did the networks and the major newspapers and news magazines. Peter Jennings, anchor for ABC's[4] "World News Tonight," was against broadcasting the Flowers story without further reporting by ABC correspondents, but says, "it was made clear to (me) . . . that if you didn't go with the story, every (ABC) affiliate in the country would look up and say, 'What the hell's going on in this place? Don't they know a story when they see it?' "

8   Some stories receive such wide visibility that to ignore them is to "play ostrich man," says Shelby Coffey, editor of the *Los Angeles Times*. "You have to give your readers some **perspective** on the information they are getting."

9   **Scrutiny** may be the price one pays for fame. But what about relatives of celebrities? Are they fair game too? And what about the average person?

10   When Sara Jane Moore pointed a gun at President Ford,[5] a man in the crowd knocked her hand, deflecting the shot. The man, Oliver W. Sipple, became an instant hero. He was thirty-three years old and a Marine veteran. What else did the public want or need to know about him? Initial reports did not mention Sipple's sexual orientation. But when a San Francisco news columnist said that local gay leaders were proud of Sipple's actions, other papers began to report it. Sipple sued the columnist and several newspapers for invading his privacy. He said that he suffered "great mental **anguish**, embarrassment, and humiliation." Lawyers argued that by becoming involved in an event of worldwide importance, Sipple had given up his right to privacy because the public has a **legitimate** interest in his activity.

11   Rosa Lopez was a maid working quietly and anonymously[6] until she became a key witness in the O. J. Simpson trial.[7] Suddenly, she was the focus of intense scrutiny. Lopez was hounded by cameras and reporters everywhere she went. Her every move was analyzed. She eventually returned to her native country to escape the pressure, only to find that the media followed her there.

12   How many witnesses will come forward in the future, knowing what kind of treatment awaits them? Do people who accidentally find themselves involved in such high-profile cases have rights, or do we deserve to know everything about them?

---

[3] **tabloid:** popular newspaper with a simple style, many photographs, and sometimes an emphasis on sensational stories

[4] **ABC:** American Broadcasting Companies, Inc.; a major television network in the United States

[5] **President Ford:** Gerald Ford, the 38th President of the United States (1974–1977)

[6] **anonymously:** namelessly, in secret

[7] O. J. Simpson is a famous former football player, actor, and sportscaster who was accused of killing his ex-wife and her friend. His trial was followed closely by the media. He eventually was found "not guilty" in criminal court, but guilty in civil court.

◖ READ FOR MAIN IDEAS

Reading One has four main ideas. What does the reading say about each idea? Circle the sentence that best summarizes the idea.

1. Reporting of facts
   a. Journalists sometimes use their own judgment and leave out certain facts when reporting a story.
   b. Journalists usually report all the facts that they know about a story.

2. Reporting about famous people
   a. In the old days, certain facts about famous people were held back from the public. This is not always true today.
   b. In the old days, certain facts about famous people were held back from the public. This is still the case today.

3. Choosing to report all stories
   a. The decision to report or not report a story is based only on the reporter's judgment.
   b. The decision to report or not report a story is influenced by many factors. The reporter's judgment is just one of these factors.

4. Respecting the right to privacy
   a. All people agree that the public has a right to know about a famous person's life.
   b. Some people believe that you lose the right to privacy when you are famous. Others disagree.

◖ READ FOR DETAILS

Complete the chart with examples or details the author uses to support each main idea.

MAIN IDEA	EXAMPLE OR DETAIL THAT SUPPORTS THE MAIN IDEA
1. Reporting of facts	retired minister
2. Reporting about famous people	
3. Choosing to report all stories	
4. Respecting the right to privacy	

◖ MAKE INFERENCES

Reading One raises questions about one's right to privacy. Read the statements and check (✓) whether you think the author would agree or disagree. Then write the number of the paragraph that supports your answer. (Note that the author does not state her opinion directly, but by reading carefully, you can infer her opinion.) Discuss your answers with a partner.

1. The public has the right to know about the sexual behavior of politicians.

   author agrees _____ author disagrees _____ paragraph _____

2. When a famous person dies, the public has a right to know all the details of the person's life and death.

   author agrees _____ author disagrees _____ paragraph _____

3. The public should know which public figures are unfaithful to their spouses.

   author agrees _____ author disagrees _____ paragraph _____

4. An average person who suddenly becomes the focus of unwanted media attention has no right to privacy.

   author agrees _____ author disagrees _____ paragraph _____

5. It was easier to be a reporter in "the old days."

   author agrees _____ author disagrees _____ paragraph _____

6. In the future, fewer witnesses will want to cooperate with the law.

   author agrees _____ author disagrees _____ paragraph _____

◖ EXPRESS OPINIONS

Discuss the questions with a partner. Then share your answers with the class. (Note that the questions are asked by the author in Reading One.)

1. When a famous person dies, does the public have a right to all the details?

2. Should the public know which public figures are unfaithful to their spouses? Are these things we need to know or just things we want to know?

3. Scrutiny may be the price one pays for fame. But what about relatives of celebrities? Are they fair game too? And what about the average person?

On July 27, 1996, during one of the first evening celebrations held at the Olympics in Atlanta, Georgia, a bomb exploded in Centennial Olympic Park. It killed one person and injured 111 others. Richard Jewell, a security guard at the park who discovered the bomb and helped numerous people to safety, was first considered a hero of the tragic incident. Later he was accused of putting the bomb there. The media then surrounded him and scrutinized his every action—past and present. They left nothing about his personal life untouched. He was later cleared of any suspicions, but his life was never the same. He received some money from lawsuits resulting from the case and worked at other law enforcement jobs. In 2005, another man confessed to the crime, and it was only then that Jewell felt the world knew the truth. Richard Jewell died in 2007 at the age of 44.

1 *Discuss the questions in a small group. Then read the article about Richard Jewell.*

    1. How do you think Richard Jewell's life changed initially after he discovered the bomb?

    2. How do you think Richard Jewell's life changed after he was accused?

    3. How do you think the media's scrutiny affected his daily life?

FOCUS ON BOMB SUSPECT BRINGS TEARS AND A PLEA

By Rick Bragg (from the *New York Times*)

1   Barbara Jewell stared into the unblinking eyes of the television cameras she has come to despise and spoke in tears today of how life had changed for her son, Richard, since he was named a month ago as a suspect in the bombing in Centennial Olympic Park.[1] "Now my son has no real life," said Mrs. Jewell, a little gray-haired woman, speaking out for the first time since her 33-year-old son was suspected—but never arrested or charged—in the bombing that killed one person and injured 111 others.

2   "He is a prisoner in my home," Mrs. Jewell said at a news conference this afternoon. "He cannot work. He cannot know any type of normal life. He can only sit and wait for this nightmare to end."

3   She begged President Clinton to clear her son's name and asked reporters to spread the word that her son was innocent of any wrongdoing in the July 27 bombing. After her tearful request, her son's lawyers said they would file civil lawsuits over reporting on the case.

4   Richard A. Jewell, a security guard in Centennial Olympic Park and a former sheriff's deputy,[2] was at first hailed as a hero for discovering the bomb and helping to clear people from the area. Then news accounts,

---

[1] **Centennial Olympic Park:** a large park and central meeting place located in Atlanta, Georgia, site of the 1996 Summer Olympic Games
[2] **sheriff's deputy:** law officer

including a special edition of the *Atlanta Journal*,[3] named him as a suspect. Since then, television and news executives have repeatedly debated the intense attention focused on Mr. Jewell, with most deciding that too many people knew he was a suspect for his name to be avoided or suppressed.

5   "Last week, a close family friend of twenty-nine years took seriously ill," Mrs. Jewell said. "While he was on his deathbed, because Richard did not want to subject him to the world attention of the media, he did not go see him. Richard was not able to see his friend before he died." Her son did go to the funeral home after his friend died, she said. "When we returned from the funeral home, for the first time I saw my son sobbing," Mrs. Jewell said, breaking into tears herself as she recounted the story. He said, "Mama, everybody was looking."

6   "I do not think any of you can even begin to imagine what our lives are like. Richard is not a murderer," said Mrs. Jewell, an insurance claims coordinator. But, she said, "He has been convicted in the court of public opinion."

7   Meanwhile, the Jewells continue to be besieged by reporters. "They have taken all privacy from us," Mrs. Jewell said. "They have taken all peace. They have rented an apartment which faces our home in order to keep their cameras trained on us around the clock. They watch and photograph everything we do. We wake up to photographers, we go to sleep with photographers. We cannot look out the windows. We cannot walk our dogs without being followed down the sidewalk."

8   Mrs. Jewell said she was not just saddened and hurt by the ordeal, but was also angry.

---

[3] **Atlanta Journal:** a newspaper

2   *Complete the chart with information about how Richard Jewell's life changed after he was named a suspect in the bombing.*

BEFORE THE BOMBING	AFTER THE BOMBING
1. Worked as a security guard	
2. Visited friends	
3. Went out; walked his dogs	
4. Had a private life	

STEP 1: Organize

You have read about three people involved in sensationalized news stories: Oliver Sipple, Rosa Lopez, and Richard Jewell. There are both similarities and differences between them. Use the words and phrases below to complete the chart. Write three things all three people share in the center box. Write two things that make each person different from the other two people on the bold lines. Write one thing that is shared between two people on the dotted lines.

ex-marine	~~security guard~~
hailed as a hero	sexual orientation revealed
hounded by media	stopped working
lost private life	suffered anguish/was very upset
maid	crime suspect
returned to native country	key witness

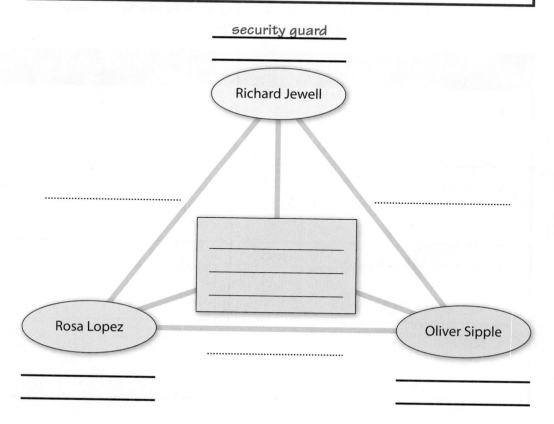

Read the statements and circle whether you agree or disagree. On a separate piece of paper, support your answers with examples from the readings and information from Step 1.

1. The public is better informed today than in the past in part because the media reports on all aspects of the lives of anyone involved in a news story.

   Agree   Disagree

2. The media should spend more time checking all the facts of a story even if it means that it cannot be published as quickly.

   Agree   Disagree

③ FOCUS ON WRITING

Ⓐ VOCABULARY

◀ REVIEW

On October 26, 1996, a U.S. Attorney cleared Richard Jewell in the Centennial Olympic Park bombing. In 2003, a man named Eric Robert Rudolph was arrested in connection with the bombings. He was convicted in 2005.

Read the imaginary letter to a newspaper from Barbara Jewell, Richard's mother, written after he was cleared of all charges in 1996. Complete the letter using the words below.

allegations	besieged	legitimate	scrutiny
anguish	judgment	~~perspective~~	suppose
beg	justified	relevant	suspect

To the Editor:

   Sensationalist reporting is very harmful and has no place in our society. I feel

strongly about this because my family has been adversely affected by the media's

sensationalism. I realize that it is the media's responsibility to supply its audience with

some ___perspective___. However, reporting unconfirmed _____ is not
　　　　　　1.　　　　　　　　　　　　　　　　　　　　　　　　　　2.

acceptable. There is no _____ reason to report facts that cannot be verified.
　　　　　　　　　　　　3.

(continued on next page)

My son, Richard Jewell, was initially considered a hero for helping people to safety after the Centennial Olympic Park bombing. Later, the police believed that he was responsible for the bombing and considered him a _____. He has recently

_{4.}

been cleared of any suspicion by the U.S. Attorney, yet the media's reporting has changed our lives forever. Our family has been _____ by reporters around

_{5.}

the clock. We have been under intense _____; now everything we do is

_{6.}

reported. Nevertheless, some of what has been published about Richard is not even

_____ as it is not related to the bombing. The media's reporting has also

_{7.}

caused Richard considerable _____. He is always sad and upset. Because

_{8.}

of his state of mind, I have gone so far as to _____ reporters to keep my

_{9.}

son's name out of their news coverage, until the U.S. Attorney settled the case, but nothing changed.

Is this type of sensationalist news ever _____? I don't think so; there is

_{10.}

no reason for it. Reporters, you need to use better _____ when deciding

_{11.}

what to publish. You need to think about consequences of what you write.

_____ you were Richard, would you approve of the way this story had been

_{12.}

reported? And wouldn't you demand a formal apology and the right to a private life?

Barbara Jewell

◖ **EXPAND**

An **idiom** is a group of words that have a special meaning that is very different from the ordinary meaning of the separate words. Look at item 1. The word *hunger* on its own usually means "a feeling that you want to eat." But *have an endless hunger for* means "have a continual need for something."

1 *Work in a small group. Read the sentences and circle the best explanation for each underlined idiom.*

1. Now, at least in part because the public seems to <u>have an endless hunger for</u> it, reporters sometimes cover these aspects of celebrities' lives more than any other.

    a. need to constantly eat
    b. have continual need for something
    c. dislike something immensely

2. In the old days, reporters <u>kept</u> some allegations and speculation about politicians and movie stars <u>to themselves</u>.

    a. didn't talk about something
    b. made a promise
    c. cared for oneself

3. Some stories receive such wide visibility that to ignore them is to "<u>play ostrich</u> man," says Shelby Coffey, editor of the *Los Angeles Times*. "You have to give your readers some perspective on the information they are getting."

    a. wear a special bird costume
    b. try to find the truth in something
    c. ignore something that is obvious

4. Scrutiny may be <u>the price one pays</u> for fame.

    a. suffering for your actions
    b. buying something you can't afford
    c. paying too much money for something

5. But what about relatives of celebrities? Are they <u>fair game</u>, too?

    a. victims of sensational writing
    b. someone that you can attack or criticize
    c. a game that is played at a fair or festival

6. She begged President Clinton to <u>clear her son's name</u> and asked reporters to spread the word that her son was innocent of any wrongdoing.

    a. erase his name
    b. declare him innocent
    c. talk to him

7. She begged President Clinton to clear her son's name and asked reporters to <u>spread the word</u> that her son was innocent of any wrongdoing.

    a. hide the fact
    b. stop reporting
    c. tell everyone

8. Even though Richard Jewell's friend was <u>on his deathbed</u>, Richard didn't visit him.

    a. in the bed you have chosen to die in
    b. extremely sick, dying
    c. in a very deep sleep

9. "Richard is not a murderer," said Mrs. Jewell . . . But . . . "he has been <u>convicted in the court of public opinion</u>."
   a. considered guilty by everyone before going to trial
   b. in a special trial in which you are found guilty
   c. forced to take part in a trial as a member of the jury

10. Reporters watched the Jewell family <u>around the clock</u>. They besieged their house.
   a. from sunrise to sunset
   b. twenty-four hours a day
   c. during the night

2 *Work in a small group or with a partner. Decide which person could have made the statements below. Write the correct letter next to each statement. In some cases, more than one person could have made the statement.*

a. Gennifer Flowers, woman alleged to have had an affair with President Clinton

b. Reporter of the minister story

c. Shelby Coffey, editor of the *Los Angeles Times*

d. Peter Jennings, ABC News anchor

e. Rosa Lopez, key witness in the O. J. Simpson trial

f. Richard Jewell, man accused of the Olympic Park bombing

_____ 1. The public seems to have an endless hunger for news, and it is our responsibility to provide valid information to the readers so they have the perspective to form their own opinions.

_____ 2. I want the public to know about my life; if the president wants to keep his private life to himself, that's his business.

_____ 3. The media can ruin your life. Reporters have no right to invade my privacy by hounding me around the clock.

_____ 4. Even though there are some stories I would rather not report, I can't play ostrich man all the time.

_____ 5. I'm glad I waited to report all the facts, because some of them were not relevant and might have been misinterpreted. I don't want anyone to be wrongly convicted in the court of public opinion.

_____ 6. Just because I'm a small part of a news story does not mean that unrelated parts of my life are fair game for reporters to write about. I'm not even a suspect.

Imagine you have seen a reporter interviewed on a television news show and are upset by his comments. On a separate piece of paper, write a response to the reporter. Use at least five of the idioms and/or vocabulary words in the box.

"I know everyone thinks reporters are sensationalist and responsible for ruining people's lives. However, if we don't report everything, and quickly, someone else will. Then my boss will want to know why our paper didn't get the story. In fact, I could lose my job!"

anguish	justify
around the clock	keep something to oneself
be convicted in the court of public opinion	legitimate
be hounded	pay the price
fair game	relevant
have an endless hunger for	scrutiny
judgment	speculation

B GRAMMAR: Passive Voice

1 *Examine the pairs of sentences and answer the questions with a partner.*

Active Voice
- A hitchhiker had killed the minister.
- Cameras and reporters hounded Rosa Lopez everywhere she went.
- At first, people hailed Richard Jewell as a hero.

Passive Voice
- The minister had been killed by a hitchhiker.
- Rosa Lopez was hounded by cameras and reporters everywhere she went.
- At first, Richard Jewell was hailed as a hero (by people).

1. The sentences in each pair have a different grammar structure, but the same meaning. The grammar structure in the active sentences is **subject** + **verb** (+ **object**). What is the grammar structure in the passive sentences?

2. Circle the words in the subject position in the active sentences.

3. Circle the words in the subject position in the passive sentences.

4. The difference in subject between an active and a passive sentence shows a change in the focus of the sentence. In the examples above, the active sentences seem to focus on *a hitchhiker, cameras and reporters,* and *people.* The subject performs the action. What seems to be the focus of the passive sentences? Do the words in the subject position perform the action?

1. To form the **passive voice,** use a form of *be* + **past participle**. When the person or thing (the agent) responsible for doing the action is used, use *by* + **the agent**:

Subject Position	Be	Past Participle	(By + Agent)
Rosa Lopez	**is**	**hounded**	**by** cameras and reporters.
Rosa Lopez	**was**	**hounded**	**by** cameras and reporters.
Rosa Lopez	**has been**	**hounded**	**by** cameras and reporters.

2. **Active sentences** focus on the person or thing that performs an action. **Passive sentences** focus on the person or thing that receives or is the result of an action. The meaning of passive and active sentences is usually similar, but the focus changes.

Active	Passive
A hitchhiker had killed the minister.	The minister had been killed by a hitchhiker.
(The hitchhiker is the focus of the sentence.)	(The minister is the focus of the sentence.)

3. Use the passive voice **without an agent** (the person or thing performing the action) when:

a. the agent is unknown or unimportant

"The minister's body **was** later **found.**"
(You don't know who found the body; it doesn't matter who found the body. What is important is that someone found the body.)

b. the agent is understood from the context

"It **was made clear** to Peter Jennings that he had to go with the story."
(It is understood that a superior, probably his boss, made it clear to him.)

c. you want to avoid mentioning the agent

"The FBI said the Richard Jewell investigation **was carried out** incorrectly."
(The FBI does not want to name exactly who in the FBI made mistakes during the investigation.)

4. Use the passive voice **with an agent** (*by* + **noun**) when:

a. you want to make the receiver of the action more important than the one who performs the action

"Lopez **was hounded** by cameras and reporters everywhere she went."
(Lopez is the focus of the sentence. She is more important than the cameras and reporters.)

b. the information is necessary to complete the meaning, or when it is new or surprising information

"Focus on Bomb Suspect Brings Tears and a Plea" **was written** by Rick Bragg.

2 *Complete the sentences. Use the active or passive voice in the past.*

1. The news columnist ___reported___ on all aspects of Oliver Sipple's life, not
   (report)
   only those related to his act of heroism.

2. The Gennifer Flowers story _____ on all the major TV networks.
   (broadcast)

3. Some of the interest in the lives of politicians _____ on the basis
   (justify)
   that character affects how people perform their jobs.

4. The retired minister _____ from his fishing trip.
   (not return)

5. A half-eaten ham sandwich, a gun, fishing tackle, and a magazine

   _____ in the minister's car.
   (find)

6. The reporter who wrote the story about the minister _____ to
   (decide)
   mention the gun and the sandwich, but not the magazine.

7. The reporter's story _____ by many people, including the
   (read)
   minister's relatives.

8. Sara Jane Moore _____ a gun at President Ford.
   (point)

9. The shot _____ when Oliver W. Sipple knocked her hand.
   (deflect)

10. Witnesses _____ about the shooting by the police.
    (question)

3 *Complete the sentences. Use the passive voice in the past. Include the agent only if it is necessary information.*

1. The local police force worked hard. The investigation _____ in
   (complete / police)
   less than 72 hours.

2. Richard Jewell _____ about where he saw the package containing
   (interview / FBI)
   the bomb and why he suspected that it contained a bomb.

3. The news was interrupted to report that the president _____.
   (shoot / an assassin)

4. Richard Jewell's mother felt Richard _____ before he even went
  (convict / media)

  to trial.

5. The celebrity _____ today at 5:00 P.M.
  (marry / a minister)

6. The newspaper story, which _____, talks about the responsibility
  (write / Peter Jennings)

  of the media in reporting the news.

7. The defendant, a news reporter, _____ of character defamation
  (find guilty / a jury)

  after a three-week-long jury trial.

C WRITING

In this unit, you read about how the media can manipulate and sensationalize the news.

You are going to **write a summary paragraph about a current or past news story and how it was sensationalized.***

◖ **PREPARE TO WRITE: Group Brainstorming**

Group brainstorming is a good way to get ideas for writing. In brainstorming, you think of as many ideas as you can. Don't think about whether the ideas are good or bad.

In small groups or as a class, complete the brainstorming activity.

1. Brainstorm news stories that have been sensationalized. The stories can be from any media source: print, television, radio, or the Internet. Don't stop to discuss the stories. Just concentrate on thinking of as many as possible.

Sensationalized News Stories

_____

_____

_____

_____

_____

_____

*For Alternative Writing Topics, see page 24. These topics can be used in place of the writing topic for this unit or as homework. The alternative topics relate to the theme of the unit, but may not target the same grammar or rhetorical structures taught in the unit.

2. Individually, choose one story that you find interesting and want to write about. Make sure you know enough about the news story to include specific details. Write the subject of your news story on a piece of paper.

(WRITE: A Summary Paragraph

A **paragraph** is a group of sentences that are related and support a controlling idea. A **summary paragraph** identifies and extracts the main idea from a text, leaving out less important details. All paragraphs have a **topic sentence** and a **controlling idea**.

TOPIC SENTENCE

The **topic sentence** is an essential part of all well-written paragraphs. The topic sentence controls the content of the rest of the paragraph. This control helps the writer focus on supporting ideas in the paragraph that are directly related to the topic sentence. The first step in writing a topic sentence is to choose a topic and find a point of view or **main idea** about it.

Topic	Main Idea
news	News is everywhere.
television	Television is a bad influence.
reading	Reading is good for you.

CONTROLLING IDEA

The next step is to narrow the main idea even more by finding a **controlling idea**. The controlling idea is the idea you want to explain, illustrate, or describe in the paragraph. It makes a specific statement about a topic. The controlling ideas in the topic sentences below are underlined.

Main Idea	Main Idea + Controlling Idea = Topic Sentence
news is everywhere	News is everywhere and <u>serves many different functions</u>.
television is a bad influence	Television has a <u>violent influence on children</u>.
reading is good for you	Reading <u>expands your mind and broadens your interests</u>.

1 *Examine the paragraph and discuss the questions on the next page with the class.*

News is everywhere and serves many different functions. The news gives instant coverage of important events. News also provides facts and information. On the other hand, news is sometimes manipulated by the government as a way to control a population. In addition, in many countries, news is business—a way to make money by selling advertising and/or newspapers and magazines. However you define news, it is all around us. You can't escape it. Every day we are bombarded by information from newspapers, magazines, television, radio, and the Internet.

1. What is the topic of this paragraph? _____

2. The first sentence is the topic sentence. What two ideas are presented in this sentence? _____

3. How does the content of the rest of the paragraph relate to the topic sentence?

   _____

   _____

2 *Each of the paragraphs is missing a topic sentence. Circle the topic sentence that best fits the paragraph. Discuss your answers with a partner.*

1.   For example, you can't pick up a newspaper these days without reading about some outrageous crime. The top television news story is usually about a murder or other violent incident. We need to read and hear about the good news stories, too. Otherwise, we will continue sending the message that only violence is worth reporting. What kind of message is that for our children?

   a. Our society is becoming more and more violent every day.
   b. Television news coverage focuses only on violent news.
   c. All of the media have become increasingly negative by focusing only on violence.

2.   As a result of live television, people can receive news as it happens. For example, during the September 11 attack on the World Trade Center in New York City, CNN viewers could see the second plane hit as the news was covering the first plane's attack. Because of "live" reporting, people feel as though they are participating in history, not just reading or hearing about it afterwards. It has changed the viewer's role completely.

   a. These days, there is more live television coverage than ever before.
   b. "Live" television reporting has changed the way we see the news.
   c. CNN changed the way we saw the news during the September 11 attacks.

3.   Experts recommend limiting viewing to one hour per day during the week and up to two hours per day on weekends. The programs should be educational and promote discussion between the parent and child. Programs on animal behavior and family values, and programs that teach basic learning skills, are highly recommended.

   a. Watching television is not bad for children and it's fine for teenagers and adults, too.
   b. Watching television is fine for children as long as you limit the hours and monitor the programs.
   c. Programs for children should be educational in content so that the time spent watching TV is not wasted.

4. What we see on the nightly news has been carefully selected by the news department at the television station. Because the station is interested in making money, the news that is selected is not necessarily the most important news but rather the news that will attract the most viewers. As a result, we may not be getting the full story.

    a. It is very important that the news make money.

    b. The news director selects the news with the help of reporters.

    c. News is not simply what we see, but what the news director at the television station wants us to see.

3 *Read the paragraphs. The underlined topic sentences are incomplete because they do not have a controlling idea. Rewrite each topic sentence, using a topic and a controlling idea.*

1. <u>Celebrities have jobs.</u> Being a movie star or sports star is their job. It is what they are good at. They should not be under the continual scrutiny of the media just because of their profession. They have a right to a private life just like you and I do.

    Rewrite: *Celebrities deserve private lives like any other person.*

2. <u>News is different.</u> In the old days, people got their news by word of mouth. As society became more literate and printing costs decreased, newspapers became more common. Radio then brought a sense of immediacy to the news, and later, television added the visual impact. Now of course, the Internet gives up-to-the-second news about any news event any time we want it. Who knows what the news medium of the future will be?

    Rewrite: _____

3. <u>Politicians are public figures.</u> As a president, one is supposed to represent the qualities of honesty and integrity. Remaining faithful to your husband or wife is the purest example of these qualities. If a president is unfaithful, how can we trust that he or she is honest in handling presidential duties? Therefore, the media have the responsibility to inform us when a public figure is unfaithful.

    Rewrite: _____

4. <u>Reading is hard.</u> As with any program of exercise, you have to discipline yourself and make reading the newspaper a part of your everyday routine. And just as exercise makes your body stronger, reading makes your mind stronger. It broadens your interests, gives you the ability to think critically about important issues, and enables you to participate in interesting conversations. In conclusion, reading the paper, like any exercise, is time well spent.

    Rewrite: _____

4 Now write the first draft of your summary paragraph. Use the information from Prepare to Write and complete the organizer below to plan your paragraph. Make sure you have a clear topic sentence and content that supports it. The topic sentence should state your opinion about how the event was sensationalized. Be sure to use grammar and vocabulary from the unit.

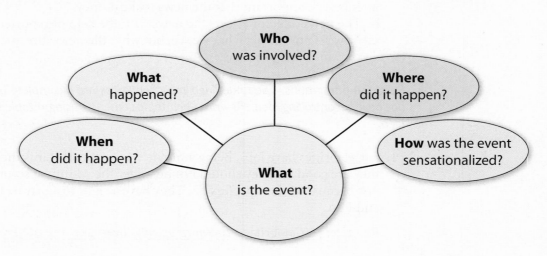

◖ REVISE: Using Time Transitions

Transitions are words and phrases that signal connections among ideas. **Time transitions** are often used to begin supporting sentences to help the reader follow the progression of examples, details, and ideas. When writing about or retelling a past event, time transitions are used to make clear what happened in the beginning, middle, and end of the event. Some of these transitions are listed here. Note that time transitions are usually not used in a topic sentence.

BEGINNING ➜	MIDDLE ➜	END
At first	Then	Finally
Initially	Next	In the end
In the beginning	Before	Lastly
First	After	Eventually
	Later	
	Subsequently	
	Some time later	
	Afterwards	

1 *Complete the paragraph with transitions from the list on page 22. Note that sometimes more than one transition could be correct.*

The news media was relentless and unfeeling in the way they covered the Centennial Olympic Park bombing case in 1996. _____, Richard

          1.
Jewell was hailed as a hero for having helped many people in Centennial Olympic Park to safety. _____, he was questioned by the police although he

       2.
was never officially named as a suspect. The media _____

               3.
surrounded him and his every action—past and present—was scrutinized, although much of what was reported was not even relevant to the case.

_____ he was considered a suspect, he had been able to have a

    4.
normal life. For example, he could walk his dog or visit friends without being hounded by the media. _____ the intense media coverage, he could

        5.
do none of those things anymore; he and his family were besieged by reporters. Despite the police's attempts to link him to the crime, he was _____

                  6.
cleared of any suspicions, but sadly his life had been changed forever.

_____, in 2003, a man named Eric Robert Rudolph was arrested in

    7.
connection with the bombings. Rudolph was convicted in 2005.

2 *Look at your first draft. Make sure you have effective time transitions.*

◖ EDIT: Writing the Final Draft

Write your final draft. Carefully edit it for grammatical problems and mechanical errors, such as spelling, capitalization, and punctuation. Make sure you used some of the vocabulary and grammar from the unit. Use the checklist to help you write your final draft. Then neatly write or type your paragraph.

✓ FINAL DRAFT CHECKLIST

- ○ Does the paragraph fully describe a sensationalized event?
- ○ Is there a topic sentence stating your opinion about the news story that was reported?
- ○ Are the time transitions used correctly?
- ○ Is the passive voice used correctly?
- ○ Has vocabulary from the unit been used?

ALTERNATIVE WRITING TOPICS

Choose one of the topics. Write a paragraph using the vocabulary and grammar from the unit.

1. Does sensational news ever have a place in our society? If yes, describe when and in what place. If no, explain why not. Be specific, and explain why you feel the way you do.

2. In Reading One, the author asks, "How many witnesses will come forward in the future (in high-profile cases), knowing what kind of treatment awaits them? Do people who accidentally find themselves involved in such high-profile cases have rights, or do we deserve to know everything about them?" What do you think? Be specific, and explain why you feel the way you do.

RESEARCH TOPICS, see page 259.

UNIT 2 Dreams Never Die

① FOCUS ON THE TOPIC

A | PREDICT

Helen Keller was born in 1880. After an illness at age two, she completely lost her ability to see and hear. Despite this loss, Helen graduated with high honors from Radcliffe College (at the time, the women's division of Harvard University). She later became a great writer and political activist.

Look at the photograph of Helen Keller and the unit title. Read the quotation. Then discuss the questions with a partner.

"Although the world is full of suffering, it is also full of overcoming it."

—Helen Keller

1. There are many different types of suffering: Physical and economic are two examples. What are some other examples of ways that people suffer?

2. What are some ways that people overcome their suffering?

3. Do you believe that "dreams never die"? What do you think the unit will be about?

1 *Match the people with the obstacles they have overcome. Then answer the questions with a partner.*

a. **Anne Frank**

b. **Lance Armstrong**

c. **Walt Disney**

d. **Amelia Earhart**

_____ 1. At age 22, this person was so poor that he "slept on cushions from an old sofa and ate cold beans out of a can." He was also fired by a newspaper editor for having no imagination.

_____ 2. This person was the first woman to fly across the Atlantic. She faced two obstacles: prejudice and lack of money.

_____ 3. This person spent over two years hiding from Nazi soldiers in an attic with her family during World War II. The diary she wrote while hiding has become one of the most widely read books in the world.

_____ 4. This person is a famous athlete who overcame cancer and went on to break sports records around the world. He also started a foundation to help people who suffer from cancer.

2 *There are many different types of obstacles. For example, being deaf is a physical obstacle. What type of obstacle did each of the people above overcome?*

3 *Can you think of other famous people who have overcome obstacles?*

1 *Read the passage on the next page about author Frank McCourt. Try to understand the boldfaced words from the context.*

Frank McCourt was born in Brooklyn, New York, in 1930. His parents, Angela and Malachy, had moved to New York from Ireland in search of a better life. Unfortunately, life was not easy in New York. His father could not earn enough money to support his family. The McCourts returned to Ireland hoping their life would improve. Again, it didn't. Life in Ireland was equally hard if not harder than in New York. Three of Frank's siblings died as babies. Eventually, his father's **abandonment** of the family forced his four sons and Angela to live a very **meager** existence.

Frank's childhood was filled with **misery**. There was never enough food. Their house was small, dirty, and very cold in the winter. When it rained, the floor would flood with water. Frank and his brothers **yearned for** a better life.

Frank did, however, have ways to escape from his **tormented** childhood. He loved to read, and because his **dilapidated** house had no electricity, he would read under the street lamp outside his home. He also had an excellent sense of humor. Humor was the McCourts' defense against their life of relentless **poverty** and **hopelessness**. Even in the worst of times, the McCourts could find something to laugh about.

In 1949, Frank returned to the United States. He was 19 years old and only had an eighth-grade education. He was full of **shame** about his past and often invented stories about his **sordid** childhood instead of telling the truth. However, Frank was never **defeated** by his obstacles; in fact, Frank eventually used his humor and his storytelling talents to overcome the challenges life had set before him.

2 *Answer the questions with a partner.*

1. Frank had a hard life growing up. What were some of the obstacles or challenges he had to overcome?

2. What did Frank enjoy doing as a child?

3. Why did Frank reinvent his past when he came to America?

3 *Find the boldfaced words in the reading passage above. Write each word next to its synonym.*

1. ___misery___ sadness

2. _____ poor, sparse

3. _____ embarrassment

4. _____ beaten, overcome by

5. _____ strongly desired, wanted

6. _____ painful

7. _____ immoral, dishonest

8. _____ having little money or few material things

9. _____ leaving someone behind

10. _____ being without hope

11. _____ falling apart, in terrible condition

A READING ONE: The Education of Frank McCourt

Read the first two paragraphs of The Education of Frank McCourt. *Work with a partner to answer the questions. Then read the rest of the article.*

1. Where is Frank McCourt now?

2. What do you think he means by "They gave me so much more than I gave them?"

3. What do you think happened to Frank between 1949 and 1997?

THE EDUCATION OF FRANK McCOURT

By Barbara Sande Dimmitt
(from *Reader's Digest*)

1 Frank McCourt sat on a stage in New York City's Lincoln Center, his white hair glistening under the lights overhead. He was still boyish of expression at 66, and smile lines radiated from hazel eyes bright with inquisitiveness. Soon he would be addressing the 1997 graduating class of Stuyvesant High School, where he had taught English for 18 years.

2 He let his mind wander as he gazed out at the great hall. *I've learned so much from kids like these,* he thought. *They gave me much more than I gave them.*

3 "Yo, Teach!" a voice boomed. Frank McCourt scanned the adolescents in his classroom. It was the fall of 1970 and his first week of teaching at Seward Park High School, which sat in the midst of **dilapidated** tenement buildings on Manhattan's Lower East Side. McCourt located the speaker and nodded. "You talk funny," the student said, "Where ya from?"

4 "Ireland," McCourt replied. With more than ten years of teaching experience under his belt, this kind of interrogation[1] no longer surprised him. But one question in particular still made him squirm[2] "Where'd you go to high school?" someone else asked.

5 If I tell them the truth, they'll feel superior to me, McCourt thought. They'll throw it in my face. Most of all, he feared an accusation he'd heard before—from himself: You come from nothing, so you are nothing.

6 But McCourt's heart whispered another possibility: Maybe these kids are **yearning for** a way of figuring out this new teacher. Am I willing to risk being humiliated in the classroom to find out?

---

[1] **interrogation**: intense questioning
[2] **squirm**: feel embarrassed or ashamed

7   "Come on, tell us! Where'd you go to high school?"

8   "I never did," McCourt replied.

9   "Did you get thrown out?"

10   I was right, the teacher thought. They're curious. McCourt explained he'd left school after the eighth grade to take a job.

11   "How'd you get to be a teacher, then?" they asked. "When I came to America," he began, "I dreamed bigger dreams. I loved reading and writing, and teaching was the most exalted profession I could imagine. I was unloading sides of beef[3] down on the docks when I decided enough was enough. By then I'd done a lot of reading on my own, so I persuaded New York University to enroll me."

12   McCourt wasn't surprised that this story fascinated his students. Theirs wasn't the kind of **poverty** McCourt had known; they had electricity and food. But he recognized the telltale signs of need in some of his students' threadbare[4] clothes, and sensed the bitter **shame** and **hopelessness** he knew all too well. If recounting his own experiences would jolt these kids out of their defeatism so he could teach them something, that's what he would do.

13   A born storyteller, McCourt drew from a repertoire of accounts about his youth. His students would listen, spellbound[5] by the gritty details, drawn by something more powerful than curiosity. He'd look from face to face, recognizing a bit of himself in each sober gaze.

14   Since humor had been the McCourts' weapon against life's **miseries** in Limerick, he used it to describe those days. "Dinner usually was bread and tea," he told the students. "Mam[6] used to say, 'We've got our balanced diet: a solid and a liquid. What more could we want?'"

15   The students roared with laughter.

16   He realized that his honesty was helping forge a link with kids who normally regarded teachers as adversaries. At the same time, the more he talked about his past, the better he understood how it affected him.

17   (While at college), a creative-writing professor had asked him to describe an object from his childhood. McCourt chose the decrepit bed he and his brothers had shared. He wrote of their being scratched by the stiff stuffing protruding from the mattress and of ending up jumbled together in the sagging center with fleas[7] leaping all over their bodies. The professor gave McCourt an A, and asked him to read the essay to the class.

18   "No!" McCourt said, recoiling at the thought. But for the first time, he began to see his **sordid** childhood, with all the miseries, betrayals and longings that **tormented** him still, as a worthy topic. *Maybe that's what I was born to put on the page,*[8] he thought.

19   While teaching, McCourt wrote occasional articles for newspapers and magazines. But his major effort, a memoir of 150 pages that he churned out in 1966, remained unfinished. Now he leafed through his students' transcribed essays. They lacked polish, but somehow they worked in a way his writing didn't. I'm trying to teach these kids to write, he thought, yet I haven't found the secret myself.

20   The bell rang in the faculty lounge at Stuyvesant High School in Manhattan. When McCourt began teaching at the prestigious[9] public high school in 1972, he joked that he'd finally made it to paradise. Some 13,000 students sought admission each year, competing for approximately 700 vacancies. Part of the fun of working with these bright students was keeping them a few degrees off-balance. McCourt asked at the beginning

---

[3] **sides of beef:** very large pieces of meat

[4] **threadbare:** very thin from being used a lot

[5] **spellbound:** very interested in something you are listening to

[6] **Mam:** a word for *mother*

[7] **fleas:** tiny insects that bite

[8] **put on the page:** to write

[9] **prestigious:** admired or respected as one of the best or most important

(continued on next page)

of a creative writing class, "What did you have for dinner last night?" The students stared at him as if he'd lost his wits.

21   "Why am I asking this? Because you need to become good observers of detail if you're going to write well." As answers trickled in, McCourt countered with more questions. "Where did you eat?" "Who else was there?" "Who cleaned up afterward?"

22   Student after student revealed families fragmented by divorce and loneliness. "We always argue at the table." "We don't eat together." As he listened, McCourt mentally catalogued the differences and similarities between his early life and theirs. He began to appreciate more the companionship that enriched the **meager** meals his mother had struggled to put on the table.

23   That night McCourt lay awake in bed, harvesting the bounty of his chronic insomnia.[10] He visualized himself standing on a street in Limerick, and took an imaginary walk about. He looked at shops and pubs, noting their names, and peered through their windows. He read street signs and recognized people walking past. Oblivious to time, he wandered the Limerick of his mind, collecting the details of scenery and a cast for the book that festered inside him.

24   Yet when he later picked up a notebook and tried to set down the previous night's travels, he stopped. McCourt knew that he was still holding back. Before, he had done it out of respect for his mother, who would have been mortified to see the darkest and most searing episodes of his childhood in print.[11] But she had died in 1981, and with her had died his excuse.

25   At least the bits and pieces that bubbled into his consciousness enlivened the stories he told in class. "Everyone has a story to tell," he said. "Write about what you know with conviction, from the heart. Dig deep," he urged. "Find your own voice and dance your own dance!"

26   On Fridays the students read their compositions aloud. To draw them out, McCourt would read excerpts from his duffel bag full of notebooks. "You had such an interesting childhood, Mr. McCourt," they said. "Why don't you write a book?" They threw his own words back at him: "It sounds like there's more to that story; dig deeper . . ."

27   McCourt was past 50 and painfully aware of the passage of time. But despite his growing frustration at his unfinished book, he never tired of his students' work.

28   These young people have been giving you lessons in courage, he thought. When will you dare as mightily as they?

29   It was October 1994. Frank McCourt, now retired, sat down and read his book's new opening, which he had written a few days before and still found satisfying. But many blank pages lay before him. *What if I never get it right?* he wondered grimly.

30   He stared at the logs glowing in the fireplace and could almost hear students' voices from years past, some angry, some **defeated**, others confused and seeking guidance. "It's no good, Mr. McCourt. I don't have what it takes."

31   Then Frank McCourt, author, heard the steadying tones of Frank McCourt, teacher: Of course you do. Dig deeper. Find your own voice and dance your own dance.

32   He scribbled a few lines. "I'm in a playground on Classon Avenue in Brooklyn with my brother Malachy. He's two, I'm three. We're on the seesaw." In the innocent voice of an unprotected child who could neither comprehend nor control the world around him, Frank McCourt told his tale of poverty and **abandonment**.

33   In September 1996 *Angela's Ashes* hit bookstores. Within weeks McCourt received an excited call from his agent: His book was getting warm reviews and selling at an unbelievable rate. The most surprising call came on April 7, 1997, when McCourt learned

---

[10] **insomnia:** sleeplessness
[11] **in print:** in a book, newspaper, or magazine

that *Angela's Ashes* had received America's most coveted literary award: the Pulitzer Prize.

34   McCourt laid his hands on the lectern, finishing his commencement address[12] at Lincoln Center. "Early in my teaching days, the kids asked me the meaning of a poem," he said. "I replied, 'I don't know any more than you do. I have ideas. What are your ideas?' I realized then that we're all in the same boat. What does anybody know?

35   "So when you go forth tonight, fellow students—for I'm still one of you—remember that you know nothing! Be excited that your whole life is before you for learning."

36   As he gave them a crooked smile, the students leapt to their feet, waving and whistling. This is too much, he thought, startled by the intensity of their response. During months of speeches and book signings, he had received many accolades.[13] But this—this left him fighting back tears. It's the culmination of everything, coming from them.

37   Their standing ovation continued long after Frank McCourt, the teacher who had learned his own lessons slowly but well, returned to his seat.

---

[12] **commencement address:** speech given at a graduation
[13] **accolades:** praise and approval for someone's work

◖ **READ FOR MAIN IDEAS**

Complete the timeline with information from Background and Vocabulary on pages 26–27 and Reading One.

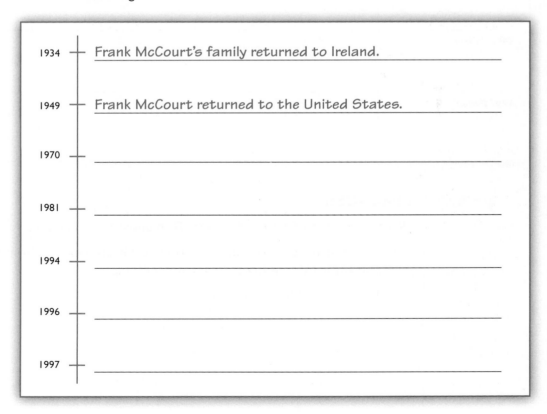

1934   Frank McCourt's family returned to Ireland.

1949   Frank McCourt returned to the United States.

1970   _____

1981   _____

1994   _____

1996   _____

1997   _____

Complete the left side of the chart using information from Read for Main Ideas on page 31. Then complete the right side of the chart with details about why the event took place and what happened as a result. Look at Background and Vocabulary on pages 26–27 and Reading One for the information.

1934 Event: Frank McCourt's family returned to Ireland.	The McCourts wanted a better life, so they returned to Ireland. Their life was still very hard. Three children died. The family remained very poor and very hungry.
1949 Event:	
1970 Event:	
1981 Event:	
1994 Event:	
1996 Event:	
1997 Event:	

◖ **MAKE INFERENCES**

Read the excerpts from Reading One. Then answer the questions.

1. "Most of all, he feared an accusation he'd heard before—from himself: You come from nothing, so you are nothing."

   What does he mean by *nothing*?

   _____

   _____

2. "His students would listen, spellbound by the gritty details, drawn by something more powerful than curiosity. He'd look from face to face, recognizing a bit of himself in each sober gaze."

What *bit of himself* does he recognize?

_____

_____

3. "He realized that his honesty was helping forge a link with kids who normally regarded teachers as adversaries. At the same time, the more he talked about his past, the better he understood how it affected him."

How do you think McCourt dealt with his past prior to working with this class?

_____

_____

4. "Write about what you know with conviction, from the heart. Dig deep," he urged. "Find your own voice and dance your own dance!"

What does he mean by *dance your own dance*?

_____

_____

5. "These young people have been giving you lessons in courage, he thought. When will you dare as mightily as they?"

What is McCourt suggesting about his current life here?

_____

_____

◖ **EXPRESS OPINIONS**

Discuss the questions with a partner. Then share your answers with the class.

1. What do you think was Frank McCourt's greatest obstacle? How did he overcome it?

2. How did Frank McCourt's students give him the courage he had been lacking to overcome his obstacles?

Diane Schuur is an accomplished jazz musician who is blind. She compares her struggles and triumphs with those of Helen Keller, the famous writer and political activist who was not only blind, but deaf as well.

1 *Discuss the questions with a partner. Then read the article by Diane Schuur.*

　1. What do you think the title, "She [Helen Keller] altered our perception of the disabled and remapped the boundaries of sight and sense" means?

　2. How do you think Diane Schuur "remapped" her boundaries?

THE MIRACLE:
She altered our perception of the disabled and remapped the boundaries of sight and sense.

By Diane Schuur (from *Time*)

Diane Schuur

1　Helen Keller was less than two years old when she came down with a fever. It struck dramatically and left her unconscious. The fever went just as suddenly. But she was blinded and, very soon after, deaf. As she grew up, she managed to learn to do tiny errands, but she also realized that she was missing something. "Sometimes," she later wrote, "I stood between two persons who were conversing and touched their lips. I could not understand, and was vexed. I moved my lips and gesticulated[1] frantically without result. This made me so angry at times that I kicked and screamed until I was exhausted." She was a wild child.

2　I can understand her rage. I was born two months prematurely and was placed in an incubator. The practice at the time was to pump a large amount of oxygen into the incubator, something doctors have since learned to be extremely cautious about. But as a result, I lost my sight. I was sent to a state school for the blind, but I flunked first grade because Braille[2] just didn't make any sense to me. Words were a weird concept. I remember being hit and slapped. And you act all that in. All rage is anger that is acted in, bottled in for so long that it just pops out. Helen had it harder. She was both blind and deaf. But, oh, the transformation that came over her when she discovered that words were related to things! It's like the lyrics of that song: "On a clear day, rise and look around you, and you'll see who you are."

3　I can say the word *see*. I can speak the language of the sighted. That's part of the first great achievement of Helen Keller. She proved how language could liberate the blind and the

---

[1] **gesticulated:** motioned
[2] **Braille:** a form of printing with raised round marks that blind people can read by touching

deaf. She wrote, "Literature is my utopia. Here I am not disenfranchised."[3] But how she struggled to master language. In her book *Midstream*, she wrote about how she was frustrated by the alphabet, by the language of the deaf, even with the speed with which her teacher spelled things out for her on her palm. She was impatient and hungry for words, and her teacher's scribbling on her hand would never be as fast, she thought, as the people who could read the words with their eyes. I remember how books got me going after I finally grasped Braille. Being in that school was like being in an orphanage. But words—and in my case, music—changed that isolation. With language, Keller, who could not hear and could not see, proved she could communicate in the world of sight and sound—and was able to speak to it and live in it. I am a beneficiary of her work. Because of her example, the world has given way a little. In my case, I was able to go from the state school for the blind to regular public school from the age of 11 until my senior year in high school. And then I decided on my own to go back into the school for the blind. Now I sing jazz.

4   I hate the word handicapped. Keller would too. We are people with inconveniences. We're not charity cases. Her main message was and is, "We're like everybody else. We're here to be able to live a life as full as any sighted person's. And it's OK to be ourselves."

5   That means we have the freedom to be as extraordinary as the sighted. Keller loved an audience and wrote that she adored "the warm tide of human life pulsing round and round me." That's why the stage appealed to her, why she learned to speak and to deliver speeches. And to feel the vibrations of music, of the radio, of the movement of lips. You must understand that even more than sighted people, we need to be touched. When you look at a person, eye to eye, I imagine it's like touching them. We don't have that convenience. But when I perform, I get that experience from a crowd. Helen Keller must have as well. She was our first star. And I am very grateful to her.

Source: © 1999 Time Inc. Reprinted by permission.

---

[3] **disenfranchised:** not having any rights; isolated from society

2   *Write answers to the questions.*

1. How is Diane Schuur similar to Helen Keller? How is she different?

_____

_____

_____

2. What does Diane Schuur mean by these statements:
   • "I hate the word handicapped. Keller would too. We are people with inconveniences. We're not charity cases."

_____

_____

_____

- "You must understand that even more than sighted people, we need to be touched. When you look at a person, eye to eye, I imagine it's like touching them. We don't have that convenience. But when I perform, I get that experience from a crowd."

_____

_____

_____

C INTEGRATE READINGS ONE AND TWO

◀ STEP 1: Organize

Both Frank McCourt and Diane Schuur faced many obstacles and challenges in their lives. These same challenges also helped them to discover and develop their talent and become successful. Complete the chart comparing Frank McCourt and Diane Schuur.

	READING ONE Frank McCourt	READING TWO Diane Schuur
1. Obstacles they faced		
2. Person or people who influenced and inspired them		
3. Personal values, traits, or characteristics that helped them face their obstacles		
4. Talent or gift that resulted from the challenges they faced		

◀ STEP 2: Synthesize

On a separate piece of paper, write a short paragraph comparing the lives of Frank McCourt and Diane Schuur using the information from Step 1. Describe their obstacles and triumphs.

③ FOCUS ON WRITING

Ⓐ VOCABULARY

◖ REVIEW

The chain diagram shows the three stages of overcoming obstacles: facing an obstacle, dealing with an obstacle, and overcoming an obstacle. Write the words from the box in the correct circle. Some of the words may be put in more than one circle. Discuss your answers with a partner.

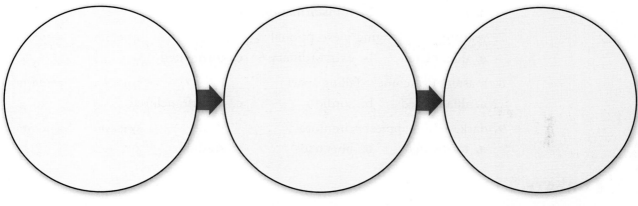

Facing an obstacle   **Dealing with an obstacle**   **Overcoming an obstacle**

achievement	exalted	isolation	paradise
confused	extraordinary	liberate	struggle
darkest	freedom	master	transformation
defeated	hopelessness	misery	utopia
disenfranchised	inquisitiveness	mortified	yearning

◖ EXPAND

An **analogy** is a comparison between two words that seem similar or are related in some way. In this exercise, the word pairs are either synonyms or antonyms. For example, in item 1, *isolated* is a synonym of *alone*; in the same way, *embarrassment* is a synonym of *shame*. Use a dictionary if you need help.

Work with a partner. Discuss the relationship between the words. Circle the word that best completes each analogy. Then circle synonym *or* antonym *for each set of words.*

1. isolated : alone = embarrassment : _____   ⟨ synonym ⟩   antonym
   a. struggle   **b.** sadness   **c.** shame

2. confusion : understanding = hopeful : _____   synonym   antonym

   a. defeated   **b.** enlivened   **c.** liberated

3. poverty : wealth = misery : _____   synonym   antonym

   a. hopelessness   **b.** happiness   **c.** yearning

4. utopia : paradise = leaving behind : _____   synonym   antonym

   a. exalted   **b.** confused   **c.** abandonment

5. meager : plentiful = failure : _____   synonym   antonym

   a. achievement   **b.** freedom   **c.** sadness

6. exalted : noble = freedom : _____   synonym   antonym

   a. isolation   **b.** transformation   **c.** liberation

7. yearning for : longing = exceptional : _____   synonym   antonym

   a. dilapidated   **b.** extraordinary   **c.** tormented

8. master : overcome = falling apart : _____   synonym   antonym

   a. dilapidated   **b.** sordid   **c.** disenfranchised

9. darkest : unhappiest = immoral : _____   synonym   antonym

   a. tormented   **b.** liberated   **c.** sordid

◖ CREATE

Choose one of the situations. On a separate piece of paper, write a letter using words and phrases from Review and Expand.

1. Imagine you are Diane Schuur. Write a letter to Helen Keller. Explain how she helped you and inspired you to overcome an obstacle.

2. Imagine you are one of Frank McCourt's former students. You have just graduated from college. Write a letter to Frank McCourt. Explain how he helped and inspired you to overcome an obstacle.

B GRAMMAR: Gerunds and Infinitives

1 *Examine the sentences and answer the questions on the next page with a partner.*

a. **Teaching** was the most exalted profession I could imagine.

b. McCourt enjoyed **writing** about his childhood.

c. McCourt had done a lot of **reading**.

d. Helen Keller learned **to deliver** speeches.

e. I persuaded New York University **to enroll** me.

f. After McCourt's mother died, he felt free **to write** his memoirs.

g. Helen Keller said the blind have the freedom **to be** as extraordinary as the sighted.

1. In sentence *a*, what is the subject?

2. In sentence *b*, what is the object of the verb *enjoyed*?

3. In sentence c, what word follows the preposition *of*?

4. Look at the boldfaced words in *a*, *b*, and *c*. They are gerunds. How are gerunds formed?

5. In sentence *d*, the main verb is *learned*. What is the verb that follows it?

6. In sentence *e*, the main verb is *persuaded*. What is the object of the main verb? What is the verb that follows it?

7. In sentence *f*, what is the verb that follows the adjective *free*?

8. In sentence *g*, what is the verb that follows the noun *freedom*?

9. Look at the boldfaced words in *d*, *e*, *f*, and *g*. They are infinitives. How are infinitives formed?

GERUNDS AND INFINITIVES	
Gerunds To form a gerund, **use the base form of the verb + -*ing*.**	read + ing = reading write + ing = writing
1. Use the gerund as the **subject** of a sentence.	**Writing** is very important to Frank McCourt.
2. Use the gerund as the **object** of a sentence after certain verbs (such as *enjoy, acknowledge, recall*).	Frank McCourt enjoys **writing**.
3. Use the gerund **after a preposition** (such as *of, in, for, about*).	Frank McCourt is interested in **writing**.

(continued on next page)

Infinitives	
To form an infinitive, use **to + the base form of the verb**.	to read to write

4. Use the infinitive **after certain verbs**.
 	
    a. some verbs are followed directly by an infinitive (such as *learn, decide, agree*)
 	
    b. some verbs are followed by an object + an infinitive (such as *urge, persuade*)
 	
    c. some verbs are followed by an infinitive or an object + an infinitive (such as *want, ask, need*)
	McCourt's students **learned to write** about their personal experiences.
	
	McCourt **urged his students to write** about their personal experiences.
	
	McCourt **wanted to write** about his personal experiences.
	
	McCourt **wanted them to write** their personal experiences.

5. Use the infinitive **after certain adjectives** (such as *free, able, hard*).	McCourt's students were **free to write** about whatever they wanted.
6. Use the infinitive **after certain nouns** (such as *ability, freedom*).	McCourt's students had the **freedom to write** about whatever they wanted.

2 *Work with a partner. Underline the gerund or infinitive in the sentences. Write the number of the grammar rule on pages 39 and 40 that applies to each sentence.*

    __1__ **a.** Learning Braille was difficult for Diane Schuur.

    _____ **b.** McCourt had the ability to describe objects from his childhood.

    _____ **c.** McCourt acknowledged not going to high school.

    _____ **d.** Helen Keller was able to live in the world of sight and sound.

    _____ **e.** A professor asked McCourt to describe an object from his childhood.

    _____ **f.** Diane Schuur decided to go back into the school for the blind.

    _____ **g.** Many people don't feel free to write about their lives.

    _____ **h.** Recounting his experiences inspired McCourt's students.

    _____ **i.** McCourt couldn't think about writing his memoirs while his mother was alive.

    _____ **j.** McCourt's students persuaded him to write a book.

3 *Read the information about Frank McCourt, Diane Schuur, and Helen Keller. Rewrite each situation using a form of the first verb given and the gerund or infinitive form of the second verb.*

1. McCourt was worried his memoirs would embarrass his mother. After she died, he didn't have to worry about this.

   <u>After his mother died, McCourt felt free to write his memoirs.</u>
   (feel free / write)

2. As a child, Helen Keller was impatient and hungry for words. She was frustrated because she couldn't talk to people.

   _____
   (want / communicate)

3. McCourt had no high school education, but he had read a lot. He told New York University it should admit him.

   _____
   (persuade / allow)

4. Diane Schuur sings and plays jazz. She likes the feeling she gets from a crowd.

   _____
   (enjoy / perform)

5. Frank McCourt hadn't gone to high school. He was afraid of what his students would think about him.

   _____
   (worry about / tell)

6. Diane Schuur first went to a school for the blind and after that to regular public school from age 11 until she was a senior in high school. Then she thought she should go back to the school for the blind.

   _____
   (decide / return)

7. McCourt's students didn't think they were able to write. He gave them lots of encouragement and told them "everyone has a story to tell."

   _____
   (urge / write)

8. Helen Keller was blind and deaf. She struggled with language.

   _____
   (be hard / learn)

9. McCourt remembered the town of Limerick. He could see and imagine what it was like when he was a child.

   _____
   (recall / live)

10. Diane Schuur could have gone to regular public school. She also could have gone to the state school for the blind.

    _____
    (be able / choose)

In this unit, you read personal accounts of people's overcoming obstacles.

You are going to *write a biographical paragraph about how you or someone you know overcame an obstacle.**

◖ PREPARE TO WRITE: Listing

Listing is a prewriting activity in which you list information about a topic or category before you begin to write a paragraph or essay.

Look back at Integrate Readings One and Two on page 36 to complete the first column of the chart. In the second column, add three or more obstacles that you and/or someone you know have faced.

OBSTACLES FACED BY FRANK McCOURT AND DIANE SCHUUR	OBSTACLES FACED BY ME OR SOMEONE I KNOW

◖ WRITE: A Biographical Paragraph

A **paragraph** is a group of sentences that are related and support a controlling idea. A **biographical paragraph** describes a person's life, and sometimes focuses on one particular aspect. All paragraphs have three parts: the **topic sentence,** the **supporting sentences,** and the **concluding sentence**.

TOPIC SENTENCE

The **topic sentence** introduces the main idea and the controlling idea which is your idea or opinion about the main idea. The topic sentence controls what you write in the rest of the paragraph. All the sentences in the paragraph must relate to, describe, or illustrate the controlling idea in the topic sentence.

---

*For Alternative Writing Topics, see page 46. These topics can be used in place of the writing topic for this unit or as homework. The alternative topics relate to the theme of the unit, but may not target the same grammar or rhetorical structures taught in the unit.

The second part of the paragraph includes **supporting sentences** that give details or examples that develop your ideas about the topic. This is usually the longest part of the paragraph, since it discusses and explains the controlling idea.

The **concluding sentence** is the last part of the paragraph. It can do one or more of the following: summarize the paragraph, offer a solution to the problem, restate the topic sentence, or offer an opinion.

1 Read the paragraph. Then answer the questions with a partner.

Helen Keller said, "Although the world is full of suffering, it is also full of overcoming it." This can be seen all around us. Many people have faced great obstacles in their lives but have found ways to overcome and actually benefit from these obstacles. For example, Greg Barton, the 1984, 1988, and 1992 U.S. Olympic medalist in kayaking, was born with a serious disability. He had club feet, his toes pointed inward, and as a result, he could not walk easily. Even after a series of operations, he still had limited mobility. Even so, Greg was never defeated. First, he taught himself to walk, and even to run. Then, he competed on his high school running team. He knew, though, he would never become an Olympic runner, so he looked for other sports that he could play. Happily, he discovered kayaking, a perfect sport for him because it required minimal leg and foot muscles. Using his upper body strength, he was able to master the sport. Finally, after many years of training and perseverance, Greg made the 1984 Olympic team. He says of his accomplishments, "Each step of the road has been made easier by looking just as far as necessary—yet not beyond that." In short, even though that road was paved with obstacles, he was able to overcome them and achieve the impossible.

1. What is the topic of the paragraph? How do you know?

_____

_____

2. What is the controlling idea?

_____

_____

3. Underline the sentences that support the topic and controlling ideas. How do they relate to the controlling idea?

_____

_____

4. What is the concluding sentence? What does it do?

_____

_____

Note: For more information on topic sentences and controlling ideas, see Unit 1.

2 *Now write the first draft of your biographical paragraph. Use the information from Prepare to Write and complete the chart below to plan your paragraph. Make sure you have a topic sentence, supporting sentences, and a concluding sentence. Be sure to use grammar and vocabulary from the unit.*

Topic Sentence:

1.

Supporting Sentences:

2.

3.

4.

5.

6.

Concluding Sentence:

7.

◀ **REVISE: Choosing Appropriate Support**

The **supporting sentences** in a paragraph help the reader to better understand the controlling idea. Supporting sentences provide examples, details, and facts, and must relate directly to the topic sentence.

1 *Read each topic sentence. Two of the ideas that follow support the topic sentence and one does not. Cross out the idea that does not support the topic sentence.*

1. Ever since Greg Barton was in high school, he longed to be an Olympic champion.
   a. Greg's sports records
   b. How Greg trained for the Olympics
   c. ~~Greg's academic achievements~~

2. The achievements of people like Helen Keller and Diane Schuur have inspired many others.
   a. Explanation of how they have inspired others
   b. How many people have read about Helen Keller and Diane Schuur
   c. About Helen Keller's and Diane Schuur's obstacles

3. The poverty-stricken lives of Frank McCourt's students deeply affected him.
   a. How Frank saw himself in his students
   b. How Frank taught his students to write
   c. How the students inspired Frank to write

4. Learning to read Braille is a very difficult and frustrating process.
   a. The patience people need to learn Braille
   b. Reasons why people should learn Braille
   c. The amount of practice and time needed to learn Braille

2 *Each of the paragraphs has one supporting sentence that does not directly relate to the topic sentence. Cross out the sentence and explain why it is unrelated.*

1.   Helen Keller was very frustrated as a child. First of all, because she could neither hear nor speak, she couldn't understand what was happening around her. She felt her mother's lips moving as she spoke, but this made no sense to her. She couldn't understand what her mother was doing. ~~Her mother could hear and speak~~. Secondly, once she learned what words were, she felt she could never communicate with them as quickly as sighted people could. As a result of all of her frustration, she would often cry and scream until she was exhausted.

   Explanation: <u>The sentence focuses on her mother's abilities, not Helen's frustrations.</u>

2.   The act of reading liberated Helen Keller, Diane Schuur, and Frank McCourt. All three of these people faced overwhelming obstacles, but literature freed them from their hardest struggles. For example, once Helen Keller and Diane Schuur learned to read Braille, a whole new world of books opened for them. In addition, Frank McCourt escaped his grim home life by reading as much as he could. They are all great writers or musicians.

   Explanation: _____

   _____

3.   Some of the world's most talented and famous people have overcome some of the hardest obstacles. For example, Ludwig van Beethoven became deaf at age 46. Franklin D. Roosevelt was paralyzed by polio and was often in a wheelchair, but he was elected president of the United States four times. Finally, Steven Hawking is a world-famous scientist who is completely paralyzed and cannot speak. Furthermore, he lives in England. These people show us that we should never give up or let obstacles defeat us.

   Explanation: _____

   _____

3 *Look at your first draft. Make sure your supporting sentences give clear examples and details that connect with and support the controlling idea.*

◀ EDIT: Writing the Final Draft

Write the final draft of your paragraph. Carefully edit it for grammatical problems and mechanical errors, such as spelling, capitalization, and punctuation. Make sure you used some of the grammar and vocabulary from the unit. Use the checklist to help you write your final draft. Then neatly write or type your paragraph.

✔ FINAL DRAFT CHECKLIST

- ○ Does the paragraph describe a person who was faced with challenges and overcame them?
- ○ Is there a topic sentence stating the obstacle that the person overcame?
- ○ Do all the supporting sentences relate directly to the topic sentence?
- ○ Is there a concluding sentence that restates the main idea of the paragraph, offers an opinion, or suggests a solution?
- ○ Are gerunds and infinitives used appropriately?
- ○ Has vocabulary from the unit been used?

ALTERNATIVE WRITING TOPICS

Choose one of the topics. Write a paragraph using the vocabulary and grammar from the unit.

1. Read the quotation.

   "When one door of happiness closes, another opens; but often we look so long at the closed door that we do not see the one which has been opened for us."

   —Helen Keller

   How does it apply to a person you have read about in the unit, another famous person, or yourself?

2. What are two of the values and personal characteristics people need in order to overcome obstacles? How do people apply these values and characteristics to their lives?

RESEARCH TOPICS, see page 259.

Dying for Their Beliefs

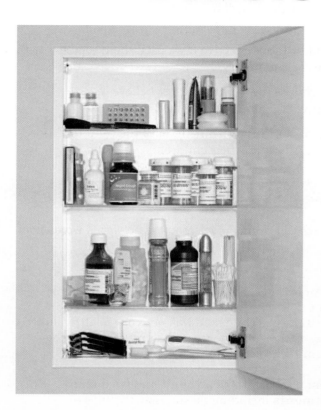

1 FOCUS ON THE TOPIC

A PREDICT

Look at the photographs and the unit title. Then discuss the questions with a partner.

1. According to your culture or background, which photograph shows conventional medical treatments?

2. Which of these treatments have you used? How do you decide which treatment to use and how much to use?

3. Do you think some beliefs are worth dying for? What do you think the unit will be about?

B SHARE INFORMATION

*Read the statements about medicine. Write **A** if you agree or **D** if you disagree. Discuss your answers in small groups.*

_____ 1. If you are sick, taking medicine is the best way to get better.

_____ 2. Praying can cure sickness.

_____ 3. People who have a positive attitude will be cured faster than people with a negative attitude.

_____ 4. Medical treatments could be more effective if we used them together with alternative (natural or herbal) remedies.

_____ 5. People have the right to choose the treatment they believe in, conventional or alternative, even if doctors do not agree.

_____ 6. Parents, rather than doctors or the government, have the right to choose the treatment they believe is best for their children.

C BACKGROUND AND VOCABULARY

1 *Read the passage about health and religion. Try to understand the boldfaced words from the context.*

Mary Baker Eddy was an American religious leader and the founder of the Christian Science movement. She was born in Bow, New Hampshire, in the United States, on July 16, 1821. As a child, she was not very healthy and suffered from various **ailments**; as a result, she missed a great deal of school. Her education came through home schooling and study of the Bible and Scriptures.[1]

She continued to suffer from poor health as an adult and tried many alternative therapies and **treatments** including mesmerism (hypnosis), hydrotherapy (water cures), and mental healing. Once, after falling on ice and suffering a severe injury, she asked for her Bible and read a Gospel[2] account of one of Jesus' healings. After reading the New Testament,[3] she was completely cured and felt she had finally found the answer to her medical problems: the Scriptures.

---

[1] **Scriptures:** the writings of the Bible

[2] **Gospel:** one of the four stories of Christ's life in the Christian Bible

[3] **New Testament:** the part of the bible that is about Jesus Christ's life and his teaching

Eddy believed that all sickness was mental rather than physical. She began the practice of healing others by reading the Bible and teaching others to be healers as well. In 1875, she published *Science and Health with Key to the Scriptures*. Eddy later wrote and published sixteen more books. In 1879, she founded the Church of Christ, Scientist, an organization she oversaw closely until her death. The **ramifications** of her writing and beliefs have been felt around the world. Today there are over 2,700 Christian Science churches worldwide.

One of the **principles** of Christian Science is that disease, as well as sin and death, do not originate with God and, therefore, are not real. They see God as the only healer. Instead of **conventional** medicinal remedies, her followers, called Christian Scientists, pray for the sick person. In addition, a church practitioner[4] prays for the sick and a church nurse gives non-medical physical care.[5] The church, however, does not **deny** its members access to doctors; it leaves the choice to the individual. Conventional treatment for "mechanical" problems such as broken bones and dental cavities does not **violate** or go against the church's beliefs.

Since Eddy first published *Science and Health with Key to the Scriptures*, there has been **debate** about the Christian Science method of healing. Followers of Christian Science **acknowledge** that their methods of treatment do not always work. Nevertheless, they feel that they are **entitled** to choose the type of treatment that *they* feel works best. In other words, they believe that prayer can be the most **effective** method of treatment.

2 *Find the boldface words in the reading passage above. Write each word next to its definition.*

1. _____ (**n.**) results of something that happens or that you do, that affects other things

2. _____ (**n.**) a discussion or argument on a subject in which people express different opinions

3. _____ (**n.**) methods that are intended to cure an injury or sickness

4. _____ (**adj.**) used or existing for a long time and considered usual (for a particular group or culture)

5. _____ (**v.**) to disobey or to do something against a law, rule, agreement etc.

6. _____ (**v.**) given the right to have or do something

---

[4] **practitioner:** a person who has been schooled and trained in praying for the sick

[5] **nonmedical physical care:** care that includes taking care of hygiene and dietary needs as well as caring for injuries; does not include giving medication

7. _____ (**adj.**) producing the result that was wanted or intended

8. _____ (**v.**) to accept or admit that something is true or official

9. _____ (**n.**) basic ideas that a plan or system is based on

10. _____ (**v.**) to refuse to allow someone to have or do something

11. _____ (**n.**) illnesses that are not very serious

2 FOCUS ON READING

A READING ONE: Dying for Their Beliefs

Read the first three paragraphs of Dying for Their Beliefs. *Work with a partner to answer the questions. Then read the rest of the article.*

1. How did Amy's life change in 1986?

2. Why did Mary Christman's husband say, "If the child does not receive medical attention, she will be dead within a week"?

3. What exactly do you think is wrong with Amy?

DYING FOR THEIR BELIEFS:
Christian Scientist Parents on Trial in Girl's Death
By Jeffrey Good (from the *St. Petersburg Times*)

1   Amy Hermanson was a sunny seven-year-old with blond hair and bubbly ways. She liked to serenade adults with her favorite song: Disney's "It's a Small World After All."

2   But Amy's world went awry[1] one Sunday in 1986. An adult friend of her family noticed the child's sunken eyes, her listless[2] manner, the way her clothes hung from her tiny bones. She tried to get the child to sing her favorite song.

3   "She used to come over and sing every verse to me. I couldn't even get her to make a comment on the song, let alone sing it," the friend, Mary Christman, would later tell investigators. She recalled her husband saying, "If the child does not receive medical attention, she will be dead within a week."

4   But Amy's parents are Christian Scientists. They decided to try to heal the child with prayer rather than seek a doctor's aid. Two days after the Christmans saw her, Amy died of diabetes.

5   On Monday, Amy's parents are scheduled to go on trial in the Sarasota County Courthouse

[1] **awry:** wrong; to not happen as planned
[2] **listless:** feeling tired and not interested in things

on charges of third-degree murder[3] and felony child abuse.[4] Prosecutors say William and Christine Hermanson committed a crime by putting religious principles ahead of protecting their daughter. The Hermansons say their accusers are wrong. If convicted, the couple could face three to seven years in jail.

6   At issue is a legal principle with national ramifications. Since 1967, no Christian Scientist in the United States has stood trial for denying children medical care for religious reasons. Six similar cases are pending, but the Hermansons are the first to go to court.

7   "The children are entitled to protection, and if the parents won't give it to them, they (the parents) will suffer the (legal) consequences," says Mack Futch, an assistant state attorney in Sarasota County.

8   The Hermansons, however, have maintained that prosecutors want to violate their constitutional right of religious freedom. And in interviews last week, their supporters maintained that the couple treated their daughter with a proven—if unconventional— method of healing.

9   Frederick Hillier, a Christian Science "practitioner" who was ministering to the child when she died, said that Christian Scientists regard prayer as a better treatment than conventional medicine. "A Christian Scientist is doing nothing any different than anyone who has found medical treatment to be effective," said Hillier, who also acts as the spokesman for Florida Christian Science churches. "Why do Christian Scientists rely on spiritual healing when they could go to a physician if they wanted to? In their experience, they found it to be effective."

10   Church members acknowledge that their methods sometimes fail, just as doctors sometimes fail, he said. But that doesn't mean the Christian Scientists deserve criminal charges any more than the doctors do, he said. "We don't claim any more than anyone else claims to be 100 percent effective," Hillier said. "Even Jesus didn't."

11   Amy's third grade report card was her last. It showed A's in reading, English, spelling, mathematics, science, and social studies. "Amy takes a keen interest in all her work," a teacher wrote.

12   But in September 1986, Amy began fourth grade as a different child. Teachers noticed her dozing off in class, shedding weight at an alarming rate, and complaining of stomachaches. At one point, she held her hands over her ears and pleaded, "Stop the noise. Stop the noise," at the sound of a pencil scratching paper.

13   "After the school year began, Amy was often upset. She would cry and say that she did not feel well," said June R. McHugh, director of the private Julie Rohr Academy attended by Amy and her older brother, Eric. McHugh told investigators that about a week before Amy's death, she told Mrs. Hermanson her daughter might be suffering from a physical ailment. McHugh recalled that Mrs. Hermanson said, "the situation was being handled."

14   On September 22, one of the practitioners began praying for the child.

15   On September 25, the Hermansons left Amy in a baby-sitter's care and went to Indiana for a Christian Science conference on spiritual healing. They returned on September 29.

16   But at 8:30 A.M. on September 30, 1986, a state social worker in Sarasota took a call from Amy's aunt. The worker's notes sketched a chilling picture: "Over the last two weeks (Amy) has lost 10 pounds, drinks constantly, eats large amounts of food, muscle tone is virtually gone, eyes are sunken and functioning

---

[3] **third-degree murder:** murder without intention
[4] **felony child abuse:** a serious crime where a child is physically or psychologically hurt

(continued on next page)

separately. Child can barely walk and has to be carried—All indications point to diabetes but parents refuse to take said child to the doctor as they are Christian Scientists."

17　A court hearing was scheduled for 1:30 P.M. and Amy's father arrived early. At 1:27 P.M., Hermanson took a phone call from home reporting that Amy had taken a turn for the worse and an ambulance was en route. Learning this, the judge ordered that a medical doctor examine Amy.

18　But it was too late. With Christian Science practitioner Hillier nearby, Amy had died in her parents' bed.

Most Important Right

19　After performing an autopsy on the child, Associate Medical Examiner James C. Wilson concluded that medical treatment up to just hours before her death probably could have saved Amy. The Hermansons have acknowledged they never sought such treatment. That does not make them criminals, say their lawyers and supporters.

20　"There isn't anyone who is more loving to their children than Christian Scientists," said Bob Drabik, chairman of the board of directors at Sarasota's First Church, Christian Science, where the Hermansons are members.

21　Florida law says parents can't be judged "abusive or neglectful" because they withhold conventional medical treatment for religious reasons. Similar laws exist in most states. They were enacted under heavy lobbying from the Boston-based church after one of its members, Dorothy Sheridan of Harwich, Massachusetts, was convicted in 1967 of manslaughter in the death of her child. "William and Christine Hermanson, at all times material[5] to the facts in this case, followed the religious teachings of their church and relied upon Christian Science healing in the care and treatment of Amy Hermanson," the court record states.

22　Within the legal community, there is considerable debate over whether that is an adequate defense when a child dies. Harvard law professor Alan Dershowitz says that such trials revolve around two important constitutional rights: parents' freedom of religion, and children's right to grow up healthy.

23　In cases where one right must take priority, Dershowitz says, the choice is clear: "It's not a difficult question. Children have a right to live and be brought up to make their own religious decisions."

24　Hillier, the Christian Science spokesman, said that church members view prayer as the best way to make sick children well. "We don't want the right to do harm to children," he said, "we only want the right to do what is good for children."

---

[5] **material:** important to, related to

◖ READ FOR MAIN IDEAS

Complete the sentences based on Reading One. Compare sentences with a partner.

1. Amy's disease was _____

_____

2. Amy might have been saved if _____

_____

3. Her parents are going on trial because _____

_____

4. Christian Scientists and other supporters defend the Hermansons because

_____

5. Some people in the legal community believe that the two main issues are:

   a. _____

   b. _____

◀ READ FOR DETAILS

*Write **T** (true) or **F** (false) for each statement. Write the number of the paragraph that supports your answer. If the statement is false, change it to make it true.*

Paragraph

_____ 1. The Hermansons knew that some people thought Amy   _____
          might have a medical problem.

_____ 2. Christian Scientists acknowledge that their methods are   _____
          not always effective.

_____ 3. Some of the symptoms of Amy's disease were: loss of weight, _____
          stomachaches, and an intense interest in schoolwork.

_____ 4. If Amy had received medical treatment just hours before   _____
          she died, she probably could have recovered.

_____ 5. Christian Scientists and their supporters believe they want _____
          only to do what is good for their children.

_____ 6. In Florida, parents can be judged "abusive or neglectful" if _____
          they choose to deny their children conventional medical care
          for religious reasons.

◀ MAKE INFERENCES

Work in a group. Match the people with the statements they could have made. In some cases, more than one person could have made the statement. Refer to Reading One to support your answers.

a. Amy Hermanson, sick child

b. Alan Dershowitz, Harvard law professor

c. Mack Futch, assistant state attorney

d. Frederick Hillier, Christian Science practitioner and spokesman

e. Dorothy Sheridan, Christian Scientist convicted of manslaughter

f. James C. Wilson, associate medical examiner

_____ 1. If parents don't give their children medical protection, then the court system or the government must get involved.

_____ 2. Prayer, although not always effective, is the best treatment available.

_____ 3. The Hermansons are responsible for Amy's death.

_____ 4. This was a senseless death. Medically, it could have been prevented.

_____ 5. The Constitution entitles us to religious freedom; this allows us to decide what is best for our children.

_____ 6. Being a good student is easy if you can concentrate on your schoolwork.

_____ 7. Children should be able to live long enough to make their own religious decisions.

_____ 8. It's worth being convicted of a crime if what we do is for the benefit of our children.

_____ 9. Spiritual healing is just as legitimate a type of medical treatment as drugs.

_____ 10. Children's right to live is more important than their parents' religious beliefs.

◖ **EXPRESS OPINIONS**

Discuss the questions in a small group. Then share your answers with the class.

1. Do you think Amy's parents are responsible for her death? Why or why not? If so, what punishment do you think they should receive?

2. Alan Dershowitz said that such trials revolve around two important constitutional rights: parents' freedom of religion and children's right to grow up healthy. What does he mean by this? How does it apply to Amy's situation?

B **READING TWO: Norman Cousins's Laugh Therapy**

Norman Cousins was a well-known American writer and editor. When he was diagnosed with a serious illness, he decided to use his own type of alternative therapy. He focused on the importance of a positive attitude in healing. After writing about his successful recovery, he received mail from all over the world. Many letters came from doctors who supported his ideas.

Norman Cousins lived for 26 years after he became ill. He died in 1990 at the age of 75.

1 _Discuss the questions with a partner. Then read the article about Norman Cousins._

1. What do you think "a positive attitude in healing" means?

2. Look at the photograph of Charlie Chaplin on page 55. Why do you think he could be associated with a positive attitude in healing?

Norman Cousins's Laugh Therapy

Charlie Chaplin

1   In the summer of 1964, well-known writer and editor Norman Cousins became very ill. His body ached and he felt constantly tired. It was difficult for him to even move around. He consulted his physician, who did many tests. Eventually he was diagnosed as having ankylosing spondylitis, a very serious and destructive form of arthritis.[1] His doctor told him that he would become immobilized[2] and eventually die from the disease. He was told he had only a 1 in 500 chance of survival.

2   Despite the diagnosis,[3] Cousins was determined to overcome the disease and survive. He had always been interested in medicine and had read the work of organic chemist Hans Selye, *The Stress of Life* (1956). This book discussed the idea of how body chemistry and health can be damaged by emotional stress and negative attitudes. Selye's book made Cousins think about the possible benefits of positive attitudes and emotions. He thought, "If negative emotions produce (negative) changes in the body, wouldn't positive emotions produce positive chemical changes? Is it possible that love, hope, faith, laughter, confidence, and the will to live have positive therapeutic value?"

3   He decided to concentrate on positive emotions as a remedy to heal some of the symptoms of his ailment. In addition to his conventional medical treatment, he tried to put himself in situations that would elicit positive emotions. "Laugh therapy" became part of his treatment. He scheduled time each day for watching comedy films, reading humorous books, and doing other activities that would bring about laughter and positive emotions. Within eight days of starting his "laugh therapy" program, his pain began to decrease and he was able to sleep more easily. His body chemistry even improved. Doctors were able to see an improvement in his condition! He was able to return to work in a few months' time and actually reached complete recovery after a few years.

4   Skeptical readers may question the doctor's preliminary diagnosis, but Cousins believes his recovery is the result of a mysterious mind-body interaction. His "laugh therapy" is a good example of one of the many alternative, or nonconventional, medical treatments people look to today.

[1] **arthritis:** a disease that causes pain and swelling in the joints of the body
[2] **immobilized:** not able to move
[3] **diagnosis:** identification of what illness a person has

2 *Write answers to the questions.*

1. What was Norman Cousins's original diagnosis and how did he respond?

_____

_____

2. What is the connection between mind and body in laugh therapy?

_____

_____

3. What are some examples of laugh therapy?

_____

_____

4. How did Cousins benefit from his laugh therapy?

_____

_____

C INTEGRATE READINGS ONE AND TWO

◀ STEP 1: Organize

You have read about the Christian Scientists' therapy through prayer and the Bible and Norman Cousins's laugh therapy. What are the similarities and differences between them? Complete the Venn diagram with information from both readings. In the left circle, write notes that are true only about the Hermansons. In the right circle, write notes that are true only about Norman Cousins. In the middle, write notes that are true for all of them.

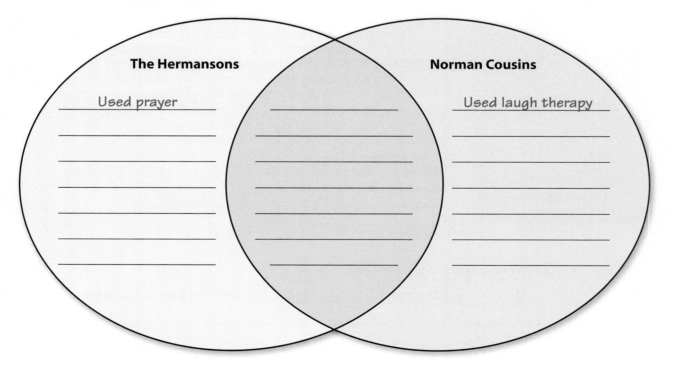

The Hermansons

Used prayer

Norman Cousins

Used laugh therapy

On a separate piece of paper, write a short paragraph explaining the similarities and differences between Amy Hermanson's story and Norman Cousins's story using the information from Step 1. (Note that neither the Hermansons nor Norman Cousins explicitly state their opinion about conventional medicine, but by reading carefully, you can infer their opinions. Include any information you were able to infer, too.)

③ FOCUS ON WRITING

Ⓐ VOCABULARY

◀ REVIEW

Work with a partner. Write **S** if the word pairs have a similar meaning and **D** if they have a different meaning.

1. ramification /effect __S__

2. ailment /symptom _____

3. elicit / produce _____

4. skeptical /doubtful _____

5. violate / disobey _____

6. principles / beliefs _____

7. treatment / diagnosis _____

8. acknowledge / admit _____

9. conventional / alternative _____

10. debate / agreement _____

11. consult / ask advice of _____

12. entitled / effective _____

◀ EXPAND

An **analogy** is a comparison between two words that seem similar or are related in some way. Sometimes the words are related because they are synonyms or antonyms, and sometimes there is another relationship. For example, in item 1, *arthritis* is an example of a diagnosis; in the same way, *achiness* is an example of a symptom.

Work with a partner. Discuss the relationship between the words. Circle the word that best completes each analogy.

1. arthritis : diagnosis = achiness : _____

    a. disease   **(b.)** symptom   **c.** cure

2. therapy : cure = treatment : _____

    a. heal   **b.** regimen   **c.** practitioner

3. consult : ask = admit : _____

   a. deny   **b.** acknowledge   **c.** suffer

4. typical : common = nonconventional : _____

   a. conventional   **b.** mainstream   **c.** alternative

5. jury : verdict = doctor : _____

   a. symptom   **b.** diagnosis   **c.** disease

6. ramification : effect = advantage : _____

   a. claim   **b.** cure   **c.** benefit

7. evidence : crime = symptom : _____

   a. jury   **b.** ailment   **c.** treatment

8. defend : accuse = allow : _____

   a. deny   **b.** elicit   **c.** recover

◖ **CREATE**

Imagine that you are going to interview the Hermansons or Norman Cousins. On a separate piece of paper, write four interview questions that you would like to ask. Use at least one of the words from the box in each question. Then, work with a partner. Answer each other's questions as if you were the Hermansons or Norman Cousins.

accuse	consult	diagnosis	entitled	symptom
acknowledge	(un)conventional	effective	principles	treatment
benefit	defend	elicit	ramifications	violate

B   **GRAMMAR: Past Unreal Conditionals**

1   *Examine the sentences with a partner. Write **T** (true) or **F** (false) for the statements that follow the sentences.*

   a. If Amy **hadn't died**, the medical examiner **wouldn't have examined** her.

   b. If Amy's parents **had seen** a doctor, Amy **could have taken** conventional medicine to control her diabetes.

   c. If Amy **had sung** her favorite song, Mrs. Christman **might not have noticed** she was sick.

1. In sentence *a:* Amy died. _____

   The medical examiner didn't examine her body. _____

2. In sentence *b:* Amy's parents didn't see a doctor. _____

   Amy didn't take conventional medicine to control her diabetes. _____

3. In sentence *c:* Amy didn't sing her favorite song. _____

   Mrs. Christman didn't notice she was sick. _____

PAST UNREAL CONDITIONALS

1. A **past unreal conditional** sentence has two clauses: the ***if* clause,** which gives the condition, and the **result clause,** which gives the result. The sentence can begin with the *if* clause or the result clause, and the meaning is the same.

2. There are two important things to notice in past unreal conditional sentences:

   - the use of the comma when the *if* clause comes at the beginning of the sentence
   - the verb forms used in each clause

If Clause	Result Clause
If + subject + past perfect,	subject + *would (not) have* + past participle *could (not) have* *might (not) have*
If Amy **hadn't died,**	Dr. Wilson **would not have examined** her.

Result Clause	*If* Clause
Subject + *would (not) have* + past participle *could (not) have* *might (not) have*	*if* + subject + past perfect
Amy **would have taken** medicine	if her parents **had brought** her to a doctor.

3. The past unreal conditional talks about past unreal, untrue, or imagined conditions and their results. Both parts of the sentence describe events that are the opposite of what happened.

Conditional statement:	Mrs. Christman **might not have noticed** if Amy **had sung.**
What really happened:	Mrs. Christman noticed. Amy didn't sing.

4. The past unreal conditional is often used to express regret about what really happened. In sentences like this, use *would have* in the result clause. To express possibility or uncertainty about the result, use ***might have*** or ***could have*** in the result clause.

2 *Read the conditional sentences. Write **T** (true) or **F** (false) for each statement that follows the sentences.*

1. If Mary Baker Eddy hadn't slipped on the ice, she wouldn't have broken her ankle.

   __T__ She slipped on the ice.

   __F__ She didn't break her ankle.

2. If Norman Cousins had been healthy, he wouldn't have had to try laugh therapy.

   _____ Norman Cousins was healthy.

   _____ He didn't have to try laugh therapy.

3. According to the medical examiner, Amy Hermanson might have lived if she had been given medication.

   _____ Amy died.

   _____ Amy wasn't given medication.

4. Amy's parents wouldn't have gone on trial for third-degree murder if she had not died.

   _____ Amy's parents didn't go on trial for third-degree murder.

   _____ Amy died.

5. If Mary Baker Eddy hadn't been so religious, she might not have turned to prayer to cure herself.

   _____ Mary Baker Eddy was religious.

   _____ She turned to prayer to cure herself.

6. If Amy's parents hadn't been Christian Scientists, they might have gotten conventional medical help for Amy.

   _____ Amy's parents are not Christian Scientists.

   _____ Amy's parents didn't get her conventional medical help.

7. If Amy had stayed awake in class, her teacher might not have noticed that something was wrong.

   _____ Amy slept in class.

   _____ Her teacher noticed that something was wrong.

8. If Norman Cousins hadn't believed in a mind-body interaction, laugh therapy might not have been effective for him.

   _____ Norman Cousins didn't believe in a mind-body interaction.

   _____ Laugh therapy didn't work for him.

3 *Write a sentence about each situation. Use the past unreal conditional.*

1. Laurie Rent had a headache. She took some aspirin. She soon felt better.

   If she hadn't taken aspirin, she might not have felt better.

2. Peter Deering had a problem with his allergies. He used conventional medical treatments. He didn't feel better. _____

   _____

3. Norman Cousins read extensively about alternative medicine. When he was diagnosed with ankylosing spondylitis, he already had some ideas about alternative treatments. _____

   _____

4. Norman Cousins was sick. He tried to cure himself by using laugh therapy. He made a complete recovery. _____

   _____

5. William Bullard was not a Christian Scientist. He believed in conventional Western medicine. He gave his daughter drugs when she was sick. _____

   _____

6. Amy began dozing off in class. Her teacher noticed that something was wrong. She called Amy's parents. _____

   _____

7. Norman Cousins wasn't satisfied with his doctor's treatment plan. He developed his own laugh therapy treatment. _____

   _____

C WRITING

In this unit, you read about the Hermansons, who were found guilty in the death of their daughter. They received a four-year suspended sentence and were placed on probation for fifteen years.[1] The sentence created a great deal of discussion both in favor of and against the verdict.

You are going to *write a three-paragraph opinion essay expressing your opinion on the initial verdict.**

---

[1] Six years after the Hermansons were found guilty, the Florida Supreme Court overturned the sentencing. The Hermansons were then found innocent of all charges.

*For Alternative Writing Topics, see page 66. These topics can be used in place of the writing topic for this unit or as homework. The alternative topics relate to the theme of the unit, but may not target the same grammar or rhetorical structures taught in the unit.

PREPARE TO WRITE: Tree Mapping

Tree mapping helps you to organize ideas about a topic. The topic is written on the top line. Your ideas are written in branches leading from the topic. You can include reasons and evidence on smaller branches.

Complete the tree map. Then discuss your tree with a partner.

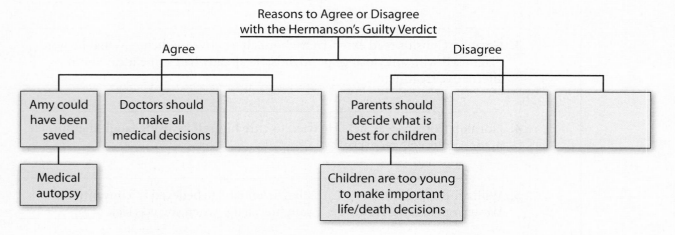

WRITE: An Opinion Essay

An **essay** is a group of paragraphs about one topic. An **opinion essay** is written to persuade or convince the reader that your opinion is "the right way of thinking." An opinion essay has three parts: the **introduction**, the **body**, and the **conclusion**.

INTRODUCTION

The **introduction** is the first paragraph of your essay. It includes a thesis statement which introduces the topic and states the main idea. The introduction should capture the readers' attention and make them want to read on. Many introductions begin with general background information on the topic and often end with the thesis statement as the last sentence of the paragraph. In an opinion essay, the thesis statement should state your opinion about the topic. *Tip:* Some writers find it helpful to write their introductory paragraph after they have completed their essay.

BODY

The **body** is one to three paragraphs. The body supports the thesis statement by giving examples, details, reasons, and facts to support the thesis statement. Each paragraph should start with a clearly stated topic sentence which relates to the thesis statement. In addition, because you are trying to convince your readers to accept your opinion, you need to give evidence to support your opinion. You also need to give reasons which explain why the evidence supports your opinion.

The **conclusion** should restate the thesis statement and include the writer's final thoughts on the topic. For example, the writer can give advice, suggest a solution to a problem, or predict what will happen in the future. The conclusion should not include new or unrelated topics.

Note: See Units 1 and 2, pages 19–24 and 42–46 for information on paragraph writing.

1 *Examine the opinion essay. Then complete the essay organizer with the parts of the essay.*

The Power of Prayer

Shocking. Disappointing. These two words come to mind when reading the word *guilty* in the Hermanson verdict. That loving and devoted parents could be convicted of negligence is against everything the United States stands for. First let me say that I am a loving and devoted parent. I am president of our local parent-teacher association. I am a Harvard graduate and a lawyer. I am also a Christian Scientist. From this personal perspective, I believe in the power of spiritual healing and the right of families to choose the treatment they feel is most effective.

I have witnessed the power of spiritual healing and its ability to cure on many occasions. When I was born, I was diagnosed with a blood disorder. The doctor said I had two hours to live. At the time, blood transfusions were not available for this disease. My mother, a Christian Scientist, brought in a practitioner and through much prayer, I was healed. I believe that if my mother hadn't been a Christian Scientist, I would probably not have survived. With my own children there have been many occasions when doctors would have prescribed antibiotics for ailments such as ear infections, colds, etc. However, with the power of prayer, my children have been healed without these medicines.

Christian Scientists are seen by some as law breaking and irresponsible caretakers. Neither of these accusations is true. First, as citizens, we are exercising our rights as guaranteed by the Constitution. If we truly believe that conventional medicine is not helpful, we have the right to say "no" and choose the treatment that we feel is appropriate and effective for our family. As far as being irresponsible, this is also false. Many scientific studies have proven that through prayer and spiritual healing, numerous people have been cured of illness and disease the medical community had declared incurable.

I hope that people won't stop looking for alternative treatments because the Hermansons have been found guilty. Do we as a society truly believe that conventional medicine is the only effective and accepted treatment? Should we allow our rights to be taken away because of this belief? Remember, children die as the result of conventional medical treatment, too, and no one accuses the parents of these unfortunate children of negligence, nor brings them to court.

THREE PARTS OF AN ESSAY	NOTES
I. Introduction	**Background Information:**
Thesis Statement:	
II. Body Paragraph 1	**Body Paragraph 1**
Topic:	Support/Evidence:
Body Paragraph 2	**Body Paragraph 2**
Topic:	Support/Evidence:
III. Conclusion	
Restate the Thesis:	
Final Thought/Wrap Up:	

2 *Make an essay organizer like the one above with information for your opinion essay about the Hermansons.*

3 *Now write the first draft of your opinion essay. Use the information from Prepare to Write and your essay organizer to plan your essay. Make sure you have four paragraphs: an introductory paragraph, two body paragraphs, and one concluding paragraph. Be sure to use grammar and vocabulary from the unit.*

◖ REVISE: Writing Introductions and Hooks

The **introductory paragraph** is very important in all essays. The reader will decide whether or not your essay is worth the time and effort to read depending on how interesting your introductory paragraph is. The introduction for an opinion essay should:

- state who you are and why your opinion matters;
- provide background information about the topic;
- provoke the reader's interest with a hook;
- include a thesis statement.

A **hook** is a sentence or two meant to grab the reader's attention. The hook could be:

- a shocking or surprising sentence;
- an anecdote (story);
- an interesting point;
- a quote.

1 *Is there a hook in the essay on page 63? What is it? Is it effective? Why or why not? Share your answer with a partner.*

2 *Read the hooks from introductions of opinion essays. Check (✓) the hooks you think are effective. Discuss your answers with a partner.*

1. _____ People are becoming more open minded about spiritual healing. Spiritual healing can really be effective if you are a true believer.

2. _____ Spiritual healing works. "People with a strong sense of spirituality and routine prayer had less pain, needed less medication, and had more social outlets that helped them cope with their disease than those who did not have a spiritual practice," says Dr. Paul Jones of Indiana State Medical Center.

3. _____ People should stick with conventional medicine because it has been proven. There is no proof spiritual healing is effective or even safe.

4. _____ There are some studies that prove meditation and prayer can help with healing. This is why prayer should be a part of your life.

5. _____ Dr. Larry Dorsey saw for himself the power of spiritual healing when his patient whose lungs were filled with cancer and who refused all medical intervention returned to his care within one year with completely clean lungs. What had the patient done? Pray.

6. _____ Stop! Don't take that pill! You can pray that headache away. Or at least that's what people who believe in spiritual healing would have you believe.

3 *Look at the introductory paragraph in your first draft. Make sure you have all the parts of an effective introduction. If you don't have a hook, add one.*

◖EDIT: Writing the Final Draft

Write your final draft. Carefully edit it for grammatical problems and mechanical errors, such as spelling, capitalization, and punctuation. Make sure you used some of the grammar and vocabulary from the unit. Use the checklist to help you write your final draft. Then neatly write or type your essay.

✓ FINAL DRAFT CHECKLIST

- ○ Does the essay have an introduction, two body paragraphs, and a conclusion?
- ○ Does the introduction include a thesis statement, background information about the topic, and a hook?
- ○ Does each paragraph have a topic sentence?
- ○ Do all the topic sentences support the thesis statement?
- ○ Does the essay have a conclusion that restates the thesis and includes a final thought?
- ○ Is the past unreal conditional used correctly?
- ○ Has vocabulary from the unit been used?

ALTERNATIVE WRITING TOPICS

Choose one of the topics. Write an essay using the vocabulary and grammar from the unit.

1. Different cultures define nonconventional medicine in different ways. What do you think nonconventional medicine is? How do you feel about the use of nonconventional medicine?

2. What do you think of Norman Cousins's laugh therapy? Do you think there is any truth to the idea of a mind-body interaction? Have you or someone you know had a medical experience where the mind was stronger than the body?

RESEARCH TOPICS, see page 260.

Animal Intelligence:
Instinct or Intellect?

Pet Pig Saves Owner

LuLu, the Vietnamese potbellied pig, receives an award for saving her owner

Beaver Falls New York—Lulu, a potbellied pig owned by Jo Ann Altsman, saved her owner from a potentially fatal heart attack late yesterday morning. Home alone with Lulu, Altsman felt sick, and tried to get a neighbor's attention by throwing an alarm clock out the window. No one responded. Lulu then took control of the situation. She squeezed through the family's dog door and threw herself into the middle of a busy road. She stopped traffic, and led a passing motorist back to her home where he found her distressed owner and called an ambulance. Doctors believe Altsman would have died within 15 minutes if Lulu had not acted on her own.

①FOCUS ON THE TOPIC

A PREDICT

Read the true news story and the unit title. Then discuss the questions with a partner.

1. Some people believe that Lulu's actions showed intelligence. Do you agree or disagree? Why or why not?

2. Other people believe that Lulu was just acting on instinct: acting without really understanding. Do you agree or disagree? Why or why not?

3. What are some ways animals show intelligence? How do they show instinct? Is the difference always clear?

1 Work in a small group. List examples of animal intelligence that you have experienced or heard about. Then number the animals in order of most intelligent (1) to least intelligent (5). Discuss your rankings and examples.

INTELLIGENCE RANK	ANIMAL	EXAMPLE

2 Based on your discussion or other experience or knowledge you have, answer the questions.

1. Do you believe that dogs might think? What about bees, rats, birds, cats, monkeys, and apes?

2. How easily do animals learn?

3. Can animals apply what they may have learned to new challenges in their lives?

4. How can people learn about and evaluate the intelligence of animals?

C BACKGROUND AND VOCABULARY

Reading One is an excerpt from the book, *How Smart Are Animals?* The sentences in the left column on page 69 are from Reading One and are grouped under themes that appear in the reading.

Read the vocabulary words and their definitions in the right column. Then, complete the sentences in the left column with the correct words. (Note: The part of speech is in parentheses.)

Views on Animal Intelligence

1. Until the 1960's the view that animals acted only on instinct _____.

2. During the nineteenth century and early twentieth centuries, people readily _____ human emotions and mental abilities to animals.

Is This Intelligence?

3. Dolphins and killer whales can perform spectacular _____ at marine parks.

4. Because dogs _____ from wolves, which are highly social animals, they are very protective.

5. Since the lives of animals are so different from ours, we can't apply human _____ to them.

On Thinking

6. Although drug sniffing dogs are good at their jobs, they have no _____ of drug illegality. They aren't thinking and then deciding what to do.

7. Some of the most trainable creatures, such as dolphins, are the most likely _____ for genuine animal thinking.

Measuring Intelligence

8. When studying animals, we must test them in situations that have meaning for their lives, not ours, and not just look to see how much they _____ us.

9. Most IQ tests do not _____ creativity and other important mental skills.

10. Finding ways to get at animals' real mental _____ can be very difficult.

11. More than a hundred _____ of intelligence have been written about in scientific literature.

12. Dogs will sniff luggage and signal when they _____ drugs or illegal food in the bags.

candidates (n.): people or animals who are perfect for a job or are suitable to do something

concept (n.): understanding of how something is

capacity (n.): the ability to do or produce something

prevailed (v.): was the most common or frequent

evaluate (v.): to judge how good, useful, or successful someone or something is

feats (n.): impressive achievements needing a lot of strength and skill

perceive (v.): to notice something, that is difficult to notice

factors (n.): things that influence or cause a situation

standards (n.): levels of quality, skill, or ability considered to be normal

evolved (v.): developed and changed over a long period of time

attributed (v.): assigned

resemble (v.): to look like or be similar to

A READING ONE: How Smart Is Smart?

Read the first paragraph of How Smart Is Smart? *Work with a partner to answer the questions. Then read the rest of the article.*

1. Summarize what happened to Andrea Anderson.

   _____

   _____

   _____

   _____

2. Did Villa's actions come from instinct or intellect?

   _____

HOW SMART IS SMART?

By Dorothy Hinshaw Patent from *How Smart Are Animals?*

1   The blizzard[1] came on suddenly, with no warning. Eleven-year-old Andrea Anderson was outside near her home when the storm struck. The sixty- to eighty-mile-per-hour winds drove her into a snowdrift, and the snow quickly covered her up to her waist. Unable to get out, she screamed desperately for help. Through the swirling[2] wind, Villa, a year-old Newfoundland dog belonging to Andrea's neighbors, heard her cries. Villa had always been content to stay inside her dog run, but now she leapt over the five-foot fence and rushed to Andrea's side. First she licked the girl, then began circling around her, packing down the snow with her paws. Next, Villa stood as still as a statue in front of the girl with her paws on the packed snow. The dog waited until Andrea grabbed her, then strained[3] forward, pulling the girl from the drift. As the storm raged[4] around them, Villa led the way back to Andrea's home.

2   Villa won the Ken-l Ration Dog Hero of the Year award for her bravery, loyalty, and intelligence. Her **feat** was truly impressive—understanding that Andrea needed help and performing the tasks necessary to save her. We can all admire Villa and envy Andrea for having such a loyal friend. But did

---

[1] **blizzard:** a long heavy storm with a lot of wind and snow
[2] **swirling:** turning around and around
[3] **strained:** pulled hard at something
[4] **raged:** continued happening with great force or violence

Villa's heroic behavior exhibit intelligence? Some scientists would say that, while Villa certainly is a wonderful animal, her behavior was unthinking, perhaps an instinctive holdover from the protective environment of the wolf pack, where the adult animals defend the pups against danger. After all, dogs **evolved** from wolves, which are highly social animals. They would say that Villa just acted, without really understanding the **concept** of danger or thinking about what she was doing. Up until the 1960s, this view of animals **prevailed** among scientists studying animal behavior. But nowadays, a variety of experiments and experiences with different creatures are showing that some animals have impressive mental abilities.

DO ANIMALS THINK?

3   If dogs might think, what about bees, rats, birds, cats, monkeys, and apes? How well do animals learn? How much of their experiences can they remember? Can they apply what they may have learned to new challenges in their lives? Are animals aware of the world around them? How might it be possible to learn about and **evaluate** the intelligence of different animals?

4   It is easy to confuse trainability with thinking. But just because an animal can learn to perform a trick doesn't mean that it knows what it is doing. In the IQ Zoo in Hotsprings, Arkansas, for example, animals perform some amazing tasks. A cat turns on a light and then plays the piano, while a duck strums on a guitar with its bill. Parrots ride tiny bicycles and slide around on roller skates. At John F. Kennedy Airport in New York, beagles[5] work for the Food and Drug Administration, sniffing at luggage and signaling when they **perceive** drugs or illegal foods in the baggage. Dolphins and killer whales at marine parks perform some spectacular feats, and their behavior is often linked into a story line so that it appears they are acting roles, as humans would in a movie or play. These animals may seem to be behaving in an intelligent fashion, but they are just repeating behavior patterns they have been trained to perform for food rewards. The drug-sniffing beagle has no concept of drug illegality, and the duck doesn't understand or appreciate music. They aren't thinking and then deciding what to do.

5   Studying the intelligence of animals is very tricky. During the nineteenth and early twentieth centuries, people readily **attributed** human emotions and mental abilities to animals. Even learned scientists had great faith in animals' minds— "An animal can think in a human way and can express human ideas in human language," said the respected Swiss psychiatrist Gustav Wolff in the early 1900s.

6   Wolff's statement was inspired by Clever Hans, a horse that appeared to show remarkable intelligence. A retired schoolteacher trained Hans as he would a child, with blackboards, flash cards, number boards, and letter boards. After four years of training, Hans was ready to perform in public.

---

[5] **beagle:** a type of dog with long ears and smooth fur   *(continued on next page)*

When asked to solve a numerical problem, Hans would paw the answer with his hoof. He shook his head "yes" and "no," moved it "up" and "down", and turned it "right" or "left." Hans would show his "knowledge" of colors by picking up a rag of the appropriate shade with his teeth. Many scientists of the time came to watch Hans and tried to figure out how he performed his

Clever Hans and his trainer

amazing feats; they went away impressed. Hans appeared to understand human language and to have mastered arithmetic.

7   Then Oskar Pfungst, a German experimental psychologist, uncovered Hans's secret by using what is now a standard scientific method—the double-blind experiment[6]. When the horse was asked a question, no one in his presence knew the answer. Under these conditions, Clever Hans was no longer so "smart;" he couldn't come up with the correct responses. By observing the horse and the audience when the answer was known, Pfungst discovered Hans was very sensitive to the smallest movements of the people watching. They would lean ever so slightly forward until he had pawed the correct number of times, then relax. He watched for that sign of relief, then stopped pawing. His trainer unknowingly moved his head from side to side or up and down just enough for Hans to take a cue as to what to do. At the end of the investigation, Pfungst was able to prove his point. He stood in front of Hans without asking any question. He nodded his head slightly, and the horse began to tap his hoof. When Pfungst straightened his head, Hans stood at attention.

8   Ever since the embarrassment of Clever Hans, psychologists have been extremely wary of falling into the same trap. They are ready to call upon the "Clever Hans phenomenon" whenever an animal seems to be exhibiting intelligent behavior. Clever Hans taught psychology some important lessons, but the incident may also have made behavioral scientists too cautious about the mental abilities of animals.

9   Animals that are easy to train may also be very intelligent. Some of the most trainable creatures, such as dolphins, are also the most likely **candidates** for genuine animal thinking. But finding ways to get at animals' real mental **capacity** can be very difficult.

---

[6] **double-blind experiment:** an experiment or study that compares two or more groups in which neither the scientists nor the people being studied know which group is being tested and which group is not. Scientists get better results in double-blind studies.

WHAT IS INTELLIGENCE?

10   We humans recognize a "smart" person when we meet one; we know who is a "brain" and who is not. In school, we take IQ tests, which are supposed to give a numerical measure of our "intelligence." But these days, the whole concept of intelligence is being reevaluated. The older, standard IQ tests measure only a limited range of mental abilities, concentrating on mathematics and language skills. Creativity, which most people would agree is a critical element in the meaningful application of intelligence, has not traditionally been evaluated by such tests, and other important mental skills have also been ignored. But things are changing. Many scientists believe that dozens of different talents are a part of intelligence. In fact, more than a hundred **factors** of intelligence have been written about in scientific literature. Psychologists are now developing tests that measure intelligence more accurately and more broadly. The SOI (Structure of Intellect) test, for example, evaluates five main factors of intelligence: cognition (comprehension), memory, evaluation (judgment, planning, reasoning, and critical decision making), convergent production (solving problems where answers are known), and divergent production (solving problems creatively). Each of these is broken down further into many subcategories.

11   But what about animals? We can't hand them a pencil and paper and give them a test, and we can't ask them what they're thinking. We must find other ways of measuring their "smarts." And that's not the only problem. Since the lives of animals are so different from ours, we can't apply human **standards** to them. We must develop different ideas of what animal intelligence might be.

12   The concept of intelligence was thought up by humans, and our thinking about it is tied up with our own human system of values. The things that are important to animals can be different than those that matter to humans. When studying animals, we must test them in situations that have meaning for their lives, not ours, and not just look to see how much they **resemble** us.

◖ **READ FOR MAIN IDEAS**

Read the main ideas. Write the paragraph or paragraphs where the main ideas are found.

1. _____ Clever Hans wasn't really exhibiting intelligence; he was acting based on cues from people around him.

2. _____ Testing animal intelligence is problematic because the idea of intelligence must be seen from the perspective of the animal.

3. _____ Scientists' ideas about exactly what animal intelligence is have changed over time.

4. _____ Scientists are reevaluating their ideas about exactly what human intelligence is.

5. _____ Trained animals are not exhibiting intelligence because they don't understand what they are doing.

◖ READ FOR DETAILS

Complete the chart with supporting ideas for the main ideas in Reading One. Share your answers with a partner.

MAIN IDEAS	SUPPORTING IDEAS
1. Scientists' ideas about exactly what animal intelligence is have changed over time.	• Before the 1960s, scientists believed _____ _____ • Nowadays, scientists think _____ _____
2. Trained animals are not exhibiting intelligence because they don't understand what they are doing.	• Many animals appear to be behaving intelligently, but they are simply _____ _____ • For example, the duck that plays the guitar does not _____ _____
3. Clever Hans wasn't really exhibiting intelligence; he was acting based on cues from people around him.	• Clever Hans was simply observing _____ _____ • If no one in the audience knew the answer to the question, Hans _____ _____
4. Scientists' ideas about exactly what human intelligence is are being reevaluated.	• Older, standard IQ tests only measure _____ and _____, but not _____ • However, more than _____ of intelligence have been written about in _____
5. Testing animal intelligence is problematic because the idea of intelligence must be seen from the perspective of the animal.	• What is important to an animal is _____ _____ than what is important to a _____ • Therefore tests of animal intelligence must involve situations that _____ _____

(MAKE INFERENCES

Read the true animal stories. How do you interpret the animal's behavior? Look again at the paragraphs listed and decide if the animals' behavior is instinct, learned behavior from training, or intelligence. How do the stories relate to the views about intelligence in Reading One?

Gracious Gorilla

1. A three-year-old boy falls into a gorilla pen at a zoo with seven gorillas. An eight-year-old female gorilla named Binti picks him up, protects him from the other gorillas, and gently brings him to emergency personnel waiting at a door to the enclosure. The boy is taken to a hospital where he recovers after a few days.

See Reading One, Paragraph 2

_____

_____

_____

Musical Monkeys

2. Some monkeys are able to recognize children's songs. One of the twelve songs they remembered is "Happy Birthday."

See Reading One, Paragraph 4

_____

_____

_____

Parlez-vous Prairie Dog

3. Scientists have discovered that prairie dogs have a highly developed communication system. These rodents have specific calls to express, "hawk ahead," "coyote alert," and "human approaching."

See Reading One, Paragraphs 11 and 12

_____

_____

_____

◖ **EXPRESS OPINIONS**

Discuss the questions with a partner.

1. Oskar Pfungst proved that Clever Hans wasn't able to solve mathematical problems. Do you still believe that Hans showed intelligence by learning to "read" the movements of his questioners and audience members?

2. The author states that in order to evaluate animal intelligence we have to test animals in situations that are meaningful for them. Is it possible for people to know what is meaningful for animals? How?

B READING TWO: Extreme Perception and Animal Intelligence

Reading Two talks about animals with extreme perception. It also discusses animal intelligence.

1 *Discuss the questions in a small group. Then read the article.*

1. What do you think *extreme perception* means?

2. Could extreme perception be a sign of animal intelligence or do you think they are unrelated? Explain.

EXTREME PERCEPTION
AND
ANIMAL INTELLIGENCE

By Temple Grandin and Catherine Johnson
(from *Animals in Translation*)

1   Many animals have extreme perception. Forensic[1] dogs are three times as good as any X-ray machine at sniffing out contraband[2], drugs, or explosives and their overall success rate is 90 percent.

2   The fact that dogs can smell things a person can't doesn't make him a genius; it just makes him a dog. Humans can see things dogs can't, but that doesn't make us smarter. But when you look at the jobs some dogs have invented for themselves using their advanced perceptual abilities, you're moving into the realm of true cognition, which is solving a problem under novel conditions. The seizure[3] alert dogs are an example of an animal using advanced perceptual abilities to solve a problem no dog was born knowing how to solve. Seizure alert dogs are dogs who, their owners say, can *predict* a seizure before it starts. There's still controversy over whether you can train a dog to predict seizures, and so far people haven't had a lot of luck trying. But there are a number of dogs who have figured it out on their own. These dogs were trained as seizure response dogs, meaning they can help a person once a seizure has begun. The dog might be trained to lie on top of the person so he doesn't hurt himself, or bring the person his medicine or the telephone. Those are all standard helpful behaviors any dog can be trained to perform.

3   But some of these dogs have gone from responding to seizures to perceiving signs of a seizure ahead of time. No one knows how they do this, because the signs are invisible to people. No human being can look at someone who is about to have a seizure and see (or hear, smell, or feel) what's coming. Yet one study found that 10 percent of owners said their seizure response dogs had turned into seizure alert dogs.

4   The *New York Times* published a terrific article about a woman named Connie Standley, in Florida, who has two huge Bouvier de Flandres dogs who predict her seizures about thirty minutes ahead of time. When they sense Ms. Standley is heading into a seizure, they'll do things like

Seizure alert dog with owner Donna Jacobs

pull on her clothes, bark at her, or drag on her hand to get her to someplace safe so she won't get hurt when the seizure begins. Ms. Standley says they predict about 80 percent of her seizures. Ms. Standley's dogs apparently were trained as seizure alert dogs before they came to her, but there aren't many dogs in that category. Most seizure alert dogs were trained to respond to seizures, not predict seizures.

5   The seizure alert dogs remind me of Clever Hans. Hans was the world-famous German horse in the early 1900s whose owner, Wilhelm von Osten, thought he could count. Herr von Osten could ask the horse questions like, "what's seven and five?" and Hans would tap out the number twelve with his hoof. Hans could even tap out answers to questions like, "If the eighth day of the month comes on Tuesday, what is the date for the following Friday?" He could answer mathematical questions posed to him by complete strangers, too.

(continued on next page)

---

[1] **forensic:** relating to methods for finding out about a crime
[2] **contraband:** goods that are brought into or taken out of a country illegally
[3] **seizure:** a short time when someone is unconscious and cannot control the movements of his/her body

6 Eventually, a psychologist named Oskar Pfungst managed to show that Hans wasn't really counting. Instead, Hans was observing subtle, unconscious cues the humans had no idea they were giving off. He'd start tapping his foot when he could see it was time to start tapping; then he'd stop tapping his foot when he could see it was time to stop tapping. His questioners were making tiny, unconscious movements only Hans could see. The movements were so tiny the humans making them couldn't even *feel* them.

7 Dr. Pfungst couldn't see the movements, either, and he was looking for them. He finally solved the case by putting Hans's questioners out of view and having them ask Hans questions they didn't know the answers to themselves. It turned out Hans could answer questions only when the person asking the question was in plain view and already knew the answer. If either condition was missing, his performance fell apart.

8 Psychologists often use the Clever Hans story to show that humans who believe animals are intelligent are deluding themselves. But that's not the obvious conclusion as far as I'm concerned. No one has ever been able to *train* a horse to do what Hans did. Hans trained himself. Is the ability to read a member of a different species as well as Hans was reading human beings really a sign that he was just a "dumb animal" who'd been classically conditioned to stamp his hoof? I think there is more to it than that.

9 What makes Hans similar to seizure alert dogs is that both Hans and the dogs acquired their skills without human help. As I mentioned, to my knowledge, so far no one has figured out how to take a "raw" dog and teach it how to predict seizures. About the best a trainer can do is reward the dogs for helping when a person is having a seizure and then leave it up to the dog to start identifying signs that predict the onset of a seizure on his own. That approach hasn't been hugely successful, but some dogs do it. I think those dogs are showing superior intelligence the same way a human who can do something few other people can do shows superior intelligence.

10 What makes the actions of the seizure alert dogs, and probably of Hans, too, a sign of high intelligence—or high talent—is the fact that they didn't have to do what they did. It's one thing for a dog to start recognizing the signs that a seizure is coming; you might chalk that up to unique aspects of canine hearing, smell, or vision, like the fact that a dog can hear a dog whistle while a human can't. But it's another thing for a dog to start to recognize the signs of an impending seizure and *then decide to do something about it*. That's what intelligence is in humans; intelligence is people using their built-in perceptual and cognitive skills to achieve useful and sometimes remarkable goals.

2 *Complete the statements.*

1. Seizure alert dogs are different from seizure response dogs because _____
_____.

2. Clever Hans and seizure alert dogs are similar because they both _____
_____.

3. Clever Hans knew when to start or stop tapping his hoof because _____
_____.

4. For Clever Hans to correctly answer a question, two conditions had to be met:

a. _____

b. _____

STEP 1: Organize

The two readings present differing interpretations of animal intelligence. In addition, the interpretations have changed over time. Complete the sequence organizer with information from the readings.

---

1. Early 1900s

Gustav Wolff believed, "an animal can _____ ." This belief was

inspired by the fact that Clever Hans, at first, seemed to _____ and _____ .

▼

2. Oskar Pfungst's view of Clever Hans

Pfungst believed Hans did not _____ .

Instead, Hans _____ .

▼

3. Before 1960

Scientists believed that animals' actions were based on _____ and not _____ .

▼

4. Current views on trained animals

Animals that are easy to train may be _____ .

▼

5. Current views on trainability of animals

Trained animals may appear to be intelligent, but _____

_____ .

▼

6. Current views on testing animal intelligence

When evaluating animal intelligence, we must test them _____

_____ not _____ .

▼

7. Temple Grandin's view of animal intelligence

If an animal can recognize signs they weren't _____ and decide

to _____, then _____ .

On a separate piece of paper, write a summary of how views on animal intelligence have changed over time using the information from Step 1. Use transitional phrases such as first, then, after that, over time, now, and today.

③ FOCUS ON WRITING

Ⓐ VOCABULARY

◖ REVIEW

Two of the three words in each row have similar meanings to the boldfaced word from the readings. Cross out the word that does not belong. If you need help, use a dictionary.

1. **evaluate**	assess	signal	test
2. **concept**	idea	answer	understanding
3. **perceive**	detect	notice	believe
4. **resemble**	look like	build	be similar to
5. **controversy**	gathering	disagreement	debate
6. **predict**	forecast	report	expect
7. **conditioned**	trained	taught	worked
8. **standards**	values	norms	characteristics
9. **capacity**	activity	ability	capability
10. **feats**	acts	accomplishments	attempts
11. **evolve**	develop	decay	progress
12. **attributed**	offered	assigned	attached

◖ EXPAND

Many academic words, especially those used in the sciences, have Latin or Greek roots. For example, the word *psychiatrist* comes from the Greek root, *psych*, meaning *mind*. A **psych**iatrist is a doctor who studies the mind.

Complete the chart with words from the readings. The first column gives the root. The second column gives the root's meaning. The next column gives the reading number and paragraph number where you can find a word with this root. Look for the words in the readings. Then guess their meanings using the roots' meanings and the context of the sentence. Finally, think of other words with the same root and write them in the last column. If you need help, use a dictionary. Share your answers with the class.

ROOT	MEANING	READING-PARAGRAPH	WORD	MEANING	OTHER WORDS WITH THE SAME ROOT
1. psych-	mind	R1-5 R1-7 R1-8	Psychiatrist	Doctor who studies the mind	Psychic
2. cogni-	know/learn	R2-2 R2-10			
3. -dict	say/tell	R2-2			
4. sign-	mark	R1-4			
5. cent-	one hundred	R1-5 R2-3			
6. numer-	number	R1-6			
7. aud-	hear/listen	R1-7			
8. spect-	see/look	R1-4			
9. sens-	feeling	R1-7 R2-4			

◖ CREATE

On a separate piece of paper, write five questions about Clever Hans. Use at least one word from the Expand or Review sections in each question. Then, exchange papers with a partner and answer the questions. You can write or discuss your answers.

B **GRAMMAR: Identifying Adjective Clauses**

1 *Examine the sentences and answer the questions with a partner.*

a. When studying animals, we must test them in situations **that have meaning for their lives.**

b. No human being can look at someone **who is about to have a seizure** and see (or hear, smell, or feel) what's coming.

c. Oskar Pfungst often thought back proudly on the afternoon **when he was finally able to figure out how Clever Hans was able to answer the questions.**

1. In sentence *a*, what kinds of situations is the writer describing?

2. In sentence *b*, what type of person does the writer say no human being can look at and see what's coming?

3. In sentence *c*, which afternoon is the writer describing?

4. What words begin the boldfaced phrases? Are the words that come just before these phrases verbs, adjectives, nouns, or adverbs?

IDENTIFYING ADJECTIVE CLAUSES

1. **Identifying adjective clauses,** sometimes called restrictive relative clauses, are groups of words (phrases) that act as adjectives to describe or identify a noun. These phrases come directly after the nouns they describe and begin with relative pronouns that refer to the noun. Sentences with adjective clauses can be seen as a combination of two shorter sentences about the same noun.

He had **a horse.** + **The horse** could answer mathematical questions.
= He had **a horse that could answer mathematical questions**.

The duck lived in **a zoo.** + **The zoo** was in Arkansas.
= **The zoo where the duck lived** was in Arkansas.

---

2. Identifying adjective clauses begin with a **relative pronoun**. The noun it describes determines the choice of pronoun.

who = person or people (and sometimes animals)
which = thing or things
that = thing, things, person, or people (less formal than which or who)
when = a time or times
where or *in which* = a place or places
whose or *in whose* = possession

---

3. Remember that the relative pronoun replaces the noun it describes; the noun is not repeated.

I saw **the horse.** + The scientist was testing **the horse**.
= I saw **the horse *that*** the scientist was testing.

INCORRECT: I saw **the horse *that*** the scientist was testing **the horse**.

---

2   *Read the sentences and circle Correct or Incorrect for the relative pronoun used. If the pronoun is correct, add an alternative that could also be used. If the pronoun is incorrect, write two pronouns that could be used.*

1. The scientist <u>which</u> observed Clever Hans wrote a book.

   Correct   Alternatives : _____

   (Incorrect)   Corrections : _____*who or what*_____

2. The zoo <u>where</u> animals are trained to perform spectacular feats is located in Arkansas.

Correct   Alternatives : _____

Incorrect   Corrections : _____

3. Seizure alert dogs are dogs <u>whose</u> can predict a seizure before it starts.

Correct   Alternatives : _____

Incorrect   Corrections : _____

4. Hans was the world-famous horse <u>which</u> owner, Wilhelm von Osten, was a retired school teacher.

Correct   Alternatives : _____

Incorrect   Corrections : _____

5. On the day <u>when</u> Villa the dog saved the little girl, I was out of town.

Correct   Alternatives : _____

Incorrect   Corrections : _____

6. Psychologists are now developing tests <u>that</u> assess human intelligence more accurately.

Correct   Alternatives : _____

Incorrect   Corrections : _____

7. Many people <u>when</u> study animals are convinced that they are able to understand some human language.

Correct   Alternatives : _____

Incorrect   Corrections : _____

8. Villa the Newfoundland pulled Andrea from the snowdrift <u>which</u> she was stuck.

Correct   Alternatives : _____

Incorrect   Corrections : _____

3 *Combine each pair of sentences into one sentence using an identifying adjective clause.*

1. **a.** Clever Hans was trained by a retired school teacher.
   b. The school teacher had taught science for many years.

   Clever Hans was trained by a retired school teacher who had taught science for many years.

2. **a.** The afternoon was cold and rainy.
   b. That afternoon Clever Hans was ready to perform in front of an audience.

   The afternoon when Clever Hans was ready to perform in front of an audience was cold and rainy.

3. **a.** Binti the gorilla is best known for an amazing incident.
   b. The incident occurred on August 16, 1996.

   _____

   _____

4. **a.** I spoke with a man.
   b. The man had trained dolphins and killer whales.

   _____

   _____

5. **a.** Psychologists study many animals.
   b. Animals live in zoos.

   _____

   _____

6. **a.** I saw my friend.
   b. Her dog could predict seizures before they started.

   _____

   _____

7. **a.** We saw the dolphin.
   b. The dolphin performed some spectacular feats.

   _____

   _____

8. **a.** The psychologist had studied at the University of Berlin.
   b. The psychologist developed a new test of animal intelligence.

   _____

   _____

9. **a.** The morning was sunny and hot.
   b. That morning Lulu the pig saved Mrs. Altsman.

   _____

   _____

10. **a.** The girl was covered in snow.
    b. She was saved by Villa the dog.

   _____

   _____

In this unit, you read two passages on animal intelligence. How would you summarize the important information from one of the readings?

You are going to **write a summary of Reading Two as if you were a journalist writing for a newspaper or magazine.***

◖ **PREPARE TO WRITE:** Asking and Answering *Wh-* Questions

To help you to plan your summary of Reading Two, you will **ask and answer the *Wh-* questions *Who, What, Where, When, Why,* and *How.*** Many writers, especially journalists, use the *Wh-* questions when they are writing a summary of an important story or news event.

Write one or two questions for each Wh- *question. Share your questions with a partner and answer them.*

Q: What: What is the main idea (paragraph) or thesis (essay or longer article)? What does the person have to say? What issues are discussed?

A: _____

_____

Q: Who: Who wrote the article or passage?

A: _____

_____

Q: Where: _____

_____

A: _____

_____

STORY

Q: When: _____

A: _____

_____

Q: Why: _____

A: _____

_____

Q: Where: _____

A: _____

*For Alternative Writing Topics, see page 90. These topics can be used in place of the writing topic for this unit or as homework. The alternative topics relate to the theme of the unit, but may not target the same grammar or rhetorical structures taught in the unit.

◖ WRITE: A Summary

A **summary** is a shortened version of a text that focuses on the thesis or main idea. It does not include many details or examples. It does not include personal opinions. Here are some important points:

1. **Read and reread the text**. As you read, think about the *Wh-* questions. Make sure you understand the text.

2. **Highlight or underline the thesis**. To find the thesis, think about the purpose of the text. What is the author's main idea?

3. **Rewrite the thesis in one sentence**. Use your own words.

4. **Continue reading**. Highlight the main idea, key words and phrases for each paragraph. Write one sentence summaries in your own words for each paragraph.

5. **Check your sentences against the text**. Again, use your own wording.

6. **Make sure you have not included irrelevant examples or your own opinion**.

7. **Write your summary**.

8. **Return later and check it again** with fresh eyes.

9. **Polish summary for flow**; it needs to read well.

1 *Read the summary of Reading One and answer the questions.*

In the excerpt from, *How Smart is Smart?*, author Dorothy Hinshaw Patent discusses how scientists in the past fifty years have changed their opinions of what animal intelligence is. Hinshaw states that through experimentation and observation, scientists now believe that many animals act in ways that show great intelligence, not just instinctual behavior. In discussing an animal's ability to think, Hinshaw believes it is first important to distinguish between intelligence and trainability. In other words, animals that are highly trained to do specific tasks or tricks may not be thinking on their own and therefore not showing a form of intelligence. On the other hand, Hinshaw does acknowledge that, "Animals that are easy to train may also be highly intelligent." Hinshaw concludes that testing an animal's intelligence is very difficult and we should not apply our own human beliefs about what intelligence is to them. Specifically, animals must be tested against measures that are important and useful to them, not just to the human world.

1. Who is the author? What is the title of the book? _____

2. What is the thesis? _____

   _____

3. How has the view of intelligence changed over time? _____

   _____

4. What is the author's conclusion about testing animal intelligence? Why does the author believe it is so difficult to test an animal's intelligence? _____

   _____

2 *Before you begin to write a summary for the whole text, practice by summarizing sections of the reading, individual paragraphs, or groups of paragraphs. For paragraphs 1–7, circle the sentence that best describes the main idea. For paragraphs 8–10, write the one-sentence summary yourself. Check your answers with a partner.*

1. Read paragraph 1 of Reading Two. Which statement best describes the main idea of the paragraph?
   a. Animals that display a deep understanding of the world around them are plentiful.
   b. There are some dogs that can sniff out dangerous materials at a very successful rate.
   c. Some forensic dogs are so good at their jobs, they are much better than X-ray machines.

2. Read paragraph 2. Which statement best describes the main idea of the paragraph?
   a. Some seizure response dogs have trained themselves to be seizure alert dogs.
   b. Dogs who are truly intelligent will apply their thinking skills to new situations.
   c. Seizure response dogs are trained to save their owner's lives.

3. Read paragraphs 3 and 4. Which statement best describes the main idea of the paragraphs?
   a. Connie Standley's dogs predict her seizures before they happen.
   b. No one knows how seizure response dogs read signs given off by humans before a seizure.
   c. Some seizure response dogs have become seizure alert dogs without any training.

4. Read paragraphs 5, 6, and 7. Which statement best describes the main idea of the paragraphs?
   a. Clever Hans was not really counting, but was able to detect and understand human signs that even humans could not see just as seizure alert dogs are.
   b. Oskar Pfungst, a psychologist, eventually proved that Clever Hans was not really counting.
   c. Clever Hans looked like he was counting but was really just tapping his foot until he knew to stop.

5. Read paragraph 8. Write a one-sentence summary of the main idea.

_____

6. Read paragraphs 9 and 10. Write a one-sentence summary of the main idea.

_____

3 *Now write your first draft of your summary of Reading Two. Use the information from Prepare to Write and Write to plan your summary. Make sure you state the thesis and eliminate any unimportant details. Be sure to use grammar and vocabulary from the unit.*

◖ REVISE: Paraphrasing

Summary writing often requires the writer to restate an author's ideas. It is very important to restate the author's ideas in your own words while keeping true to the author's ideas. This is called **paraphrasing**. (*Note:* When you choose to use author's direct words, you must use quotation marks.)

AUTHOR'S OWN WORDS	PARAPHRASED TEXT
"The things that are important to animals can be different than those that matter to humans. When studying animals, we must test them in situations that have meaning for their lives, not ours, and not just look to see how much they **resemble** us."	Hinshaw concludes that testing an animal's intelligence is very difficult and we should not apply our own human beliefs about what intelligence is to them. Specifically, animals must be tested against measures that are important and useful to them, not to the human world.
When using a direct quote, use these punctuation rules:	When paraphrasing or quoting, use a variety of reporting verbs to introduce an author's ideas:
1. Lift the quote directly as is from the text. Do not change the capitalization or punctuation.	*says* *notes* *tells* *mentions* *acknowledges* *thinks* *concedes* *writes* *states* *believes* *explains* *concludes*
2. Place a comma before the quote: Hinshaw does however acknowledge that**,** "Animals that are easy to train may also be highly intelligent."	
3. Place the final punctuation mark at the end of the sentence before the final quotation mark: Hinshaw does however acknowledge that, "Animals that are easy to train may also be highly intelligent**."**	

When paraphrasing, first think of the main idea or what the author is trying to tell you. Think of ways to say the same thing using your own words. Do not just replace words in a sentence with synonyms.

Original	**Paraphrase**
Many animals have extreme perception.	~~Many animals have excellent awareness.~~

Rules for Paraphrasing

1. Read the original text. Make sure you understand it. Highlight the main idea and key words or phrases.

2. Read the text again. Put the text aside.

3. Write the idea in your own words without looking at the text. Try to use different words than the text.

4. Try to reorder the ideas in the sentence. Start with the middle or the end. Put the paraphrased text aside for a while.

5. With fresh eyes, check your paraphrased sentence against the original. Make sure it is not too close to the original.

Original	**Paraphrase**
Many animals have extreme perception.	Animals that display a deep understanding of their world are not hard to find.

1 *Paraphrase the sentences from Reading One in your own words.*

1. Ever since the embarrassment of Clever Hans, psychologists have been extremely wary of falling into the same trap. They are ready to call upon the "Clever Hans phenomenon" whenever an animal seems to be exhibiting intelligent behavior.

_____

_____

_____

2. Some scientists would say that, while Villa certainly is a wonderful animal, her behavior was unthinking, perhaps an instinctive holdover from the protective environment of the wolf pack, where the adult animals defend the pups against danger.

_____

_____

_____

3. Many scientists believe that dozens of different talents are a part of intelligence. In fact, more than a hundred factors of intelligence have been written about in scientific literature.

_____

_____

_____

2 Look at your first draft. Make sure you have paraphrased the author of Reading Two using your own words. Check against the original text and make any changes necessary. Add a quote if you think it will be effective. Watch your punctuation with your quote!

◀ EDIT: Writing the Final Draft

Write the final draft of your essay. Carefully edit it for grammatical problems and mechanical errors, such as spelling, capitalization, and punctuation. Make sure you used some of the grammar and vocabulary from the unit. Use the checklist to help you write your final draft. Then neatly write or type your essay.

✓ FINAL DRAFT CHECKLIST

- ○ Does the summary include the author's name and the title of the reading?
- ○ Does the summary include a thesis statement?
- ○ Does the summary answer some of the 5W and 1H questions?
- ○ Is the summary in your own words?
- ○ Did you use a variety of reporting verbs?
- ○ If you are using quotes, are they properly punctuated?
- ○ Did you use identifying adjective clauses?
- ○ Has vocabulary from the unit been used?

ALTERNATIVE WRITING TOPICS

Choose one of the topics. Write an essay using the vocabulary and grammar from the unit.

1. In Reading One, the author states, "The things that are important to animals can be different than those that matter to humans. When studying animals, we must test them in situations that have meaning for their lives, not ours, and not just look to see how much they resemble us." Think of a specific animal or group of animals. What do you think are situations that would have meaning for them? Why? How could you test them in these situations?

2. Two differing views of Clever Hans' intelligence were presented in the unit. Do you agree with either one or do you have an alternative explanation?

RESEARCH TOPICS, see page 261.

Longevity: Too Much of a Good Thing?

off the mark.com   by Mark Parisi

©2005 MARK PARISI DIST. BY UFS INC.

1 FOCUS ON THE TOPIC

A PREDICT

Look at the cartoon and the unit title. Then discuss the questions with a partner.

1. What was Ponce de Leon searching for?

2. Immortality means living forever. Do you know stories or myths about the desire or search for immortality?

3. What do you think "too much of a good thing" means? What do you think the unit will be about?

Throughout history, people have sought immortality. People today are living longer than at any time in history; however, we are still a long way from reaching immortality.

Work with a partner or in a small group and discuss the questions.

1. If scientists could create a pill that would allow you to live twice as long while staying healthy, would you take it?

2. How would life be different if you lived longer? How would it be better? How would it be worse? Think about how such issues as relationships, marriage, family structure, and career might be affected.

C **BACKGROUND AND VOCABULARY**

Reading One is a story about Marilisa and her husband, Leo. Read the letter Marilisa wrote to a friend about Leo. Choose the definition that best defines the boldfaced word.

1. **a.** mean
   b. energetic
   c. lazy

2. **a.** on time
   b. well dressed
   c. considerately

3. **a.** understandably
   b. incredibly
   c. to some extent

4. **a.** difficult
   b. fascinating
   c. different

5. **a.** slightly
   b. always
   c. completely

6. **a.** complicated
   b. impressive
   c. terrible

7. **a.** doing things slowly after thinking about them
   b. doing things because somebody told you to
   c. doing things quickly without thinking

8. **a.** annoying
   b. friendly
   c. interesting

Dear Susannah,

I know you are worried about my marrying Leo, but please realize he has many good qualities. For example, he is quite **(1) vigorous**. Despite his age, he still exercises for hours and then works in the garden. In addition, he is very thoughtful. Unlike some of my friends, he always arrives **(2) punctually**. If he says he will meet me at 10 o'clock, he will be there exactly at 10.

He is also **(3) immeasurably** wise. He has so much knowledge and experience and is interested in so many **(4) disparate** subjects such as Greek history, diamond mining, dinosaurs, and alternative medicine. Even though they are not related, he enjoys them all. I find this quality **(5) utterly** fascinating. I am totally amazed by his vast knowledge. Leo really has had an **(6) awesome** life when you think about everything he has done. It is so exciting living with someone who has had so many incredible experiences.

However, I'm not claiming Leo is perfect. For one thing, he can be very **(7) impetuous**. Just last week, he bought a new car. He didn't even think about the fact that we needed that money to pay our credit card bills!

Furthermore, at times, he can be **(8) insufferable**. I was trying to watch television last night and he was constantly interrupting me to ask questions. Couldn't he understand that I was trying to concentrate on the show? His family is another problem. Take his ex-wife, Katrin, for example. I don't understand why he ever married her. Leo, of course, is very nice and friendly to everyone.

9. **a.** pleasant
   b. very unfriendly
   c. unhappy

10. **a.** rude or arrogant
    b. modest or shy
    c. admired or respected

11. **a.** accustomed to
    b. feeling love or affection for
    c. discovered

12. **a.** maybe
    b. currently
    c. in the end

She, however, always seems very **(9) chilly**, especially toward me. Also, one of his sons from a previous marriage can be very **(10) presumptuous**. He expects me to do things for him just because I am now married to his father . . . even though I barely know him! His daughter, however, is lovely. I am really quite **(11) fond of** her. I think you would really like her, too.

Despite my complaints, I know that Leo is **(12) ultimately** the best first husband I could ever wish for, so don't worry. I'm sure we'll always be happy together.

Susannah, I hope all is well with you.

Love,

Marilisa

2 FOCUS ON READING

A READING ONE: Death Do Us Part

The story you are about to read is science fiction. Science fiction is a genre of writing that describes imaginary future developments in science and technology and their effect on people. It often includes elements that seem familiar to our lives today, making it seem "real."

Read the first two paragraphs of Death Do Us Part. *Work with a partner to answer the questions. Then read the rest of the story.*

1. What do you think was "her first, his seventh"?

2. What is happening with Marilisa and Leo?

3. Where and when do you think this story takes place?

4. What seems real?

5. What seems unreal?

6. What do you think "the Process" is?

DEATH DO US PART

By Robert Silverberg

1   It was her first, his seventh. She was thirty-two, he was three hundred and sixty-three: the good old May/December[1] number. They honeymooned in Venice, Nairobi, the Malaysia Pleasure Dome, and one of the posh[2] L-5 resorts, a shimmering glassy sphere with round-the-clock sunlight and waterfalls that tumbled like cascades of diamonds, and then they came home to his lovely sky-house suspended on tremulous guy-wires[3] a thousand meters above the Pacific to begin the everyday part of their life together.

2   Her friends couldn't get over it. "He's ten times your age!" they would exclaim. "How could you possibly want anybody that old?" Marilisa admitted that marrying Leo was more of a lark[4] for her than anything else. An impulsive thing: a sudden **impetuous** leap. Marriages weren't forever, after all—just thirty or forty years and then you moved along. But Leo was sweet and kind and actually quite sexy. And he had wanted her so much. He genuinely did seem to love her. Why should his age be an issue? He didn't appear to be any older than thirty-five or so. These days you could look as young as you like. Leo did his Process faithfully and **punctually**, twice each decade, and it kept him as dashing and **vigorous** as a boy.

3   There were little drawbacks, of course. Once upon a time, long, long ago, he had been a friend of Marilisa's great-grandmother: They might have even been lovers. She wasn't going to ask. Such things sometimes happened and you simply had to work your way around them. And then also he had an ex-wife on the scene, Number Three, Katrin, two hundred and forty-seven years old and not looking a day over thirty. She was constantly hovering[5] about. Leo still had warm feelings for her. "A wonderfully dear woman, a good and loyal friend," he would say. "When you get to know her, you'll be as **fond of** her as I am." That

one was hard, all right. What was almost as bad, he had children three times Marilisa's age and more. One of them—the next-to-youngest, Fyodor—had an **insufferable** and **presumptuous** way of winking[6] and sniggering[7] at her. "I want you to meet our father's newest toy," Fyodor said of her once, when yet another of

---

[1] **May/December:** term used to describe a romantic relationship where there is a big difference between the ages of the two people

[2] **posh:** expensive and used by rich people

[3] **tremulous guy-wires:** shaking cables (metal ropes)

[4] **lark:** something you do to amuse yourself or as a joke

[5] **hovering:** staying in the same place especially because you are waiting for something

[6] **winking:** closing and opening one eye quickly, usually to show that you are joking, being friendly, or telling a secret

[7] **sniggering:** laughing quietly in a way that is not nice

Leo's centenarian sons, previously unsuspected by Marilisa, turned up. "We get to play with her when he's tired of her." Someday Marilisa was going to pay him back[8] for that.

4   Still and all, she had no serious complaints. Leo was an ideal first husband: wise, warm, loving, attentive, and generous. She felt nothing but the greatest tenderness for him. And then too he was so **immeasurably** experienced in the ways of the world. If being married to him was a little like being married to Abraham Lincoln or Augustus Caesar, well, so be it: They had been great men, and so was Leo. He was endlessly fascinating. He was like seven husbands rolled into one. She had no regrets, none at all, not really.

5   In the spring of eighty-seven they go to Capri for their first anniversary. Their hotel is a reconstructed Roman villa on the southern slope of Monte Tiberio: alabaster wall frescoed in black and red, a brilliantly colored mosaic of sea-creatures in the marble bathtub, a broad travertine terrace that looks out over the sea. They stand together in the darkness, staring at the **awesome** sparkle of the stars. A crescent moon slashes across the night. His arm is around her; her head rests against his breast. Though she is a tall woman, Marilisa is barely heart-high to him.

6   "Tomorrow at sunrise," he says, "we'll see the Blue Grotto[9]. And then in the afternoon we'll hike down below here to the Cave of the Mater Magna. I always get a shiver when I'm there. Thinking about the ancient islanders who worshipped their goddess under that cliff, somewhere back in the Pleistocene. Their rites and rituals, the offerings they made to her."

Blue Grotto

7   "Is that when you first came here?" she asks, keeping it light and sly. "Somewhere in the Pleistocene?"

8   "A little later than that, really. The Renaissance, I think it was. Leonardo and I traveled down together from Florence-"

9   "You and Leonardo, you were like *that*?"

10   "Like that, yes. But not like *that*, if you take my meaning."

11   "And Cosimo di'Medici. Another one from the good old days. Cosimo gave such great parties, right?"

12   "That was Lorenzo," he says. "Lorenzo the Magnificent, Cosimo's grandson. Much more fun than the old man. You would have adored him."

13   "I almost think you're serious when you talk like that."

14   "I'm always serious. Even when I'm not." His arm tightens around her. He leans forward and down, and buries a kiss in her thick dark hair. "I love you," he whispers.

15   "I love you," she says. "You're the best first husband a girl could want."

16   "You're the finest last wife a man could ever desire."

(continued on next page)

---

8 **pay (someone) back:** to do something unpleasant to someone as a punishment because they have done something unpleasant to you

9 **Blue Grotto:** a famous sea cove on the coast of the Italian island of Capri

17   The words skewer[10] her. *Last* wife? Is he expecting to die in the next ten or twenty or thirty years? He is old—ancient—but nobody has any idea yet where the limits of the Process lie. Five hundred years? A thousand? Who can say? No one able to afford the treatments has died a natural death yet, in the four hundred years since the Process was invented. Why then does he speak so knowingly of her as his last wife? He may live long enough to have seven, ten, fifty wives after her.

18   Marilisa is silent a long while.

19   Then she asks him, quietly, uncertainly. "I don't understand why you said that."

20   "Said what?"

21   "The thing about my being your last wife."

22   He hesitates[11] a moment. "But why would I ever want another, now that I have you?"

23   "Am I so **utterly** perfect?"

24   "I love you."

25   "You loved Tedesca and Thane and Iavilda too," she says. "And Miaule and Katrin." She is counting on her fingers in the darkness. One wife is missing from the list. "And . . . Syantha. See, I know all their names. You must have loved them but the marriage ended anyway. They have to end. No matter how much you love a person, you can't keep a marriage going forever."

26   "How do you know that?"

27   "I just do. Everybody knows it."

28   "I would like this marriage never to end," he tells her. "I'd like it to go on and on and on. To continue to the end of time. Is that all right? Is such a sentiment[12] permissible, do you think?"

29   "What a romantic you are, Leo!"

30   "What else can I be but romantic, tonight? This place, the spring night, the moon, the stars, the sea, the fragrance of the flowers in the air. Our anniversary. I love you. Nothing will ever end for us. Nothing."

31   "Can that really be so?" she asks.

32   "Of course. Forever and ever, as it is this moment."

33   She thinks from time to time of the men she will marry after she and Leo have gone their separate ways. For she knows that she will. Perhaps she'll stay with Leo for ten years, perhaps for fifty; but **ultimately**, despite all his assurances to the contrary,[13] one or the other of them will want to move on. No one stays married forever. Fifteen, twenty years, that's the usual. Sixty or seventy tops.

34   She'll marry a great athlete, next, she decides. And then a philosopher; and a political leader; and then stay single for a few decades, just to clear her palate, so to speak, an intermezzo[14] in her life, and when she wearies of that she'll find someone entirely different, a simple rugged man who likes to hunt, to work in the

---

[10] **skewer:** to hurt
[11] **hesitates:** pauses before doing or saying something because you are uncertain
[12] **sentiment:** an opinion or feeling that you have about something
[13] **to the contrary:** showing that the opposite is true
[14] **intermezzo:** a short period of time between two longer periods

fields with his hands, and then a yachtsman with whom she'll sail the world, and then maybe when she's about three hundred she'll marry a boy, an innocent of eighteen or nineteen who hasn't even had his first Prep yet, and then—then a childish game. It always brings her to tears, eventually. The unknown husbands that wait for her in the misty future are vague **chilly** phantoms, fantasies, frightening, and inimical[15]. They are like swords that will inevitably fall between her and Leo, and she hates them for that.

35   The thought of having the same husband for all the vast expanse[16] of time that is the rest of her life, is a little disturbing—it gives her a sense of walls closing in, and closing and closing and closing—but the thought of leaving Leo is even worse. Or of his leaving her. Maybe she isn't truly in love with him, at any rate not as she imagines love at its deepest to be, but she is happy with him. She wants to stay with him. She can't really envision parting with him and moving on to someone else.

36   But of course she knows that she will. Everybody does in the fullness of time. *Everybody*.

37   Leo is a sand-painter. Sand-painting is his fifteenth or twentieth career. He has been an architect, an archeologist, a space-habitats developer, a professional gambler, an astronomer, and a number of other **disparate** and dazzling things. He reinvents himself every decade or two. That's as necessary to him as the Process itself. Making money is never an issue, since he lives on the compounding interest of investments set aside centuries ago. But the fresh challenge—ah, yes, always the fresh challenge.

38   Marilisa hasn't entered on any career path yet. It's much too soon. She is, after all, still in her first life, too young for the Process, merely in the Prep stage yet. Just a child, really. She has dabbled[17] in ceramics, written some poetry, composed a little music. Lately she has begun to think about studying economics or perhaps Spanish literature. No doubt her actual choice of a path to follow will be very far from any of these. But there's time to decide. Oh, is there ever time.

---

[15] **inimical:** harmful
[16] **vast expanse:** large, wide area
[17] **dabbled:** did something in a way that wasn't very serious

◖ READ FOR MAIN IDEAS

Reading One discusses Marilisa's and Leo's views on marriage, family structure/ relationships, careers, and longevity. Write sentences about how their views are different from the present-day society views described.

Marriage

Present-day society: *Marriage is seen as a life long commitment although in some societies divorce is common. Some people may have more than one or two marriages.*

"Death Do Us Part": _____

_____

_____

Family structure / Relationships

Present-day society: *Three or four generations of a family living at the same time is normal.*

"Death Do Us Part": _____

_____

_____

Careers

Present-day society: *Although many people have many different jobs throughout their lives, they don't frequently change careers.*

"Death Do Us Part": _____

_____

_____

Longevity

Present-day society: *The average lifespan varies around the world, but in developed countries the average lifespan is mid-seventies.*

"Death Do Us Part": _____

_____

_____

◖ **READ FOR DETAILS**

Marilisa and Leo have different perspectives on the topics in the chart. Complete the chart with examples of their differing views.

TOPIC	MARILISA	LEO
Marriage	First marriage Assumes she'll be married again to a variety of men	
Family Structure / Relationships		
Careers		
Longevity		

◖ MAKE INFERENCES

*Write **T** (true) or **F** (false) for each statement. The answer is not explicitly stated, but rather implied by other information in the text. Write the supporting evidence from the text. Share your answers with the class.*

_____ **1.** Marilisa didn't know exactly how many children Leo had before she married him.

Supporting evidence: _____

_____ **2.** Leo's son, Fyodor, does not believe in the Process.

Supporting evidence: _____

_____ **3.** Leo has a good sense of humor.

Supporting evidence: _____

_____ **4.** The Process is expensive.

Supporting evidence: _____

_____ **5.** Leo cares very much about his personal appearance.

Supporting evidence: _____

_____ **6.** Fyodor expects his father will eventually leave Marilisa for someone else.

Supporting evidence: _____

_____ **7.** The physical aspects of the Process seem to have been perfected, but its psychological ramifications are still being dealt with.

Supporting evidence: _____

◖ EXPRESS OPINIONS

Discuss the questions with a partner.

1. Do you think it was acceptable for Marilisa to marry Leo even though she wasn't truly in love with him?

2. Leo was "ten times her age." Would you marry someone older than you? By how much? What possible advantages/disadvantages are there to marrying someone much older than you?

3. The story mentions that with the Process "these days you can look as young as you like." What age would you choose to look if you were having the Process? Why?

4. Leo has had many different careers. "He reinvents himself every decade or two. That's as necessary to him as Process itself." Why do you think he changes careers so often? Would you want to reinvent yourself every decade or two? Why or why not?

READING TWO: Toward Immortality: The Social Burden of Longer Lives

Scientific understanding of aging at the cellular and molecular level may be the key to a longer lifespan. More and more scientists now believe that the human lifespan could be increased to 140 or more in the future. This may be achieved through genetic manipulation or caloric restriction (eating less). These strategies have proved effective with worms, flies, and mice. Maybe someday they will work on humans.

1 *Discuss the question with a partner.*

Do you think living longer will be good for society? Why or why not?

TOWARD IMMORTALITY: THE SOCIAL BURDEN OF LONGER LIVES

By Ker Than LiveScience Staff Writer

A doubled lifespan

1   If scientists could create a pill that let you live twice as long while remaining free of infirmities,[1] would you take it?

2   If one considers only the personal benefits that longer life would bring, the answer might seem like a no-brainer[2]: People could spend more quality time with loved ones; watch future generations grow up; learn new languages; master new musical instruments; try different careers or travel the world.

3   But what about society as a whole? Would it be better off if life spans were doubled? The question is one of growing relevance, and serious debate about it goes back at least a few years to the Kronos Conference on Longevity Health Sciences in Arizona. Gregory Stock, director of the Program on Medicine, Technology, and Society at UCLA's School of Public Health, answered the question with an emphatic "Yes." A doubled lifespan, Stock said, would "give us a chance to recover from our mistakes, lead us towards longer-term thinking and reduce healthcare costs by delaying the onset of expensive diseases of aging. It would also raise productivity by adding to our prime years."

4   Bioethicist Daniel Callahan, a cofounder of the Hastings Center in New York, didn't share Stock's enthusiasm. Callahan's objections were practical ones. For one thing, he said, doubling life spans won't solve any of our current social problems. "We have war, poverty, all sorts of issues around, and I don't think any of them would be at all helped by having people live longer," Callahan said in a recent telephone interview. "The question is, 'What will we get as a society?' I suspect it won't be a better society."

5   Others point out that a doubling of the human lifespan will affect society at every level. Notions[3] about marriage, family, and work will change in fundamental ways, they say, as will attitudes toward the young and the old.

---

[1] **infirmities:** sicknesses, diseases

[2] **no-brainer:** something that you do not have to think about because it is easy to understand

[3] **notions:** ideas, beliefs, or opinions

Marriage and family

6   Richard Kalish, a psychologist who considered the social effects of life extension technologies, thinks a longer lifespan will radically change how we view marriage.

7   In today's world, for example, a couple in their 60s who are stuck in a loveless but tolerable marriage might decide to stay together for the remaining 15 to 20 years of their lives out of inertia[4] or familiarity. But if that same couple knew they might have to suffer each other's company for another 60 or 80 years, their choice might be different. Kalish predicted that as life spans increase, there will be a shift in emphasis from marriage as a lifelong union to marriage as a long-term commitment. Multiple, brief marriages could become common.

"I'll have someone from my generation get in touch with someone from your generation."

8   A doubled lifespan will reshape notions of family life in other ways, too, says Chris Hackler, head of the Division of Medical Humanities at the University of Arkansas. If multiple marriages become the norm as Kalish predicts, and each marriage produces children, then half-siblings will become more common, Hackler points out. And if couples continue the current trend of having children beginning in their 20s and 30s, then eight or even ten generations might be alive simultaneously, Hackler said. Furthermore, if life extension also increases a woman's period of fertility, siblings could be born 40 or 50 years apart. Such a large age difference would radically change the way siblings or parents and their children interact with one other.

9   "If we were 100 years younger than our parents or 60 years apart from our siblings, that would certainly create a different set of social relationships," Hackler told *LiveScience*.

The workplace

10   For most people, living longer will inevitably mean more time spent working. Careers will necessarily become longer, and the retirement age will have to be pushed back, not only so individuals can support themselves, but to avoid overtaxing a nation's social security system.

11   Advocates of anti-aging research say that working longer might not be such a bad thing. With skilled workers remaining in the workforce longer, economic productivity would go up. And if people got bored with their jobs, they could switch careers.

12   But such changes would carry their own set of dangers, critics say. Competition for jobs would become fiercer as "mid-life re-trainees" beginning new careers vie with young workers for a limited number of entry-level positions. Especially worrisome is the problem of workplace mobility, Callahan said. "If you have people staying in their jobs for 100 years, that is going to make it really tough for young people to move in and get ahead," Callahan explained.

13   Callahan also worries that corporations and universities could become dominated by a few individuals if executives, managers and tenured professors refuse to give up their posts[5]. Without a constant infusion of youthful talent and ideas, these institutions could stagnate[6].

---

[4] **inertia:** the feeling that you do not want to do anything at all
[5] **give up their posts:** leave their jobs
[6] **stagnate:** to stop developing or improving

(continued on next page)

Time to act

14   While opinions differ wildly about what the ramifications for society will be if the human lifespan is extended, most ethicists agree that the issue should be discussed now, since it might be impossible to stop or control the technology once it's developed. "If this could ever happen, then we'd better ask what kind of society we want to get," Callahan said. "We had better not go anywhere near it until we have figured those problems out."

2 *Discuss the questions with the class.*

1. Some people in Reading Two think a longer life span is a good idea. Discuss the reasons. Do you agree?

2. Some people in Reading Two don't think a longer life span is a good idea. Discuss the reasons. Do you agree?

C INTEGRATE READINGS ONE AND TWO

◀ STEP 1: Organize

Readings One and Two discuss both positive and negative effects of longer lifespans. Complete the cause and effect diagram with information from the readings.

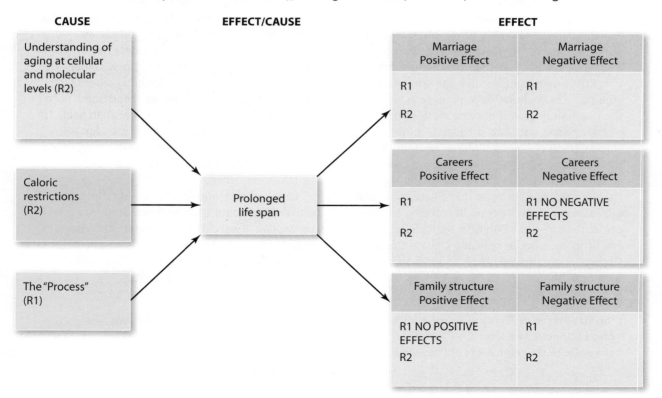

CAUSE	EFFECT/CAUSE	EFFECT	

Marriage Positive Effect	Marriage Negative Effect
R1	R1
R2	R2

Careers Positive Effect	Careers Negative Effect
R1	R1 NO NEGATIVE EFFECTS
R2	R2

Family structure Positive Effect	Family structure Negative Effect
R1 NO POSITIVE EFFECTS	R1
R2	R2

Understanding of aging at cellular and molecular levels (R2)

Caloric restrictions (R2)

The "Process" (R1)

Prolonged life span

STEP 2: Synthesize

Bioethicist Daniel Callahan asked, when talking about the potential for doubled life spans, "What will we get as a society? I suspect it won't be a better society." On a separate piece of paper, write a paragraph about whether you agree or disagree with his statement. Support your answer with at least three pieces of information from Step 1.

③ FOCUS ON WRITING

Ⓐ VOCABULARY

REVIEW

Work with a partner. Discuss the meanings of the adjectives and adverbs below. Decide if the words give you positive, negative, or neutral feelings. Note that some words can be interpreted more than one way. Discuss why.

awesome	immeasurably	presumptuous	ultimately
chilly	impetuous	punctually	utterly
disparate	insufferable	simultaneously	vigorous
fond	loveless	tolerable	worrisome

POSITIVE	NEGATIVE	NEUTRAL

Many adjectives are formed by combining a base word with a suffix.
(vigor + ous = vigorous). Look at the boldfaced adjectives.

- They stand together in the darkness, staring at the **awe<u>some</u>** sparkle of the stars.
- A couple in their 60s who are stuck in a loveless but **toler<u>able</u>** marriage might decide to stay together.
- Fyodor had a **presumptu<u>ous</u>** way of winking and sniggering at her.

Suffixes can change the meaning of the base word.

- love → loveless (without love)
- care → careful (with care)
- tolerate → tolerable (able to be tolerated)

In addition, suffixes change the form of the word.

- vigor (noun) → vigorous (adjective)

Common Adjective Suffixes					
-al	-ous	-ful	-able	-less	-ive
-ed	-ing	-ant	-ic	-ent	-ial
-ible	-ar	-en	-ical	-y	-ary
-ese	-ish	-some			

Adjective suffixes can be added to nouns or verbs

vigor → vigorous
fascinate → fascinating
disparity → disparate

Suffixes can also be added to base/root words
Sometimes there are spelling changes when a suffix is added

- Leave out the final *e*
- Leave out the final *s* before *al*
- Double the final consonant

measure → measurable
politics → political
sun → sunny

Complete the chart with synonyms from Readings One and Two that have the suffixes listed. Then, think of your own example of an adjective with that suffix.

	READING ONE: DEATH DO US PART		
Suffixes	Example from Text	Definition or Synonym	Example of a New Adjective with the Same Suffix
Paragraphs 1–2			
-ing	shimmering	sparkling	speeding
-ive		impetuous	
Paragraphs 3– 5			
-able		intolerable	
-al		perfect	
Paragraphs 6–15			
-ent		very old	
-ous		sincere	
Paragraphs 26–33			
-ible		allowable	
-ic		passionate	
Paragraphs 34–38			
-y		foggy	

Suffixes	Example from Text	Definition or Synonym	Example of a New Adjective with the Same Suffix
Paragraphs 1–2			
-al		individual	
Paragraphs 3–4			
-ical		sensible	
Paragraphs 5–7			
-less		without love	
-ing		still left	
Paragraphs 11–13			
-ed		restricted	
-some		troublesome	
-ant		steady	
-ful		young	

◖ **CREATE**

Imagine that you are the bioethicist Daniel Callahan or Gregory Stock of UCLA's School of Public Health. On a separate piece of paper, write five questions for Leo about his extended lifespan. Use at least one word from the Review or Expand section in each question. Then, exchange papers with a partner and answer the questions as if you were Leo.

GRAMMAR: Contrasting the Simple Past, Present Perfect, and Present Perfect Continuous

1 *Examine the sentences and answer the questions with a partner.*

a. Marilisa and Leo **went** to Nairobi and Venice on their honeymoon three years ago.

b. Leo **has been** an architect, an archeologist, a space-habitats developer, a professional gambler, an astronomer, and a number of other disparate and dazzling things.

c. People **have been searching** for the "fountain of youth" since the beginning of recorded history.

1. In sentence *a*, is Leo and Marilisa's honeymoon over? How do you know?

2. In sentence *b*, is Leo still an architect, an archeologist . . . ? How do you know?

3. In sentence *c*, are people still searching for the fountain of youth? How do you know? When did people start searching?

4. What verb tenses are used in sentences *a*, *b*, and *c*?

CONTRASTING THE SIMPLE PAST, PRESENT PERFECT, AND PRESENT PERFECT CONTINUOUS	
The Simple Past 1. Use the simple past for things that happened in the past and were completed.	Leo **watched** the movie. *(Leo is no longer watching the movie. He finished watching the movie.)*
2. Use past time expressions such as: *last, ago, in, on, at, yesterday, when* . . . to indicate that an action or event was completed at a definite time in the past.	Leo **watched** the movie **yesterday**. *(Leo is no longer watching the movie. He finished watching the movie yesterday.)*
The Present Perfect 3. Use the present perfect for completed actions that happened at an indefinite time in the past.	Marilisa **has eaten** breakfast. *(She has finished her breakfast, but we don't know exactly when she ate it, or it is not important.)*
4. You can also use the present perfect for repeated actions that were completed in the past, but that may happen again in the future.	Leo **has visited** Paris six times. *(Those six visits are finished. However, he may visit Paris again in the future.)*

(continued on next page)

5. Use the present perfect with *for* or *since* for actions that began in the past, but were not completed, and have continued up to the present and may continue into the future. Use *for* or *since* for this meaning especially with non-action verbs, such as *be, feel,* and *know. For* is followed by a length of time, for example, *six years. Since* is followed by a specific point in time, for example, *2099.*	Leo **has been** a sand painter **for** six years. *(Leo began to be a sand painter six years ago. He is still a sand painter today, and may continue to be a sand painter in the future.)* Leo **has been** a sand painter **since** 2099. *(Leo began to be a sand painter in 2099. He is still a sand painter today, and may continue to be a sand painter in the future.)*
6. Compare the present perfect without *for* or *since.*	Leo **has been** a sand painter. *(Leo was a sand painter at some time in the past, but he is not anymore. We don't know exactly when he was, or it is not important.)*
The Present Perfect Continuous **7.** Use the present perfect continuous for actions that began in the past but were not completed, and have continued up to the present and may continue into the future. The use of *for* or *since* with the present perfect continuous is optional. Using *for* or *since* gives additional information about when the action began or how long it has been in progress, but it does not change the meaning of the verb.	Daniel Callahan **has been studying** about the ramifications of increasing human life spans. *(Daniel Callahan began studying sometime in the past. He is still studying and will probably continue to study in the future.)*
8. Non-action verbs are not usually used in the continuous. Use the present perfect with *for* or *since* for this meaning with a non-action verb.	Callahan **has been** at the Hastings Center **for** many years. Callahan **has been** at the Hastings Center **since** 1969.

2 *Complete the conversations by circling the correct form of the verb.*

Conversation 1

REPORTER: Our readers may already know about the "fountain of youth," but can you give us some historical perspective? Also, do you think scientific advancements will turn out to be a "fountain of youth," allowing people to live forever?

Daniel Callahan: People (1) **have been searching/searched** for the "fountain of youth" since the beginning of recorded history. People believed that drinking from this fountain would allow them to be healthy and vigorous forever. They would never get sick and would be full of energy. So far, the "fountain" (2) **has been/was** impossible to find. People (3) **have not been/were not** able to truly achieve eternal life. Human life spans have been increasing, but we are still far from reaching immortality. Even considering the scientific advancements that (4) **have taken/took** place in the twentieth century, I, as a scientist, believe that ultimately the limit of human life will be no more than 150 years.

Conversation 2

Dr. Kalish: I know you have been very busy attending conferences this month. I believe you have recently attended a conference on longevity. Did you learn a lot?

Dr. Gregory Stock: What a month! The conference on longevity I (5) **attended/ have been attending** last week did not begin very punctually. It was supposed to begin at 9:00 AM but (6) **didn't actually start/hasn't actually started** until 9:45! On top of that, the first speaker was insufferable; he finished every sentence with, "you know." Luckily, I (7) **have gone/have been going** to three other conferences this month that had awesome speakers who provided us with lots of interesting facts and ideas about longevity. At the first conference, the speaker (8) **discussed/has been discussing** how restricting the amount of food eaten may increase life spans. At the next conference, I learned about some ongoing research that Dr. Clynes (9) **did/has been doing** with mice that has ramifications for human longevity.

Conversation 3

Marilisa's Friend, Susannah: Leo has such a large family. Now that you are married, how are you getting along with them?

Marilisa: Not as well as I would like, but I suppose the problems I am having are quite normal for a newlywed. I (10) **have had/had** problems with Leo's son, Fyodor, since the first time I met him, but I am willing to tolerate him for Leo's sake. Other than Fyodor, and one or two of Leo's ex-wives, I (11) **have enjoyed/enjoyed** getting to know Leo's family. I really like Leo's brother, Max. Max is a writer and scientist who (12) **has completed/completed** a book on "the process" two years ago. Ever since that was published, he (13) **worked/has been working** on his autobiography.

3 *Complete the sentences with the verb in the correct tense: simple past, present perfect, or present perfect continuous. Note that some sentences have more than one correct answer.*

1. Leo (**met**) _____ many important historical figures during his life and he looks forward to meeting many more.

2. Marilisa is not happy about the new car Leo (**buy**) _____ last week.

3. Marilisa and Leo (**visit**) _____ Capri in '87 on their first anniversary.

4. Leo (**have**) _____ at least 10 different careers so far.

5. Marilisa (**talk**) _____ to Fyodor for at least 30 minutes. Do you think they will be done soon?

6. Leo (**meet**) _____ Leonardo da Vinci over 500 years ago.

7. Doctors at the Hastings Center (**study**) _____ longevity for many years.

8. Daniel Callahan doesn't believe that scientists should continue working on extending life spans until they (**figure**) _____ out the ramifications longer life will have for society.

9. The conference that Dr. Kalish (**attend**) _____ last August dealt with the future of marriage in a society with prolonged lifespans.

10. Dr. Chris Hackler (**do**) _____ research concerning how family structure will be affected if siblings are born 40–50 years apart. He expects to finish his research next year.

11. Although it is only March, Gregory Stock (**write**) _____ _____ four papers on how increased lifespans can decrease healthcare costs. He is expecting to write at least two more papers before the end of the year.

C WRITING

In this unit, you read about immortal life in the future. Now imagine that scientists have discovered a way to make you immortal and it is now the year 2175. What is your life like? What jobs have you had? What relationships have you had? Who have you married? What is your family like? What have been the advantages of living so long? What have been the disadvantages?

You are going to **write a descriptive essay about the positive and negative aspects of your life in 2175.***

◖ PREPARE TO WRITE: Using an Idea Web

An **idea web** helps you see how different topics are related to one central theme.

Imagine your life in the year 2175. Look at the topics in the idea web. Close your eyes and try to create a mental picture of yourself and your life. Think about the topics in the circles as they relate to your life. Write your ideas about each topic in the circles. Be sure to include details and adjectives.

---

*For Alternative Writing Topics, see page 114. These topics can be used in place of the writing topic for this unit or as homework. The alternative topics relate to the theme of the unit, but may not target the same grammar or rhetorical structures taught in the unit.

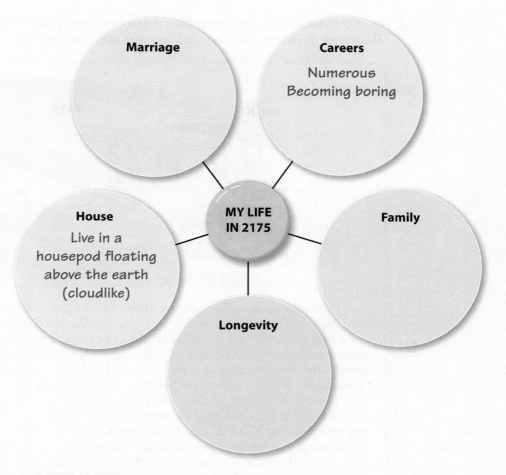

Marriage

Careers
Numerous
Becoming boring

House
Live in a
housepod floating
above the earth
(cloudlike)

MY LIFE
IN 2175

Family

Longevity

◖ **WRITE: A Descriptive Essay**

A **descriptive essay** describes a place, person, or situation using such vivid or descriptive language that the reader can create a clear mental picture of the description. Here are some important points:

1. **Have an introduction.** Capture the reader's attention by telling an interesting anecdote or story.
2. **Use strong imagery**. Try to create mental pictures for your reader by using descriptive adjectives and details.
3. **Rely on sensory details**. Create strong sensory images by describing smells, sights, sounds, tastes, and senses of touch.
4. **Have a conclusion**. Bring the ideas of the essay to a close by providing final thoughts or predictions.

1 *Read the introductory paragraph from a descriptive essay about life in the future. Then, answer the questions and share your answers with a partner.*

I sleepily open my eyes as my alarm robot vigorously shakes me awake. I can smell the usual insufferable morning smells: bitter coffee made with sour milk and burnt toast. I haven't had time to reprogram my breakfast robot since the electric meteor shower last week blew out its motherboard with a loud *crack* that sounded as if my housepod had split in half. It's during these times that I fondly remember the simple days decades ago when I made my own breakfast and lived on the earth, not floating above it like a lonely cloud. No matter. I'll glide through a convenient coffee shop's hovercraft window on the way to work. Work. I used to be so punctual. "As utterly dependable as a Swiss watch," my bosses always said, even with a half a world commute everyday. After over 150 years of work it's hard to get excited. But I am getting ahead of myself. In the past 200 years I have had numerous wives, careers, countless numbers of children, and awesome experiences. My life has been an endless rollercoaster ride filled with immeasurable happiness and sadness.

1. Circle the thesis statement. What do you expect the next paragraphs of the essay will be about?

2. What are some examples of sensory details?

TOUCH	SMELL	SIGHT	TASTE	SOUND

3. What mental picture does this writing create? Underline the words or sentences that create these images for you.

2 *Now write the first draft of your descriptive essay. Use your notes from Prepare to Write. Make sure you have multiple paragraphs and use descriptive language through the use of adjectives and sensory details. Be sure to use grammar and vocabulary from the unit.*

◖ **REVISE: Using Figurative Language**

Many descriptive essays and stories include **figurative language**, such as **similes, metaphors,** and **personification** to add depth and imagery.

A **simile** is a way of describing something through a comparison using *like* or *as*. The comparison is with something not normally connected with the subject.

Simile: *The snow was like a blanket.*

Explanation: The subject, snow, is being compared to a blanket because it covers the ground in the same way a blanket covers a bed.

---

1 *Look at the introductory paragraph in Write: A Descriptive Essay. Find the two similes and complete the information.*

_____ is being compared to _____ because

_____

_____ is being compared to _____ because

_____

2 *Look at Reading One. Find the similes and complete the information.*

Paragraph 1: _____ are being compared to _____

because _____

Paragraph 2: _____ is being compared to _____

because _____

Paragraph 34: _____ are being compared to _____

because _____

A **metaphor** is another way of describing something through a comparison but without using *like* or *as*; instead the metaphor explicitly states what a thing "is." The subject and its complement are the same.

Metaphor: *The setting sun is a red ball of fire falling into the sea.*

Explanation: The sun is not *like* a red ball of fire, it *is* a red ball of fire.

---

3 *Look at Reading One, paragraph 34. What metaphor does Marilisa use to describe her unknown future husbands? Why does she use this metaphor?*

> **Personification** gives human qualities to animals or objects. This helps the reader better connect with the image.
>
> | **Without Personification** | **With Personification** |
> |---|---|
> | The leaves blew around in the wind. | The leaves danced in the wind. |
> | The sun was shining in the sky. | The sun sang its happy summer song. |

4 Look at Reading One, paragraph 17. Find an example of personification. With a partner discuss how, with personification, the description comes alive.

5 Look at your first draft. Are your descriptions clear? Do they create vivid mental imagery? Add at least one simile, one metaphor, or one example of personification.

◀ **EDIT: Writing the Final Draft**

Write your final draft. Carefully edit it for grammatical problems and mechanical errors, such as spelling, capitalization, and punctuation. Make sure you used some of the grammar and vocabulary from the unit. Use the checklist to help you write your final draft. Then neatly write or type your essay.

✓ FINAL DRAFT CHECKLIST

- ○ Does the essay have an interesting introduction?
- ○ Does the essay have multiple paragraphs?
- ○ Does the essay include clear descriptive language including lots of adjectives?
- ○ Does the essay include vivid mental imagery including sensory details and a simile, a metaphor, or an example of personification?
- ○ Does the essay have a conclusion?
- ○ Does the essay use tenses correctly?
- ○ Has the vocabulary from the unit been used?

ALTERNATIVE WRITING TOPICS

Choose one of the topics. Write an essay using the vocabulary and grammar from the unit.

1. If scientists created a pill that would allow you to live twice as long while remaining free of infirmities, would you take it? Why or why not?

2. What would the effects of increased longevity be on society? Think about how population, food, and housing, for example, would be affected.

RESEARCH TOPICS, see page 261.

Give and Learn

Angelina Jolie

Oprah Winfrey

Bill Gates

Mother Teresa

 1 FOCUS ON THE TOPIC

A PREDICT

Look at the photographs and the unit title. Then discuss the questions with a partner.

1. Philanthropy is a way of showing concern for other people by giving money or volunteering (working without pay) to help people in need or organizations which help people in need. Match the people with the descriptions of how they have helped others.

This 1979 Nobel Peace Prize winner spent many years working with the extremely poor in India. Though not a rich person, _____ was able to personally help thousands of people.	This business person is one of the richest people in the world. _____ is also a very generous philanthropist and has created a foundation[1] focusing on education and healthcare.	This movie star is reported to give away 1/3 of his/her income to several charities. _____ is also the Goodwill Ambassador for the United Nations High Commission for Refugees.	This wealthy talk show host has created a foundation "to support the education and empowerment of women, children and families." _____ has also established a school for girls in South Africa.

2. What do people learn by giving? What do you think the unit will say about this?

---

[1] **foundation:** an organization that collects money to be used for special purposes

115

Work in a small group. The quotations represent a philosophy, or a certain way of thinking, about philanthropy. Read the quotations and answer the questions.

"It is better to give than to receive."

—Acts 20:35, Bible, Revised Standard Version

"A person's true wealth is the good he or she does in the world."

—Mohammed

"He who bestows[1] his goods upon the poor,
Shall have as much again, and ten times more."

—John Bunyan, *Pilgrim's Progress,* Part Two, Section VII

1. What is similar about the philosophy expressed in these three quotations?

   _____

   _____

2. Do you know anyone (including yourself) who incorporates this philosophy into his or her life? Describe something this person does.

   _____

   _____

1 *Two of the three words in each row have meanings similar to the boldfaced word. Cross out the word that doesn't belong. If you need help, use a dictionary.*

1. **passion**	enthusiasm	~~decision~~	interest
2. **proudly**	modestly	self-satisfyingly	contentedly
3. **challenge**	pride	test	demand
4. **satisfaction**	happiness	pleasure	amusement
5. **determined**	insistent	stubborn	uncertain
6. **proposal**	suggestion	order	recommendation
7. **donate**	contribute	give	sell
8. **admiring**	complimentary	approving	boring
9. **devote**	dedicate	appreciate	commit
10. **inspired**	saddened	encouraged	motivated
11. **manage**	handle	cope with	respond
12. **thrilled**	happy	scared	excited

---

[1] **bestows:** gives someone something important

Across the United States, more and more organizations—including corporate, educational, religious, and government groups—are supporting volunteer programs. In addition, more people are volunteering in a wide range of ways. People volunteer for many different reasons: some for political or religious reasons; some for personal or social reasons. Others volunteer because it's mandatory, or required, in certain situations; for example, as part of a school's curriculum or as a requirement for graduation.

2 *Read what people say about volunteering. Complete each statement with the words in the boxes. Then write the reasons why you think they volunteer. (Note: Not all words are used, and some people may have more than one reason.)*

Reasons for Volunteering		
environmental	medical research	political
mandatory	personal	religious

1. Doug Steinberg, age 42 : Raised $2,000 for AIDS research in the annual Boston-to-New York AIDS bicycle ride

admiring	challenge	donate	manage

"I'm trying to raise money for AIDS research in memory of my brother. I'm hoping to _____ donate _____ more than $1,000 this year. Maybe this way what happened to him won't happen to others. The ride is certainly a physical _____, especially since I hurt my leg last weekend. However, I still think I can _____ to finish the ride. In any case, I enjoy biking and this way I can combine my favorite sport with a good cause."

Reasons: _personal and medical research_ _____

2. Steve Hooley, age 36 : Donates his time as a Boy Scout leader

inspired	manage	passion	thrilled

"I've always loved the outdoors and camping. In fact, preserving the environment is a _____ for me. Therefore, I'm _____ to be a Scout leader. By being a Scout leader, I can do something I like and share my love of nature with the next generation. If they are _____, maybe they'll take care of it better than our generation has.

Reasons: _____

3. Hannah Bullard, age 27 : Volunteers in a shelter for homeless women

inspired	passion	proudly	satisfaction

"I've always been taught that we should help those who are less fortunate than we are. Reverend Woodson spoke at church last Sunday about all the good work being done here. He spoke with such _____ that I knew I wanted to participate. It gives me a lot of _____ to work with these women. Some of them have been through so much: alcoholism, drug addiction, and in many cases, abuse. I am very _____ by how far some of them have come. Despite their many problems, many of these women have now _____ taken back control of their lives."

Reasons: _____

4. Jake Hutchings, age 17 : Spends three hours a week playing guitar for senior citizens in a nursing home

determined	devote	proposal	satisfaction

"I started coming here last year because it was a school requirement. After I completed my requirement, I didn't want to stop. In order to continue volunteering, I made a _____ to the director of the program; I asked him if I could come back again this year after school and on weekends because I really have a good time with these people. I want to continue to _____ time to them because I truly enjoy being with them and I think they like to listen to my music, too."

Reasons: _____

5. Ted Sirota, age 58 : Spends five hours a week volunteering at a politician's office

admiring	determined	donate	inspire

"I feel that this person is the best candidate. I find her truly amazing; she's someone I can really look up to and want to be like. However, I'm not *just* one of her _____ supporters. I also volunteer for her. By volunteering, I can do more than just vote. I am _____ to help her get elected. That way I can be more involved in the whole political process."

Reasons: _____

Ⓐ READING ONE: Justin Lebo

Justin Lebo is a boy who volunteers his time and energy to help others in a unique way.

Read the first two paragraphs of Justin Lebo. *Work with a partner to answer the questions. Then read the rest of the article.*

1. What condition is the bicycle in?

2. Why do you think Justin would be interested in a bike in that condition?

3. What do you think Justin will do with the bicycle?

JUSTIN LEBO

BY PHILLIP HOOSE (from *It's Our World, Too*)

1   Something about the battered old bicycle at the garage sale[1] caught ten-year-old Justin Lebo's eye. What a wreck! It was like looking at a few big bones in the dust and trying to figure out what kind of dinosaur they had once belonged to.

2   It was a BMX bike with a twenty-inch frame. Its original color was buried beneath five or six coats of gunky paint. Everything—the grips, the pedals, the brakes, the seat, the spokes—was bent or broken, twisted and rusted. Justin stood back as if he were inspecting a painting for sale at an auction. Then he made his final judgment: perfect.

3   Justin talked the owner down to $6.50 and asked his mother, Diane, to help load the bike into the back of their car.

4   When he got it home, he wheeled the junker into the garage and showed it **proudly** to his father. "Will you help me fix it up?" he asked. Justin's hobby was bike racing, a **passion** the two of them shared. Their garage barely had room for the car anymore. It was more like a bike shop. Tires and frames hung from hooks on the ceiling, and bike wrenches dangled from the walls.

5   Now Justin and his father cleared out a work space in the garage and put the old junker up on a rack. They poured alcohol on the frame and rubbed until the old paint began to yield, layer by layer. They replaced the broken pedal, tightened down a new seat, and restored the grips. In about a week, it looked brand new.

(continued on next page)

---

[1] **garage sale:** a sale of used furniture, clothes, toys, etc. that you no longer want, usually held in your garage

6   Soon he forgot about the bike. But the very next week, he bought another junker at a yard sale² and fixed it up, too. After a while it bothered him that he wasn't really using either bike. Then he realized that what he loved about the old bikes wasn't riding them: it was the **challenge** of making something new and useful out of something old and broken.

7   Justin wondered what he should do with them. They were just taking up space in the garage. He remembered that when he was younger, he used to live near a large brick building called the Kilbarchan Home for Boys. It was a place for boys whose parents couldn't care for them for one reason or another.

8   He found "Kilbarchan" in the phone book and called the director, who said the boys would be **thrilled** to get two bicycles. The next day when Justin and his mother unloaded the bikes at the home, two boys raced out to greet them. They leapt aboard the bikes and started tooling around the semicircular driveway, doing wheelies and pirouettes, laughing and shouting.

9   The Lebos watched them for a while, then started to climb into their car to go home. The boys cried after them, "Wait a minute! You forgot your bikes!" Justin explained that the bikes were for them to keep. "They were so happy," Justin remembers. "It was like they couldn't believe it. It made me feel good just to see them happy."

10   On the way home, Justin was silent. His mother assumed he was lost in a feeling of **satisfaction**. But he was thinking about what would happen once those bikes got wheeled inside and everybody saw them. How could all those kids decide who got the bikes? Two bikes could cause more trouble than they would solve. Actually they hadn't been that hard to build. It was fun. Maybe he could do more . . .

11   "Mom," Justin said as they turned onto their street, "I've got an idea. I'm going to make a bike for every boy at Kilbarchan for Christmas." Diane Lebo looked at Justin out of the corner of her eye. She had rarely seen him so **determined**.

12   When they got home, Justin called Kilbarchan to find out how many boys lived there. There were twenty-one. It was already June. He had six months to make nineteen bikes. That was almost a bike a week. Justin called the home back to tell them of his plan. "I could tell they didn't think I could do it," Justin remembers. "I knew I could."

13   Justin knew his best chance to build bikes was almost the way General Motors or Ford builds cars: in an assembly line. He figured it would take three or four junkers to produce enough parts to make one good bike. That meant sixty to eighty bikes. Where would he get them?

14   Garage sales seemed to be the only hope. It was June, and there would be garage sales all summer long. But even if he could find that many bikes, how could he ever pay for them? That was hundreds of dollars.

---

² **yard sale:** another phrase for garage sale

15   He went to his parents with a **proposal**. "When Justin was younger, say five or six," says his mother, "he used to give away some of his allowance[3] to help others in need. His father and I would **donate** a dollar for every dollar Justin donated. So he asked us if it could be like the old days, if we'd match every dollar he put into buying old bikes. We said yes."

16   Justin and his mother spent most of June and July hunting for cheap bikes at garage sales and thrift shops.[4] They would haul the bikes home, and Justin would start stripping them down in the yard.

17   But by the beginning of August, he had **managed** to make only ten bikes. Summer vacation was almost over, and school and homework would soon cut into his time. Garage sales would dry up when it got colder, and Justin was out of money. Still he was determined to find a way.

18   At the end of August, Justin got a break. A neighbor wrote a letter to the local newspaper describing Justin's project, and an editor thought it would make a good story. In her **admiring** article about a boy who was **devoting** his summer to help kids he didn't even know, she said Justin needed bikes and money, and she printed his home phone number.

19   Overnight, everything changed. "There must have been a hundred calls," Justin says. "People would call me up and ask me to come over and pick up their old bike. Or I'd be working in the garage, and a station wagon would pull up. The driver would leave a couple of bikes by the curb. It just snowballed[5]."

20   The week before Christmas Justin delivered the last of the twenty-one bikes to Kilbarchan. Once again, the boys poured out of the home and leapt aboard the bikes, tearing around in the snow.

21   And once again, their joy **inspired** Justin. They reminded him how important bikes were to him. Wheels meant freedom. He thought about how much more the freedom to ride must mean to boys like these who had so little freedom in their lives. He decided to keep on building.

---

[3] **allowance:** money you are given regularly or for a special reason
[4] **thrift shops:** stores that sell used goods, especially furniture, clothes, and toys, often in order to raise money for a charity
[5] **snowballed:** got bigger quickly or got harder to control

(continued on next page)

22   "First I made eleven bikes for the children in a foster home[6] my mother told me about. Then I made bikes for all the women in a battered women's shelter. Then I made ten little bikes and tricycles for children with AIDS. Then I made twenty-three bikes for the Paterson Housing Coalition."

23   In the four years since he started, Justin Lebo has made between 150 and 200 bikes and given them all away. He has been careful to leave time for his homework, his friends, his coin collection, his new interest in marine biology, and of course, his own bikes.

24   Reporters and interviewers have asked Justin Lebo the same question over and over: "Why do you do it?" The question seems to make him uncomfortable. It's as if they want him to say what a great person he is. Their stories always make him seem like a saint, which he knows he isn't. "Sure it's nice of me to make the bikes," he says, "because I don't have to. But I want to. In part, I do it for myself. I don't think you can ever really do anything to help anybody else if it doesn't make you happy."

25   "Once I overheard a kid who got one of my bikes say, 'A bike is like a book; it opens up a whole new world.' That's how I feel, too. It made me happy to know that kid felt that way. That's why I do it."

---

[6] **foster home:** a home where a child is taken care of for a period of time by someone who is not a parent or legal guardian

(READ FOR MAIN IDEAS

Work with a partner. Read the statements and decide which three represent the main ideas of Reading One. Then discuss the reasons for your choices.

1. Justin paid $6.50 for the first bike he fixed up.

2. Justin needed to find a way to get a lot of used bikes.

3. Justin was able to fix up and donate hundreds of bikes because of the support of his parents and community.

4. Justin's hobby was bike racing.

5. Justin is a special boy because he likes to help others.

6. After the newspaper article, people called Justin and offered him their old bikes.

(READ FOR DETAILS

The chart lists some benefits of doing community service. Complete the chart with examples of how Justin Lebo benefited from his experience.

THE BENEFITS OF COMMUNITY SERVICE	EXAMPLE OF JUSTIN LEBO
Encourages people to use their free time constructively	Justin spent his free time in the summer making bicycles for the children at the Kilbarchan Home for Boys.
Gives a sense of satisfaction and builds self-esteem	
Opens people's eyes to the great variety of people in need	
One successful community service experience leads to performing other services	
Helps people to find out who they are, what their interests are, and what they are good at	

◖ MAKE INFERENCES

Read the questions and circle the best answer. If necessary, refer back to the reading to support your answer. Compare answers with a partner and give reasons to support your choice.

1. Why do you think Justin's reaction to the first bike was "perfect"?
   a. He knew immediately that the bike could be fixed up and used by someone who needed a bike.
   b. It was an inexpensive BMX bike.
   c. He only knew he wanted to fix up the bike.

2. How do you think the two Kilbarchan boys felt after Justin gave them the first two bikes?
   a. They thought Justin was very good at fixing bikes.
   b. They wished he had made bikes for all the other boys at Kilbarchan.
   c. They were surprised at how generous Justin was.

3. When Justin suggested making a bike for each boy at Kilbarchan, he felt the director's reaction was that he couldn't do it. Why might the director have felt that way?
   a. He didn't really want all the boys to have bicycles.
   b. He thought that Justin was very generous but too young to accomplish such a task.
   c. He was surprised and believed that Justin would never be able to find enough bicycles to fix up.

4. Which statement best describes Justin's motivation for continuing to build and give away bikes?

    a. He loves bicycles and wants other people to experience the happiness bicycles can bring.

    b. He loves the challenge of repairing and restoring bicycles that would otherwise be thrown away.

    c. He would rather build bikes than do his homework.

5. Which statement best describes Justin Lebo?

    a. He has a wide range of interests and hobbies.

    b. His interests are centered on bike racing and repair.

    c. He is continually changing his interests and hobbies.

6. Which statement best describes why Justin Lebo does what he does?

    a. His parents have encouraged him to help others.

    b. It makes him happy to help others.

    c. Helping others is mandatory at his school.

◀ EXPRESS OPINIONS

Discuss the questions with a partner.

1. Justin was able to combine something he loved to do with philanthropic work. Is it very important to love what you are volunteering to do? Why?

2. Who do you think received more from Justin's philanthropic work, Justin or the people that he gave the bikes to? Explain.

3. No one forced Justin to do what he did. Do you believe this makes Justin an exceptional young man? Explain.

B READING TWO: Some Take the Time Gladly / Mandatory Volunteering

Many educational organizations in the United States require high school students to devote a certain number of hours outside of the classroom to community service in order to graduate. Supporters of mandatory volunteering believe that the school's role should include both preparing children to be academically successful and helping them to be responsible citizens who are active participants in their communities.

However, not everybody believes that mandatory volunteering is a good idea. Those opposed to the requirement believe that the term "mandatory volunteering" is an oxymoron, a contradiction; they believe that volunteering should be something you do of your own free will. It is not something that is forced on you.

1 *Discuss the question with a partner. Then read the editorials about mandatory volunteering.*

Do you believe mandatory volunteering is a good idea? Why or why not?

SOME TAKE THE TIME GLADLY

By Mensah Dean (from the *Washington Times*)

1   Mandatory volunteering made many members of Maryland's high school class of '97 grumble with indignation.

2   Future seniors,[1] however, probably won't be as resistant now that the program has been broken in. Some, like John Maloney, already have completed their required hours of approved community service. The Bowie High School sophomore[2] earned his hours in eighth grade[3] by volunteering two nights a week at the Larkin-Chase Nursing and Restorative Center in Bowie.

3   He played shuffleboard, cards, and other games with the senior citizens.[4] He also helped plan parties for them and visited their rooms to keep them company.

4   John, fifteen, is not finished volunteering. Once a week he videotapes animals at the Prince George County animal shelter in Forestville. His footage is shown on the Bowie public access television channel in hopes of finding homes for the animals.

5   "Volunteering is better than just sitting around," says John, "and I like animals; I don't want to see them put to sleep."[5]

6   He's not the only volunteer in his family. His sister, Melissa, an eighth grader, has completed her hours also volunteering at Larkin-Chase.

7   "It is a good idea to have kids go out into the community, but it's frustrating to have to write essays about the work," she said. "It makes you feel like you're doing it for the requirement and not for yourself."

8   The high school's service learning office, run by Beth Ansley, provides information on organizations seeking volunteers so that students will have an easier time fulfilling their hours.

9   "It's ridiculous that people are opposing the requirements," said Amy Rouse, who this summer has worked at the Ronald McDonald House[6] and has helped to rebuild a church in Clinton.

10   "So many people won't do the service unless it's mandatory," Rouse said, "but once they start doing it, they'll really like it and hopefully it will become a part of their lives—like it has become a part of mine."

---

[1] **seniors:** students in the last year of high school, approximately 17–18 years old

[2] **sophomore:** a student in the second year of high school, approximately 15–16 years old

[3] **eighth grade:** The U.S. public school system begins with kindergarten and continues with grades 1–12. A student in eighth grade is approximately 13–14 years old.

[4] **senior citizens:** people over the age of 65

[5] **put to sleep:** to give an animal drugs so that it dies without pain

[6] **Ronald McDonald House:** a residence, usually near a hospital, which provides a home and other support services for the family of children who require a lot of time in the hospital because of serious illness

MANDATORY VOLUNTEERING FOR HIGH SCHOOL DIPLOMA NOT A GOOD IDEA

(from the *Sun Sentinel*)

11   Re: Proposals for mandatory service hours in order to graduate from high school

I am an active participant in the high school service program, and chairperson of a tutoring program run primarily by high school students such as myself. Volunteering is a personal choice and an extracurricular activity such as the debate team or school-sponsored sports.

12   Mandatory volunteering is not a good idea. First, many students do volunteer, and most do it with full force. By the time a volunteering student becomes a senior, that student could earn as many as 1000+ service hours. If an entering freshman[1] is told that he or she must volunteer for a pre-set number of hours, the student might become resentful, complete the required hours, and never volunteer again. The volunteered hours would end up being less than the hours being volunteered now.

13   Many students do not have the time to volunteer. School goes from a set starting time to a set ending time. If the student's busy after-school schedule does not allow for extracurricular[2] activities, that is the student's own business. With the exception of homework, there is nothing that a student is required to do after school hours.

14   Finally, mandatory volunteering is an oxymoron. If students are required to volunteer, it is no longer volunteering. The performed service becomes one more thing to do in order to graduate from high school. The quality of work can suffer greatly. If a student enjoys volunteering, he or she will volunteer without having to be told.

---

[1] **freshman:** a student in the first year of high school, approximately 14–15 years old
[2] **extracurricular:** not part of the usual work for school

2 Both writers give reasons to support their opinions in the editorials. Complete the chart with reasons found in the editorials. Share your list with the class.

FOR MANDATORY VOLUNTEERING	AGAINST MANDATORY VOLUNTEERING
1.	1. Volunteering is a personal choice
2.	2.
3.	3.
	4.
	5.
	6.

C INTEGRATE READINGS ONE AND TWO

◀ STEP 1: Organize

Each reading addresses four issues relating to philanthropy. Go back to the readings and find quotes or statements that relate to these issues. Underline them in the text and then write the paragraph number in the correct box. Some issues may have more than one answer.

ISSUES	READING ONE	READING TWO
1. Personal enrichment	Paragraph 24	
2. Time commitment		
3. Personal choice		
4. Dedication to work		

◀ STEP 2: Synthesize

Imagine you are Justin Lebo. On a separate piece of paper, write a letter to one of the two writers of the editorials in Reading Two. Be sure to clearly state your opinion about mandatory volunteering. Use Justin's experience as a volunteer to either disagree with or support the position stated in the editorial and explain why. Use quotes or statements from Step 1.

③ FOCUS ON WRITING

Ⓐ VOCABULARY

◀ REVIEW

1 *Look at the word forms chart. The vocabulary from the unit is boldfaced.*

NOUN	VERB	ADJECTIVE	ADVERB
admiration	admire	**admiring**	admiringly
devotion	**devote**	devoted	devotedly
challenge	challenge	challenging	X
determination	determine	**determined**	X
donation	**donate**	donated	X
fulfillment	**fulfill**	fulfilled fulfilling	X
resentment	resent	**resentful**	resentfully

indignation	X	indignant	indignantly
inspiration	**inspire**	inspired inspirational	inspirationally
management	**manage**	manageable	manageably
opposition	**oppose**	opposite opposing	X
passion	X	passionate	passionately
proposal	propose	proposed	X
pride	X	proud	**proudly**
ridicule	ridicule	**ridiculous**	ridiculously
satisfaction	satisfy	satisfied satisfying satisfactory	satisfactorily
thrill	thrill	**thrilled** thrilling	thrillingly
hope	hope	hopeful hopeless	hopefully hopelessly

2 Complete the sentences using words from the word form chart. Pay attention to verb tense and subject-verb agreement.

1. Justin Lebo had to rely on _____ from people in order to
(donate)
complete the bicycles for the children at Kilbarchan.

2. Justin felt _____ when he saw how the boys enjoyed the first two
(inspire)
bicycles he had made.

3. Many people hope that after experiencing mandatory volunteering, students

will become _____ about volunteering in general.
(passion)

4. Justin Lebo met the _____ of making a bike for each boy at
(challenge)
Kilbarchan.

5. When Justin _____ that his parents give a dollar for every dollar
(proposal)
he donated, they agreed.

6. Critics worry that students who are forced to volunteer and have a bad

experience may become _____ and never volunteer again.
(resent)

7. Although many people support mandatory volunteering, there is still a lot of

_____ to it.
(oppose)

◖ **EXPAND**

A **phrasal verb** consists of a verb and a particle. The combination often has a meaning that is different from the meaning of the separate parts.

Work in a small group. Read the sentences. Circle the best explanation for each underlined phrasal verb.

1. Supporters of mandatory volunteering say volunteering for community service is time better spent than <u>sitting around</u> all day watching television or playing computer games.
   a. doing nothing special or useful
   b. sitting with friends in a circle
   c. not taking part in something

2. Justin Lebo has <u>fixed up</u> between 150 and 200 bikes and has given them all away.
   a. arranged a date for someone
   b. repaired or restored something to working order
   c. bought at a low price

3. Supporters of mandatory volunteering hope that students will <u>keep on</u> volunteering after they have fulfilled their requirement.
   a. hold
   b. consider
   c. continue

4. At first, Justin could not <u>figure out</u> what to do with his two bikes.
   a. satisfy
   b. make a plan for
   c. take part in

5. Justin had so many bikes that he had to <u>clear out</u> his basement and start building them there.
   a. make room on a table
   b. clean an area or place
   c. empty an area or place

6. When the students <u>found out</u> the new graduation requirements, they were indignant and completely opposed to them.
   a. created something
   b. discovered something lost
   c. learned new information about something

7. After the newspaper article was published, many people <u>called</u> Justin <u>up</u> and offered him their old bikes.
   a. discussed a situation
   b. spoke disrespectfully to someone
   c. telephoned

8. People fear that if students do not do community service, they will <u>end up</u> being uncaring and unsympathetic individuals.
   a. complete a project
   b. be in a situation without planning it
   c. stop something

9. When people donate old clothes to a community center, the center staff will often come to the house and <u>pick up</u> the donations.
   a. start to increase
   b. clean something
   c. collect something

10. Justin was afraid that the garage sales would <u>dry up</u> by the end of the summer.
   a. be dull and uninteresting
   b. slowly come to an end
   c. become useless

Imagine you are a reporter interviewing the people below. How would they respond to the questions? Write answers using the words given. Change the word form or tense if necessary.

devote	determined	keep on	proudly

1. **REPORTER:** Your son Justin is quite remarkable, isn't he?

   DIANE LEBO: Yes, he is. After Justin saw the boys having so much fun on their bicycles, he became devoted to the project. He was determined to get every boy on a bicycle, so he kept on working hard. I'm very proud of him.

challenge	inspired	passion	sit around

2. **REPORTER:** After fixing the first bike, did you ever think you would end up repairing and donating over 150 more?

   JUSTIN LEBO: _____

   _____

   _____

end up	manage	proposal	thrilled

3. **REPORTER:** What did you think when Justin first told you he was planning on building a bicycle for every boy at Kilbarchan?

   DIRECTOR OF THE KILBARCHAN SCHOOL: _____

   _____

   _____

admiring	fix up	hope	inspired

4. **REPORTER:** How did you feel when you rode one of Justin's bikes?

   A BOY AT KILBARCHAN: _____

   _____

   _____

| donate | figure out | fulfilling | satisfaction |

5. REPORTER: Why do you support mandatory volunteering?

STUDENT SUPPORTING MANDATORY VOLUNTEERING: _____

_____

_____

| find out | indignant | oppose | ridiculous |

6. REPORTER: Why are you opposed to mandatory volunteering?

STUDENT OPPOSING MANDATORY VOLUNTEERING: _____

_____

_____

B GRAMMAR: Concessions

1 *Examine the sentences and answer the questions with a partner.*

   a. **Even though** Justin was not required by his school to volunteer, he chose to work on bikes and donate them.

   b. **In spite of the fact that** many students initially don't want to volunteer, they learn to love it and continue after the school requirements are fulfilled.

   c. It is a good idea to get students to go out into the community **although** it can be frustrating to have to write about it.

   1. Each of the sentences is composed of two clauses[1]. What are the clauses in each sentence?

   2. Do the concessions *although, even though,* and *despite the fact* introduce a positive or negative opinion of mandatory volunteering?

   3. Do the three sentences have the same punctuation? If not, why not?

   4. Which clauses express the writer's main idea: the clauses with the concessions *although, even though,* and *in spite of the fact that* . . . or the other clauses?

---

[1] **clause:** a group of words containing a subject and verb which forms part of a sentence. Clauses can be dependent or independent.

1. Use **concessions** when expressing an opinion, where you need to support your opinion but, at the same time recognize and describe the opposing opinion. Presenting similarities and differences in contrasting points of view makes your argument stronger.

2. Use these words to concede or acknowledge similarities or differences between two contrasting ideas.

   although   in spite of the fact that
   though   despite the fact that
   even though

   Note that these words do not introduce a complete thought—they introduce **dependent clauses.** A dependent clause cannot stand alone as a sentence. It must be joined to an independent (main) clause.

3. The **main clause** usually describes the point that is more important.

   a. **Even though Justin was not required by his school to volunteer**, he chose to work on bikes and donate them.

   <u>Writer's opinion:</u> Justin's school had no requirement for volunteering, but he still wanted to use his time to help others.
   <u>Acknowledging the opposite view:</u> You would expect Justin not to volunteer unless he was forced to.

   b. It is a good idea to get students to go out into the community **although it can be frustrating to have to write about it**.

   <u>Writer's opinion:</u> There may be problems with assignments relating to mandatory volunteering, but students should still be required to go out into the community.
   <u>Acknowledging the opposite view:</u> Being forced to write about your volunteering takes away from any benefit you may receive from it.

4. When a sentence begins with a dependent clause, use a comma to separate it from the main clause.

   Even though garage sales had dried up by the end of August, Justin got enough old bikes as the result of a letter to the newspaper.

5. When the sentence begins with an independent clause, do not use a comma.

   Justin got enough old bikes as the result of a letter to the newspaper **even though garage sales had dried up by the end of August**.

2 *Combine each pair of sentences using the words in parentheses. Does your new sentence support mandatory volunteering or oppose mandatory volunteering?*

1. Supporters of mandatory volunteering say that it is a good way for students to get valuable work experience. Critics say students should be paid if they are doing work. (even though)

   Supporters of mandatory volunteering say it is a good way for

   students to get valuable experience even though they are not paid.

   (supports mandatory volunteering)/ opposes mandatory volunteering

2. Critics of mandatory volunteering maintain that a school should not require a student to do anything after school except homework. Supporters of mandatory volunteering say that volunteering is better than just sitting around watching TV or playing video games. (though)

   _____

   _____

   _____

   supports mandatory volunteering / opposes mandatory volunteering

3. Opponents argue that volunteering is a personal choice, so it shouldn't be mandatory. Supporters note that schools have many required classes that may not be a student's personal choice. (although)

   _____

   _____

   _____

   supports mandatory volunteering / opposes mandatory volunteering

4. Critics worry that a bad volunteering experience will stop people from volunteering again in the future. Supporters maintain that most student volunteers have successful experiences and many continue to volunteer later in life. (in spite of the fact that)

   _____

   _____

   _____

   supports mandatory volunteering / opposes mandatory volunteering

5. Supporters believe mandatory volunteering can benefit the community. Critics feel that mandatory volunteers may do a bad job and therefore cause more harm than good. (despite the fact that)

_____

_____

_____

supports mandatory volunteering / opposes mandatory volunteering

3 *Write sentences expressing your opinion about each educational issue. Use the concession words in the box. Does your sentence support mandatory volunteering or oppose mandatory volunteering?*

although	even though	though
despite the fact that	in spite of the fact that	

1. **busy after-school schedules**

   Although many students do have busy after school schedules, with planning, most should be able to find some time to volunteer either after school or during free class periods.

   supports mandatory volunteering / opposes mandatory volunteering

2. **personal choice**

   _____

   _____

   _____

   supports mandatory volunteering / opposes mandatory volunteering

3. **good to get students out into the community**

   _____

   _____

   _____

   supports mandatory volunteering / opposes mandatory volunteering

4. **volunteer may do a bad job**

_____

_____

_____

supports mandatory volunteering / opposes mandatory volunteering

5. **builds self-esteem**

_____

_____

_____

supports mandatory volunteering / opposes mandatory volunteering

C WRITING

In this unit, you read about the pros and cons of mandatory volunteering. Imagine that your school has proposed a mandatory community service program. Students can choose an organization to volunteer for, and are required to give at least five hours of time a month. Students must volunteer after school but will receive academic credit.

You are going to **write a persuasive essay explaining your opinion about the volunteering program**.*

◀ PREPARE TO WRITE: Using a T-Chart

A **T-chart** is a prewriting tool that helps you examine two aspects of a topic, such as the pros and cons associated with it. When you want to persuade someone to agree with your point of view, you need to have strong reasons to support your opinion (pros). You also need to acknowledge and address possible arguments against your opinion (cons).

---

*For Alternative Writing Topics, see page 144. These topics can be used in place of the writing topic for this unit or as homework. The alternative topics relate to the theme of the unit, but may not target the same grammar or rhetorical structures taught in the unit.

1 *Work in a small group. Complete the T-chart with reasons to support a mandatory community service program (pros) and reasons against it (cons). Share your ideas with the class.*

PROS	CONS

2 *Use your T-chart to decide if this program should be implemented or not. Write a thesis statement stating your opinion.*

◀ **WRITE: A Persuasive Essay**

In a **persuasive essay**, your goal is to convince the reader to agree with your position. Here are some important points:

1. **State your position in the thesis statement.** The reader must know how you feel at the start of the essay.
2. **Present strong arguments to support your position.**
3. **Present strong support for your arguments.** Provide detailed examples, anecdotes, quotes, and statistics.
4. **Acknowledge the counter arguments presented by the opposing side.** Then, refute the counter arguments by showing why the counter arguments are weak or strong. This will make your argument stronger.

1 *Examine the persuasive essay and answer the questions.*

Cutting Our Sports Teams Is Not a Healthy Decision

Obesity rates are escalating! Students are more stressed than ever before! These are just a couple of recent news headlines. At the same time, ironically, our school administration has recently proposed eliminating all sports teams citing a decrease in team participation, low attendance, and overall high cost of maintaining these teams. While cutting team sports from the budget would save money, the immediate and long term negative results would not be worth the money saved.

First, though it is true that many teams have not had high numbers of participants, this is not a reason to cut *all* teams. A few teams still do have high participation rates and very dedicated players. One solution is to keep one or two high participation sports per season. For example, fall football, winter basketball and swimming, and spring track and baseball.

Second, the school is concerned about poor audience attendance at the games and uses this argument to support the idea that there is a decreasing interest in our teams. Although there may be lower audience numbers than in the past, the students who do go are loyal fans. Moreover, this devoted fan base has helped build a community that promotes school spirit across the campus. This school spirit affects all students whether or not they attend each game. For example, after last year's baseball finals, more baseball hats were sold in the campus store than ever before even though most of the students wearing the hats had not attended one game! Adam Deering, a student, stated, "Even though I don't go to all of the games, I am still supportive of my school and proud of it. School can be really stressful, and the teams help reduce that stress and give students something else to focus on and bring them together besides academics."

Finally, the administration states that the cost of keeping team sports is just too costly. Though the cost of sports teams may be high, the price paid for cutting the teams in the long term is even higher. Sports teams are a daily reminder of the importance of maintaining a balanced, healthy life style. School sports help promote life-long healthy habits. With this in mind, shouldn't the school be putting more money into sports rather than taking it away?

1. What is the student's main position in regards to cutting school sports?

_____

2. What are the three main arguments the school uses to support cutting school sports? Complete the left side of the chart.

3. What are the counter arguments the student presents? Complete the right side of the chart.

ARGUMENTS TO CUT SCHOOL SPORTS	COUNTER ARGUMENTS

4. Do you think the counter arguments are convincing? Why or why not?

_____

_____

_____

5. What examples are used to strengthen the student's argument? Underline them.

2 *Start planning your essay by looking at your list of pros and cons in Prepare to Write. Choose three of the strongest arguments you will use to support your position and write them in sections 2–4 in the brace map below. Add details to support your arguments on the lettered lines.*

1. Introduction and Thesis Statement:

2.

    a. _____

    b. _____

    c. _____

3.

    a. _____

    b. _____

    c. _____

4.

    a. _____

    b. _____

    c. _____

5. Conclusion:

3 Look at your arguments in support of your position in your brace map. Write them in the left column. What are the possible counter arguments? Write them in the middle column. Why are those counter arguments weak? Write the reasons in the right column. You will acknowledge the counter arguments in your essay using a concession clause and then refute them.

ARGUMENTS FOR / AGAINST COMMUNITY SERVICE PROGRAMS	COUNTER ARGUMENTS	REFUTATION (Reasons why the counter argument is weak)

4 Now write the first draft of your persuasive essay. Use the information in Prepare to Write and your brace map to plan your essay. Include an introductory and a concluding paragraph. When writing the body, be sure to acknowledge the counter arguments by using a concession clause. Be sure to use vocabulary and grammar from the unit.

◖**REVISE: Writing Introductions and Conclusions**

The Introduction

The **introduction** to an essay can have several functions. It states the thesis, or controlling idea, and gives the reader an idea of what will be discussed. It can also provide background information on the topic. However, one of the most important functions is to provoke the reader's interest and make the reader want to continue reading. Here are three common techniques used in introductions:

a. State why the topic is important.

b. Ask a provocative question.

c. Tell a relevant story or anecdote.

1 *Work in pairs. Read the three introductions. Underline the thesis statements. Then label each introduction with the letter of the technique used.*

Introduction 1   **Technique:** _____

Society today is obsessed with commercialism. People think only about making money and buying more and more possessions. Many college students choose their majors by deciding which careers will pay the most money. Young people today are not learning enough about the nonfinancial rewards in life. They are not learning about the joy and fulfillment of helping others. This is a very serious problem with education today. It is important to support the proposal for a mandatory community service program so that young people will learn the value of giving to others.

Introduction 2   **Technique:** _____

When I was in high school, I was required to take part in a community service project. At first, I really didn't want to do it. I thought it would be boring and a waste of time. The school let us choose our project, and I decided to work at an animal shelter. I like animals, and I thought the work wouldn't be too difficult. I worked all semester helping the veterinarian take care of sick and abandoned animals. I was surprised to find that by the end of the semester, I really liked my community service job. In fact, it was my favorite part of the week, and I signed up to work another semester. So I am a perfect illustration of the benefits of mandatory community service programs in school. This is why I support a program of mandatory community service in our university.

Introduction 3   **Technique:** _____

We all want to live in a better world, don't we? Poor children do not get enough to eat. The school system is not educating our kids. The environment is getting more and more polluted. What would happen if we all did something to solve the problems around us? Well, we can do something, and we should. A mandatory community service program in our school will give students a valuable experience and also help solve important problems in our community.

2 *Look at the introduction of your essay. Make sure you have a thesis statement and use one of the three techniques for writing an effective introduction.*

The Conclusion

The **conclusion** of an essay should bring the ideas of the essay to a close. Most commonly, the conclusion restates the thesis of the essay and offers the writer's final thoughts on the topic. Here are three common techniques used in conclusions:

a. Tell a relevant story or anecdote.

b. Ask a final question that the reader can think about.

c. Make a prediction about the future.

3 Read the three conclusions. Underline the sentences that restate the thesis of the essay. Label the conclusion with the letter of the technique used.

Conclusion 1   Technique: _____

I urge everyone to support the mandatory community service program in our university. It has many benefits for both students and the community, including teaching students new skills, building bridges between students and community members, and exposing students to new experiences. I believe that if students try volunteering, many of them will discover that community service can be an enjoyable and rewarding experience.

Conclusion 2   Technique: _____

As you can see, community service benefits everyone. I know my life will never be the same after my experience in the veterinary clinic. Before I did my service, I wasn't sure what I wanted to do for a career. This experience has broadened my future and helped shape my goals. Now I know for certain that I want to do something in the animal sciences. Without this experience, I'm not sure I would have known what I wanted to do. Isn't this called a win-win situation?

Conclusion 3   Technique: _____

On a final note, I'd like to share a personal experience. Last year I started tutoring an elementary school student whose parents don't speak English. At first, he was resentful that he had to stay after school and do more schoolwork. Truthfully, it was also hard for me knowing he did not want to be there. But as the year progressed, I got to know him and the kind of books he liked to read. He began to look forward to our weekly sessions and was eager to see what books I had brought for him. Now we are not just reading friends but we are real friends. I know I have made a difference in his life and he has certainly made a difference in mine. If I hadn't had to do community service I know I would not have had this experience. And I would not have discovered what a difference I can make.

4 Look at the first draft of your essay. Make sure you have restated the thesis and have included your final thoughts by using one of the three conclusion techniques.

◀ EDIT: Writing the Final Draft

Write your final draft. Carefully edit it for grammatical problems and mechanical errors, such as spelling, capitalization, and punctuation. Make sure you use some of the vocabulary and grammar from the unit. Use the checklist to help you write your final draft. Finally, give your essay a title, and neatly write or type your final draft.

✓ FINAL DRAFT CHECKLIST

- ○ Does the essay have an introduction, three body paragraphs, and a conclusion?
- ○ Does the introduction include a thesis statement? Does it provoke the interest of the reader?
- ○ Does each body paragraph have a topic sentence? Do all the topic sentences support the thesis statement?
- ○ Do the body paragraphs present your arguments for or against mandatory volunteering? Did you acknowledge and then refute possible counter arguments?
- ○ Did you use concessions to introduce the counter argument?
- ○ Does the conclusion restate the thesis and offer final thoughts?
- ○ Has vocabulary from the unit been used?

ALTERNATIVE WRITING TOPICS

Choose one of the topics. Write an essay using the vocabulary and grammar from the unit.

1. Imagine you are responsible for setting up a community service program in your city. What kind of program would you start? Who would it serve? Would there be volunteers? Who would the volunteers be? What would you hope to accomplish? Be specific.

2. Read the quotation from John Bunyan on page 116. There are many different ways to "bestow your goods upon the poor." What are some of these ways and why do you think people perform these acts?

RESEARCH TOPICS, see page 262.

Homing in on Education

1 FOCUS ON THE TOPIC

A PREDICT

Read the cartoon and the unit title. Then discuss the questions with a partner.

1. How do you think the boy in the cartoon feels about school? Why is he frustrated?

2. Did you ever complain to your parents about school? Did they agree with you?

3. The unit title mentions "home" along with education. How do you think home and education are related? What do you think the unit will be about?

The term homeschooling *means teaching children at home instead of sending them to school. Look at the information about homeschooling in the graph and discuss the questions in a small group. Then report your ideas back to the class.*

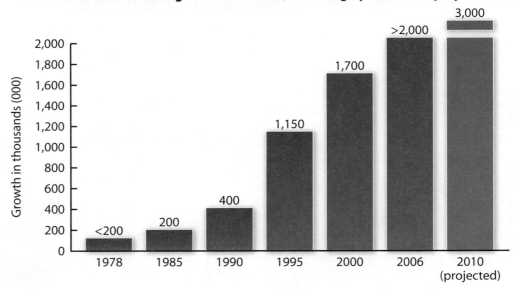

Growth of homeschooling in United States, including updates, and projections

1. How many homeschoolers were there in the United States in 1978? In 2006? How many are projected in 2010?

2. Why do you think people choose to homeschool?

3. What do you think are the pros and cons of homeschooling?

1 *Read the information about homeschooling. Try to understand the boldfaced words from the context.*

Over two million children now being homeschooled in the United States!

The practice of homeschooling has been steadily increasing in popularity over the past 25 years. Today, in the United States alone, it is estimated that close to two million children are being homeschooled. Supporters of homeschooling claim it is a **viable** alternative to traditional school; however, critics question whether it really meets the needs of students academically, emotionally, and socially. Why are some parents in favor of homeschooling their children? They believe that in traditional schools:

- Their children will be bullied or harassed (physically and/or emotionally harmed) by other students.
- Negative influences of other students may lead their children to smoke, drink alcohol, or take drugs.

- The course of studies that traditional schools have **dictated** isn't interesting.
- These courses are not **stimulating** for students.
- As a result, **avid** learners will not be motivated.
- The religious education in traditional schools isn't satisfactory.

Critics of homeschooling feel, however, that traditional schools provide a much more complete education. They feel that the criticism of traditional schools is based on **misconceptions**. They believe:

- Many students go to traditional schools and most are not bullied or harassed.
- Homeschooling can lead to social **isolation**; homeschoolers will not have enough contact with people outside of their family.
- In traditional schools, children learn to interact with an **eclectic** group of people; this is an important skill for life in the multicultural twenty-first century.
- Ongoing **consultation** between schools and government agencies ensures that curriculum is up to date and engaging.
- Students in traditional schools are taught what they need to fulfill their academic and professional **ambitions**.
- Although students must have **persistence** and not give up when they encounter difficult course work, at least traditional school settings offer support services to help when there are difficulties.
- Teachers in traditional schools are professionals with advanced degrees and have the **expertise** to teach complex subjects and make them interesting.

Still the number of homeschoolers continues to increase. What will this mean for traditional schools? How will schooling change in the future? Will we see high schools offering online courses, as many colleges already do? Will schooling look the same 50 years from now as it does today? The possibilities seem endless.

2 *Find the boldfaced words in the reading passage above. Write each word next to its synonym.*

1. _____ discussion, meeting
2. _____ loneliness, separation
3. _____ different from each other, varied
4. _____ required, ordered
5. _____ objectives, goals
6. _____ reasonable, feasible, able to succeed
7. _____ wrong or untrue ideas
8. _____ interesting, exciting
9. _____ eager, enthusiastic
10. _____ special skill or knowledge
11. _____ not giving up, determination

Read the title of the article and the first paragraph. Work with a partner to answer the questions. Then read the rest of the article.

1. The first paragraph mentions two possible reasons for the increasing popularity of homeschooling. What are they?

    a. _____

    b. _____

2. The first paragraph also mentions four mistaken ideas about homeschooling. What are they?

    a. _____

    b. _____

    c. _____

    d. _____

3. The title of the article is *The Satisfied Learner: How Families Homeschool Their Teens*. What do you think they do?

    _____

    _____

    _____

The Satisfied Learner:
How Families Homeschool Their Teens by Cafi Cohen

Mothering, March-April 2000 p74   COPYRIGHT 2000 Mothering Magazine

1   Maybe it's the fear of school violence or the lack of **stimulating** courses, but the number of homeschooling teenagers is on the rise. Some parents balk[1] at the very thought of homeschooling their teen. After all, it's one thing to teach your daughter how to read. It's quite another to teach her trigonometry. But the idea that parents are solely responsible for instruction is just one of the many

[1] **balk:** to not want to do something because it seems difficult

misconceptions about home education. Some other incorrect notions include that homeschooling inevitably leads to social **isolation**, decreased participation in music and sports, and college rejection letters. The following families' stories speak the truth: Socially and intellectually satisfying, homeschooling is an extremely **viable** option—for both parent and child.

Nikki—The Long-Distance Learner

2   Nikki Davis, a 16-year-old A and B student in San Diego, California, hated school. Her number one complaint: There was no time for making friends. Ten minutes in the hall between classes and occasional after-school visits was just not enough. Academics were also frustrating. She loved biology and longed to experiment with local marine ecosystems,[2] but this year's curriculum **dictated** that she memorize plant parts instead. In addition, typical school activities seemed childish to Nikki. A dedicated surfer, she was not interested in cheerleading, fund-raisers, or dances. Since seventh grade, she begged her parents to homeschool her. While Susan, Nikki's mother, agreed with the idea, her father—not unlike many parents who attended public school—resisted. Finally, just before her junior year, Nikki's **persistence**, as well as her continued unhappiness with school, convinced her father. The Davises decided to try home education.

3   To begin homeschooling, Nikki enrolled in American School, a fully-accredited[3], independent—study correspondence institution[4]. Based in Illinois, the school enrolls students from around the world. Just like any high school accepting a transfer student, American School gave Nikki credit for work completed during her freshman and sophomore years in public school. Then they outlined[5] the courses she would need to earn a diploma. For each course, American School supplied a textbook, study guide, and other necessary materials, such as lab supplies for biology or tapes for foreign language. The study guide provided reading assignments, teacher lectures (in written form), quizzes, tests, and answers. With occasional reminders from her parents to buckle down[6], Nikki worked entirely on her own. For subject matter **expertise**, answering questions about geometry proofs or science experiments, she corresponded with teachers at American School. For each course, she submitted anywhere from six to twelve written tests, the scores of which were averaged to obtain grades for her transcript.

4   And what was Susan's primary responsibility? Writing checks to American School—a reasonable $250 per year—and providing transportation for other activities. Susan did not need to dredge up[7] long-forgotten lessons in algebra or American government because the materials that Nikki used were, unlike typical classroom texts, designed for self-instruction. When she needed help, Nikki phoned or wrote the teachers at American School for **consultation**.

5   Within a month, Nikki found that she could complete her academic work in less than two hours each day. That left free time for anything and everything: paying work, volunteering, reading, surfing. She found a job bagging groceries, and spent many hours happily riding the waves at a nearby beach. Having always loved marine animals, she convinced a local museum to give her a volunteer job. She also rediscovered a childhood joy—reading for hours on end—books selected without regard to high school reading lists or requirements. Another advantage of her new schedule: plenty of time for a social life. She continued to see old school buddies, and began making new friends just as adults do—through

---

[2] **marine ecosystem:** all the animals and plants in the ocean and the way in which they are related to each other and their environment

[3] **accredited:** having official approval; certified, licensed

[4] **institution:** a school (*as used in this article*)

[5] **outlined:** gave the main ideas or facts about something

[6] **buckle down:** start working seriously

[7] **dredge up:** remember

(continued on next page)

existing acquaintances and new outside activities. Within six months, she said, "I can't believe it. I have more friends now than when I attended school."

6   Less than a year after she began homeschooling—and a full year before her former classmates—Nikki graduated from American School. People hearing this say, "She must be very smart. My teenagers could never do that." Yes, Nikki is bright. Nevertheless, her timetable and results are typical. Most homeschoolers complete traditional high school (grades 9 to 12) in two to three years. What takes conventionally schooled students a week to accomplish, most homeschoolers achieve in two to four days, working two to three hours each day. This is because homeschooling eliminates "administrivia" such as passing out supplies, correcting papers, announcements, waiting while a teacher handles discipline problems, and general busywork. Homeschooling is efficient—in fact, it's very efficient.

David Unschools

7   Nikki's approach to homeschooling—an approach many would call "traditional academics"—worked well for her. In contrast, David Jackson, a

15-year-old homeschooler from Louisville, Kentucky, says, "We never use textbooks and have no typical days. Every day is different." David's father is a mechanic with United Parcel Service. His mother Gail's formal education ended with her high school diploma. She homeschools David and his three younger brothers, ages seven, ten, and twelve, using an approach called unschooling.

8   Traditionalists and curriculum-oriented homeschoolers believe that kids learn best with schedules, textbooks, and tests. Unschoolers say just the opposite—that children are more **avid** learners when their interests direct their education. Unschooling parents provide educationally rich home environments and encourage their children to study whatever appeals to them. "Curriculum" is usually determined after the fact. Watching a film like Shakespeare's *Henry V* becomes a lesson in history and literature. Reading books selected from the library is English or language arts. Bird-watching is science, and helping with church bookkeeping is math. In life, the opportunities for education are endless.

9   This year David's science lessons are taking place at the local Natural History Museum, where he works. In the Hands-On Children's Room, he cleans the reptile cages, feeds the snakes, helps with the demonstration beehive, rotates the microscope exhibits, and conducts tours for school groups. Gail says, "He's getting so much more hands-on biology doing this than he would in any classroom. Not only that, his confidence in public speaking improves every week."

10   When he is not handling reptiles, David, like many lifelong unschoolers, reads voraciously[8]. His tastes range from science fiction and the Civil War to the *Guinness Book of World Records* and a

---

[8] **voraciously:** with unusual enthusiasm

host of news magazines, including *Time*, *Newsweek*, and *U. S. News & World Report*. He also writes—letters to friends, articles for a family newsletter, heart-felt journal entries, and even poetry. Math lessons are a by-product of running his own small computer-consulting business.

11   Interested in keeping his body in shape, as well as his mind, David began running in community races at age 13. He now runs three to five miles daily and regularly competes in 5 to 10K races (approximately three to six miles). In addition, he plays basketball with a homeschool team in the fall and Little League baseball in the spring.

Andy's Eclectic Approach

12   While David explores his world, 17-year-old Andy Herndon from rural Texas has a singular goal: He wants to attend the United States Air Force Academy and train to fly Air Force jets. Andy knows that math and science are important, and that his physical conditioning must be top-notch[9] if he is to fulfill his **ambition**. Without access to a high school sports program, Andy devised his own physical conditioning regimen[10], including running and weight training.

13   Andy's parents, Debra and Tom, are involved in the homeschooling movement, participating in support groups, writing articles, and organizing conferences. They've thought long and hard about the best way to homeschool. Debra says, "While traditionalists say kids learn best with schedules and texts, and unschoolers say kids learn best when their interests direct the learning, **eclectic** home educators say that there's no one way that all kids learn best all the time." Tom adds, "As eclectic homeschoolers, we use anything that encourages enthusiasm for learning. Sometimes that means traditional materials like textbooks. Sometimes we unschool and allow Andy unlimited free time to pursue his interests. And sometimes we fall somewhere in the middle. We always take full advantage of community resources, and, like unschoolers, we find ways to identify most of Andy's activities as school."

14   So how do Debra and Tom handle advanced math and science—topics that Andy needs to cover but in which they lack expertise? They've found several solutions to this problem. First, they located an exemplary[11] self-instructional math course that allows Andy to teach himself advanced mathematics, including trigonometry and calculus. Second, they enrolled him in physics and geology courses at the community college. This gives him the chance to earn some college credit during his high school years, while also providing access to professors and other resources at the college. He enjoys the classes and says, "I am keeping up and don't feel at any disadvantage." Third, Andy takes private pilot license lessons through a local Civil Air Patrol Cadet Program squadron (CAP is an auxiliary of the United States Air Force). In addition to contributing to his study of aviation and aerospace, CAP, as well as 4-H, provides plenty of opportunities for Andy to socialize with other teens.

15   To round out his education, Andy takes private piano lessons and, like many homeschooled teenagers, volunteers; he works in a local soup kitchen and at a nearby hospital. Volunteering opportunities abound in any community—libraries, museums, drama groups, radio and television stations, churches, even schools. And they always provide remarkable educational experiences.

[9] **top-notch:** having the highest quality or standard
[10] **regimen:** a special plan for eating, exercising, etc. that is intended to improve your health
[11] **exemplary:** excellent and providing a good example to follow

◖ READ FOR MAIN IDEAS

*Write **T** (true) or **F** (false) for each statement. If the statement is false, change it to make it true.*

_____ **1.** Homeschoolers approach their schooling in many different ways.

_____ **2.** Homeschooling takes less time than traditional schooling.

_____ **3.** Homeschooling prevents students from integrating into their community.

_____ **4.** Parents must be highly educated to homeschool their children.

_____ **5.** All homeschoolers follow the same curriculum.

◖ READ FOR DETAILS

Circle the correct answer.

1. What was Nikki 's main problem with school?
   a. She had no time for making friends.
   b. She didn't like studying about plants.
   c. She felt many of the school activities were childish.

2. Which statement best describes Nikki's independent study?
   a. All of her credits were completed through American School which supplied her with the necessary study materials and tapes.
   b. When she had academic problems, Nikki could phone teachers for consultation.
   c. Nikki viewed teacher lectures at home.

3. What role did her mother, Susan, play in Nikki's homeschooling?
   a. She provided Nikki with subject matter expertise.
   b. She gave Nikki tests.
   c. She drove Nikki to her activities.

4. According to the reading, one of the reasons why homeschooling is more efficient than conventional schooling is:
   a. Homeschooled students spend less time waiting for teachers to handle discipline problems.
   b. Homeschooled students spend less time socializing during their "school day."
   c. Homeschooled students put in more hours a day but fewer days a week.

5. What is true about David's parents?
   a. They use textbooks to teach David.
   b. They are highly educated.
   c. They vary David's schooling each day.

6. What determines "curriculum" for unschoolers?
   a. textbooks that students choose to study
   b. films and books chosen by parents
   c. life experience inside and outside the home

7. What is one result from David's "unschooling"?
   a. He gets more hands-on experience.
   b. He studies more Shakespeare.
   c. He does more reading, writing, and math than he used to.

8. How has Andy prepared for his goal?
   a. He has taken courses at the United States Air Force Academy.
   b. He has trained to fly Air Force jets.
   c. He has established his own physical conditioning program.

9. Which aspect of homeschooling do Andy's parents prefer?
   a. the use of schedules and texts
   b. the use of Andy's interests to direct his learning
   c. the use of an eclectic approach

10. How do Andy's parents help him deal with advanced math and science topics?
    a. They have the expertise to teach him.
    b. They enrolled him in courses at the community college.
    c. He gets help from other teens at the Civil Air Patrol.

11. What additional schooling does Andy get to round out his education?
    a. He takes piano lessons.
    b. He takes courses at a nearby hospital.
    c. He takes drama classes.

◖ MAKE INFERENCES

1 *Read the quotes from Reading One. The author has a strong opinion about homeschooling and uses specific vocabulary to make her opinion clear. Underline the specific word or words that convey either positive or negative feelings. Then answer the questions.*

1. "She . . . spent many hours happily riding the waves at a nearby beach . . . She also rediscovered a childhood joy—reading for hours on end . . ."

2. " . . . but this year's curriculum dictated that she memorize plant parts instead."

3. "Writing checks to American School—a reasonable $250 per year . . ."

4. "Maybe it's the fear of school violence or the lack of stimulating courses . . ."

5. " . . . typical school activities seemed childish to Nikki."

6. "Unschooling parents provide educationally rich home environments and encourage their children to study whatever appeals to them."

7. "First, they located an exemplary self-instructional math course that allows Andy to teach himself . . ."

8. "Volunteering opportunities abound in any community . . . And they always provide remarkable educational experiences."

2 *Answer the questions.*

1. What was the author's purpose in writing this article?

_____

_____

2. What is the author's attitude about traditional schooling versus homeschooling?

_____

_____

_____

3. How do the homeschoolers the author chose reflect her attitude about homeschooling?

_____

_____

_____

◖ EXPRESS OPINIONS

Discuss the questions in a small group. Then, share your ideas with the class.

1. Did anything surprise you about Nikki, David, and Andy? How would you describe them? In your opinion, are they unique or special compared to traditional students?

2. What kind of lives do you think Nikki, David, and Andy will lead?

3. Would you be successful at homeschooling? Why or why not? Be specific.

This story was written by Isaac Asimov in 1951. It addresses the question of homeschooling using a computer. At that time, the idea of this type of homeschooling was science fiction; having a home computer was unimaginable. Most people did not even own a television set at the time!

Discuss the question with a partner. Then read the story.

What do you think the author will say was fun about school?

THE FUN THEY HAD

By Isaac Asimov (from *Earth Is Room Enough*)

1   Margie even wrote about it that night in her diary. On the page headed May 17, 2157, she wrote, "Today Tommy found a real book!"

2   It was a very old book. Margie's grandfather once said that when he was a little boy, his grandfather told him that there was a time when all stories were printed on paper.

3   They turned the pages, which were yellow and crinkly,[1] and it was awfully funny to read words that stood still instead of moving the way that they were supposed to—on a screen, you know. And then, when they had turned back to the page before, it had the same words on it that it had had when they read it the first time.

4   "Gee," said Tommy, "what a waste. When you're through with the book, you just throw it away, I guess. Our television screen must have had a million books on it and it's good for plenty more. I wouldn't throw it away."

5   "Same with mine," said Margie. She was eleven and hadn't seen as many books as Tommy had. He was thirteen.

6   She said, "Where did you find it?"

7   "In my house." He pointed without looking, because he was busy reading. "In the attic."

8   "What's it about?"

9   "School."

10   Margie was scornful.[2] "School? What's there to write about school? I hate school."

---

[1] **crinkly:** having many folds or wrinkles; dried out

[2] **scornful:** critical of someone or something that you think is not good

(continued on next page)

11   Margie had always hated school, but now she hated it more than ever. The mechanical teacher[3] had been giving her test after test in geography and she had been doing worse and worse until her mother had shaken her head sorrowfully and sent for the County Inspector.

12   He was a round little man with a red face and a whole box of tools with dials and wires. He smiled at Margie and gave her an apple, then took the teacher apart. Margie hoped he wouldn't know how to put it together again, but he knew how all right, and after an hour or so, there it was again, large and square and ugly, with a big screen on which all the lessons were shown and the questions were asked. That wasn't so bad. The part Margie hated most was the slot[4] where she had to put homework and test papers. She always had to write them out in a punch code[5] they made her learn when she was six years old, and the mechanical teacher calculated the mark[6] in no time.

13   The Inspector had smiled after he was finished and patted Margie's head. He said to her mother, "It's not the little girl's fault, Mrs. Jones. I think the geography sector[7] was geared a little too quick. Those things happen sometimes. I've slowed it up to a ten-year level. Actually, the overall pattern of her progress is quite satisfactory." And he patted Margie's head again.

14   Margie was disappointed. She had been hoping they would take the teacher away altogether. They had once taken Tommy's teacher away for nearly a month because the history sector had blanked out[8] completely.

15   So she said to Tommy, "Why would anyone write about school?"

16   Tommy looked at her with very superior eyes. "Because it's not our kind of school, stupid. This is the old kind of school that they had hundreds and hundreds of years ago." He added loftily, pronouncing the word very carefully, "Centuries ago."

17   Margie was hurt. "Well, I don't know what kind of school they had all that time ago." She read the book over his shoulder for a while, then said, "Anyway, they had a teacher."

18   "Sure they had a teacher, but it wasn't a regular teacher. It was a man."

19   "A man? How could a man be a teacher?"

20   "Well, he just told the boys and girls things and gave them homework and asked them questions."

21   "A man isn't smart enough."

22   "Sure he is. My father knows as much as my teacher."

23   "He can't. A man can't know as much as a teacher."

24   "He knows almost as much, I betcha."[9]

---

[3] **mechanical teacher:** a computer (in this story)

[4] **slot:** an opening for a paper

[5] **punch code:** a pattern of holes put on a card that was used in past times for putting information in a computer

[6] **mark:** a number score or letter grade

[7] **sector:** an area

[8] **blanked out:** been erased

[9] *I betcha*: "I'll bet you", "I'm sure"

25   Margie wasn't prepared to dispute that. She said, "I wouldn't want a strange man in my house to teach me."

26   Tommy screamed with laughter. "You don't know much, Margie. The teachers didn't live in the house. They had a special building and all the kids went there."

27   "And all the kids learned the same thing?"

28   "Sure, if they were the same age."

29   "But my mother says a teacher has to be adjusted to fit the mind of each boy and girl it teaches and that each kid has to be taught differently."

30   "Just the same, they didn't do it that way then. If you don't like it, you don't have to read the book."

31   "I didn't say I didn't like it," Margie said quickly. She wanted to read about those funny schools.

32   They weren't even half-finished when Margie's mother called, "Margie! School!"

33   Margie looked up. "Not yet, Mama."

34   "Now!" said Mrs. Jones. "And it's probably time for Tommy, too."

35   Margie said to Tommy, "Can I read the book some more with you after school?"

36   "Maybe," he said nonchalantly.[10] He walked away whistling, the dusty old book tucked beneath his arm.

37   Margie went into the schoolroom. It was right next to her bedroom and the mechanical teacher was on and waiting for her. It was always on at the same time every day except Saturday and Sunday, because her mother said little girls learned better if they learned at regular hours.

38   The screen was lit up, and it said: "Today's arithmetic lesson is on the addition of proper fractions. Please insert yesterday's homework in the proper slot."

39   Margie did so with a sigh. She was thinking about the old schools they had when her grandfather's grandfather was a little boy. All the kids from the whole neighborhood came, laughing and shouting in the schoolyard, sitting together in the schoolroom, going home together at the end of the day. They learned the same things, so they could help one another on the homework and talk about it.

40   And the teachers were people . . .

41   The mechanical teacher was flashing on the screen: "When we add the fractions 1/2 and 1/4—"

42   Margie was thinking about how the kids must have loved it in the old days. She was thinking of the fun they had.

_____

[10] **nonchalantly:** calmly, in an informal way

2 *Discuss the questions in a small group. Then share your ideas with the class.*

1. What does Tommy discover in his attic and why is it such an important discovery?

2. What does Margie think about the discovery?

3. How does Margie feel about the "old days"?

4. How do you think the writer feels about the future of books?

C INTEGRATE READINGS ONE AND TWO

STEP 1: Organize

Reading One and Reading Two describe different models of homeschooling. Complete the chart comparing the readings.

	READING ONE	READING TWO
1. Is there a teacher? If yes, describe the teacher.		
2. Where does the "school" take place?		
3. Who determines what the students learn and at what pace they learn?		
4. What happens if students don't understand or can't do something?		
5. When and where do students socialize with friends?		
6. What do the students think about being homeschooled?		
7. What do the students think about traditional school?		

Choose one of the scenarios. For number one, write a response from Margie. For number two, write a response from David. Write on a separate piece of paper using information from Step 1.

1. **From Nikki to Margie:** "You are really lucky that you have been homeschooled your whole life. I had to beg my parents to allow me to be homeschooled and now I am so happy. You must be, too."

2. **From Tommy to David:** "Margie and I hate being homeschooled. We don't understand why you would choose to be homeschooled. Wouldn't you have more fun and friends in a school? Also, wouldn't you learn more?"

③ FOCUS ON WRITING

Ⓐ VOCABULARY

◀ REVIEW

Read the imaginary letter to a newspaper from a parent describing her family's experience with homeschooling. Complete the letter using the words below. Note that some verbs are in the past and some nouns may be plural.

dictate	dispute	isolation	persistence	stimulating

To the Editor:

For the past few years, our daughter, Anna, had been more and more involved in competitive figure skating. Her demanding practice schedule has _____ that she be at the skating rink six hours a day. Her high school curriculum was too inflexible, so for the last couple of years, she had been asking us to homeschool her. At first we were completely against the idea, but because of her _____ and continued conflicts between school and practice schedules, she finally persuaded us. We were originally against the idea because we had many concerns about homeschooling. For one thing, we thought Anna would experience social _____. That is, if we homeschooled her, she would have fewer friends. Since Anna is shy, we knew it would be a lot of work to keep her social life active especially given her practice schedule. Nevertheless, we gave in.

| ambition | avid | eclectic | misconception |

After much research, we decided on a plan that was _____; sometimes Anna studied at set times and followed a structured curriculum provided by an online school, but at other times, she spent an entire week just working on one high-interest subject by visiting museums, watching movies, and going on field trips. Because of her _____ to be an Olympic skater, she is highly motivated to finish her studies as quickly as possible. Because Anna has always been a(n) _____ learner, it seemed possible that she could finish high school in two to three years.

| adjust | consultation | expertise | nonchalantly | viable |

Everything was going well until we needed subject matter _____; obviously, her father and I couldn't help her in all subjects. We tried a few strategies. Anna contacted her online teachers for _____. If she was still having difficulty, we would hire a tutor to help. Unfortunately, the online help was minimal and often the online teacher answered questions _____ without any real thought. The tutor was not a(n) _____ option as each tutoring session cost over $60.00 an hour!

disappoint	dispute	misconception	stimulating

One problem was that our family entered into homeschooling with many
_____; for example, that it would be relatively easy because of Anna's
discipline and motivation. While there were positive outcomes, there certainly were
negative ones. The biggest surprise was the way our relationship with Anna
changed. We had always been on good terms with Anna, but when we started
homeschooling, we had to be more than parents. We had to be teachers,
homework-checkers, grade-givers, disciplinarians, and test-givers. Anna often
_____ our authority and this led to many tearful fights.

After a year, Anna decided to go back to public school. She missed the
_____ class discussions and the time hanging out with her friends. We
do not regret our try at homeschooling, but we also do not miss the stress of being
both parent and teacher.

Jan Burstein

Mountainview, California

◖EXPAND

1 *Complete the chart on the next page with the forms of the words from the readings. If
you need help, use a dictionary. (Note: Not all words have all forms.)*

NOUN	VERB	ADJECTIVE	ADVERB
1. stimulation	stimulate	stimulating	X
2. consultation			X
3.		scornful	
4.	dictate	X	X
5. persistence			
6. misconception			X
7.	dispute		
8. expertise	X		
9. isolation			X
10. X	X	avid	
11. ambition	X		
12.	X	eclectic	
13.		disappointed	
14.	adjust		X
15.	X	viable	

■ CREATE

Imagine you are a reporter interviewing the students and parents from Readings One and Two. How would they respond to the questions? Write answers using the words given. Change the word form or tense if necessary.

| avidly | consultation | expert | persistent |

1. **REPORTER:** What do you do if you have a problem with a subject you are studying?

   DAVID: If I need help and have to find outside expertise, I can consult with other homeschoolers either in person, by phone, or online. I have done this in the past, but because I am very persistent, I often am able to figure out the solution to my problem by myself. Also, because I am an avid reader, I am often able to find answers to my questions in books.

| adjustment | dispute | isolate | misconception |

2. **REPORTER:** You were unhappy with public school because you didn't have enough time for your friends. Don't you feel even more alone now?

   NIKKI: _____

   _____

   _____

| ambitious | disappointed | persistence | viable |

3. **REPORTER:** You want to attend the United States Air Force Academy. Do you really believe that homeschooling will enable you to do this?

   ANDY: _____

   _____

   _____

isolation	misconceive	scorn	stimulation

4. REPORTER: What concerns did you originally have about homeschooling?

NIKKI'S MOTHER, SUSAN: _____

_____

_____

consult	dictation	eclectic	stimulate

5. REPORTER: Why did you decide to use an unschooling approach for David and his brothers?

DAVID'S MOTHER, GAIL: _____

_____

_____

disappoint	expertly	isolation	viability

6. REPORTER: What do you think about schools today compared to your school?

TOMMY: _____

_____

_____

1 *Examine the pairs of sentences and answer the questions with a partner.*

Direct Speech	**Indirect Speech**
• Nikki's mother, Susan, said, "My primary responsibility is writing checks for the American School and providing transportation for my daughter's other activities."	• Nikki's mother, Susan, said her primary responsibility was writing checks for the American School and providing transportation for her daughter's other activities.
• David said, "We never use textbooks and have no typical days. Every day is different."	• David said they never used textbooks and had no typical days. Every day was different.
• Tom Herndon said, "Andy did very well in his community college classes and in the fall will take college calculus."	• Tom Herndon said Andy had done very well in his community college classes and in the fall would take college calculus.

1. What are the differences in punctuation between direct and indirect speech?

2. What other differences are there between direct and indirect speech? Which words are different? How do they change?

DIRECT AND INDIRECT SPEECH

Speech (and writing) can be reported in two ways:

Direct speech (also called *quoted speech*) reports the speaker's exact words.
Indirect speech (also called *reported speech*) reports what the speaker said without using the exact words.

Punctuation

For direct speech, put quotation marks before and after the words being quoted. Use a comma to separate the words in quotation marks from the reporting verbs such as *say, tell,* and *report.*

For indirect speech, there is no special punctuation.

(continued on next page)

Verb Tense Changes

For indirect speech, when the reporting verb is in the past tense (*said, told, reported*), the verbs inside the quotation marks change.

Direct Speech		Indirect Speech
Margie said, "I **do** my homework at night."		Margie said she **did** her homework at night.
do/does (simple present)	→	**did** (simple past)
am/is/are doing (present progressive)	→	**was/were doing** (past progressive)
did (simple past)	→	**had done** (past perfect)
was/were doing (past progressive)	→	**had been doing** (past perfect progressive)
has/have done (present perfect)	→	**had done** (past perfect)
will (modal)	→	**would** (past modal)
can (modal)	→	**could** (past modal)
may (modal)	→	**might** (past modal)

Time and Location Word Changes

For indirect speech, time and location words may change to keep the speaker's original meaning.

Direct Speech		Indirect Speech
Tommy said, "I don't have to study **now**."		Tommy said he didn't have to study **at that time**.
now	→	**then/at that time**
tomorrow	→	**the next (following) day**
ago	→	**before/earlier**
here	→	**there**
this	→	**that**

Pronoun and Possessive Changes

For indirect speech, pronouns, and possessives change to keep the speaker's original meaning.

Direct Speech	Indirect Speech
Mrs. Jackson said, "**I** ..."	Mrs. Jackson said **she** ...
Mrs. Jackson said, "**Our** children ..."	Mrs. Jackson said **their** children ...

2 *Read the first sentence in each item. It is reported speech. Then, circle the speaker's exact words.*

1. Andy said that he learned more outside of school than he did in traditional school.
   a. "I have learned more outside of school than I have in traditional school."
   b. "I had learned more outside of school than I did in traditional school."
   c. "I learn more outside of school than I do in traditional school."

2. Mrs. Jackson reported that David's youngest brother had never attended school.
   a. "David's youngest brother has never attended school."
   b. "David's youngest brother never attends school."
   c. "David's youngest brother may never attend school."

3. Andy said that in order to get into the USAF Academy, he had to be in top-notch physical condition.
   a. "In order to get into the USAF Academy, I will have to be in top-notch physical condition."
   b. "In order to get into the USAF Academy, I have to be in top-notch physical condition."
   c. "In order to get into the USAF Academy, I have had to be in top-notch physical condition."

4. David's father told us that David would take two courses at the community college the next year.
   a. "David takes two courses at the community college next year."
   b. "David took two courses at the community college next year."
   c. "David will take two courses at the community college next year."

5. Tommy said that he didn't think that a man could know as much as a teacher.
   a. "I didn't think that a man could know as much as a teacher."
   b. "I don't think that a man can know as much as a teacher."
   c. "I don't think that a man could have known as much as a teacher."

6. Margie said that they hadn't had time to think about the book.
   a. "We didn't have time to think about the book."
   b. "We don't have time to think about the book."
   c. "We may not have time to think about the book."

7. Nikki said that many of her new friends were studying at home, too.
   a. "Many of my new friends were studying at home, too."
   b. "Many of her new friends are studying at home, too."
   c. "Many of my new friends are studying at home, too."

3 Write the direct speech statements in indirect speech. Remember to keep the speaker's original meaning.

1. Tommy said, "My father knows as much as my teacher."

   Tommy said his father knew as much as his teacher.

2. The inspector told Margie's mother, "I think the geography sector was a little too difficult."

3. He added, "I've slowed it up to a ten-year level."

4. Tommy said, "This is the old kind of school that they had hundreds and hundreds of years ago."

5. Margie told Tommy, "My mother says a teacher has to be adjusted to fit the mind of each boy and girl it teaches."

6. Tommy told Margie, "You can read the book with me again tomorrow."

C WRITING

In this unit, you read about different models of homeschooling. What choices have you had to make in your educational experience? Have you made choices about the type of school to attend, the field of study to major in, extracurricular activities to participate in (drama, sports, clubs), or any other aspects of your education?

You are going to **write a classification essay describing an important choice you have made about your schooling.***

*For Alternative Writing Topics, see page 174. These topics can be used in place of the writing topic for this unit or as homework. The alternative topics relate to the theme of the unit, but may not target the same grammar or rhetorical structures taught in the unit.

Classifying is a way of analyzing a large topic by breaking it down into parts, called categories. There is often more than one way to choose categories. For example, if the topic is *schooling options*, the categories can be *public, private,* and *homeschooling* (or something else, such as *academic, religious,* and *technical*).

The categories can be further divided into subcategories. For example, the category *public* can be divided into *traditional, magnet,* and *vocational.*

TOPIC	CATEGORIES	SUBCATEGORIES
Schooling options	public	traditional magnet[1] vocational
	private	boarding day school religious
	homeschooling	traditional unschooling eclectic

Choose a topic about education for your classification essay. You can use one of the topics below or think of your own idea. Make a chart like the one above. Then work in a small group and brainstorm categories for each student's topic. Think of as many categories as possible.

cities to study in	extracurricular activities	schools
classes	majors	teachers
countries to study in	schedules	your own idea

---

[1] **magnet school**: a type of American public school that specializes in one area of study such as science and technology or arts.

◖ WRITE: A Classification Essay

In a **classification essay**, each body paragraph describes a separate subcategory of the category. It is helpful to the reader if the information about the subcategories is parallel—that is, the same points are discussed for each of the items. However, the information in each paragraph does not have to be identical. You should decide what to include by thinking about what your audience expects to read or hopes to learn. Here are some important points:

> 1. **Have an introduction that provokes the reader's interest in the topic**. Include a thesis statement that identifies the subcategories in your classification.
>
> 2. **Make sure each body paragraph explains one subcategory**. Try to keep the information parallel by discussing the same points in each paragraph. Include a topic sentence in each paragraph.
>
> 3. **Have a conclusion**. Restate the thesis of the essay and add your final thoughts on the topic: why you made the choice you did and how you feel about it.

1 *Read the outline for the three body paragraphs of a classification essay on types of homeschooling from Reading One. In a classification essay, each body paragraph describes a separate subcategory of the category (in this case, homeschooling options). Notice how the paragraphs are parallel because they discuss many of the same points, such as the type of curriculum. Look at the outline and answer the questions.*

> Topic: School Options Available Today
> Category: Types of Homeschooling
>
> **I. Traditional**
>
>   **A.** Follows traditional curriculum
>
>   **B.** Uses texts, materials from accredited institution
>
>   **C.** Requires parents or tutors or online teachers for guidance and instruction
>
>   **D.** Best for students who still need structure and clear goals
>
> **II. Unschooling**
>
>   **A.** Student's interests determine the curriculum
>
>   **B.** Uses rich home and local environment; no textbooks
>
>   **C.** Self-directed, self-taught learning; little parent/teacher involvement
>
>   **D.** Best for students who are more independent and have strong personal academic interests

1. One subcategory discussed in all three paragraphs is the curriculum. List the other subcategories discussed in each paragraph.

   _____

   _____

2. Think of one more subcategory that could be added for each paragraph.

   _____

2 *Read the beginning of a classification essay about types of homeschooling and answer the questions.*

When you choose to homeschool, there are many things to consider: the source of your curriculum, the source of your texts and materials, and whether or not you will have a parent, tutor or other form of guidance. However, another important point to think about is the kind of learner you are. There is a proverb that says, "A square peg cannot fit into a round hole." This is true for learners as well. The type of learner you are will determine the style of homeschooling best suited for you. Do you need structure and plans to follow? Do you prefer to let your own interests guide you? Or are you a combination depending on the subject matter? Answers to these questions may help you decide whether the traditional, unschooling, or eclectic homeschooling model is best for you.

One common type of homeschooling is traditional homeschooling. In this model, the student follows an established curriculum provided by the government or by an online institution using recommended or approved texts and materials. Some students may enroll in an online or correspondence school that provides them with their curriculum and materials. These students can communicate with teachers online and take tests much like any other traditionally educated student does. Other traditionally homeschooled students are often taught by a parent and/or tutor who use a local or government curriculum. This type of homeschooling is best for students who like to work independently and at their own pace, but still need a set curriculum and guidance along the way.

1. Look at the introduction paragraph. What is the thesis of the essay? Who is the audience? Where does the author introduce the subcategories of the essay?

_____

_____

2. Look at the first body paragraph. What subcategory is discussed in the paragraph? What details does the writer use to explain the subcategory?

_____

_____

3. List the information the writer could include in the next paragraph on unschooling. Include details to support the subcategory.

_____

_____

_____

3 *Now write the first draft of your classification essay. Use the information in Prepare to Write to plan your essay. Look at your topic and the categories you have listed. Choose a category you would like to write about. Add three separate subcategories of the category you have chosen to your chart. These will become the body paragraphs of your essay. Make the paragraphs parallel by including information about the same points for each subcategory. Be sure to use vocabulary and grammar from the unit.*

◀ **REVISE: Using Parallel Structure**

Coordinating conjunctions such as *and, but, and or* are used to combine ideas in a sentence. The words or phrases that are linked with a conjunction must be **parallel**, that is, function as the same part of speech.

- There are three types of homeschooling: <u>traditional</u>, <u>unschooling</u>, or <u>eclectic</u>. (*adjectives*)
- A dedicated surfer, Nikki was not interested in <u>cheerleading</u>, <u>fund-raisers</u>, or <u>dances</u>. (*nouns*)
- In traditional homeschooling, students are usually expected <u>to read coursebooks</u> and <u>to take tests</u>. (*infinitive phrases*)
- When students need help with their coursework they <u>e-mail their teachers</u> or <u>phone their friends</u> for help. (*verb phrases*)
- Aside from e-mail, students can also communicate <u>through newsgroups</u> and <u>in chat rooms</u>. (*prepositional phrases*)

1 Check (✓) the sentences that show correct parallel structure. *For the incorrect sentences, identify the parts of speech of each word or phrase, and correct them to make them parallel.*

_____ 1. Every morning before studying, Andy <u>runs 5 miles</u> and <u>is trying</u> to do 50 sit-ups and 20 push ups.

_____ 2. Communicating on the Internet with teachers is <u>quick</u> and <u>easy</u> but also <u>impersonal</u>.

_____ 3. Nikki checks her e-mail <u>after breakfast</u>, <u>the early afternoon</u>, or sometimes <u>before bed</u>.

_____ 4. Many students enjoy traditional schooling because they can <u>see their friends throughout the day</u>, <u>talk to their advisors</u>, and <u>staying after school for extra help</u>.

_____ 5. <u>To take classes</u> on line and <u>getting credit</u> for them is becoming more common.

_____ 6. David gets his education through <u>online classes</u>, <u>the local community college</u>, and <u>self study book</u>s.

_____ 7. Nikki gets <u>frustrated</u>, <u>upset</u>, and <u>impatient</u> when her e-mail stops working or her Internet connection is down.

2 Complete the sentences with parallel structure. *Use your own ideas.*

1. Students taking a seminar class must speak up and _____ in class discussions.

2. Some homeschoolers feel they have more time for studying, volunteering, and _____.

3. While science class is mostly hands on with lots of interesting lab experiments, English class is lecture based so students must have good listening and _____ skills to take good notes.

4. Registering for a course is easy. You just have to _____ your course from the course catalog, fill out the registration card, and bring it to your advisor or guidance counselor.

5. Starting a new school year is exciting but also _____ at the same time.

6. Margie could not believe that schools in the past had special buildings, books, and _____.

3 Look at your first draft. *Make sure you used correct parallel structure.*

◖EDIT: Writing the Final Draft

Write your final draft. Carefully edit it for grammatical problems and mechanical errors, such as spelling, capitalization, and punctuation. Make sure you used some of the grammar and vocabulary from the unit. Use the checklist to help you write your final draft. Then neatly write or type your essay.

✔ FINAL DRAFT CHECKLIST

❍ Does the essay have an introduction, three body paragraphs, and a conclusion?

❍ Does the introduction provoke the reader's interest in the topic and include a thesis statement that introduces the subcategories in the classification?

❍ Does each body paragraph have a topic sentence? Do all the topic sentences support the thesis statement?

❍ Do the body paragraphs explain the subcategories in the classification? Is the information in each paragraph parallel?

❍ Does the conclusion restate the thesis of the essay and give the writer's final thoughts on the topic?

❍ Does the essay include correct use of parallel sentence structure?

❍ Are word forms used correctly?

❍ Does the essay include an appropriate quotation in direct speech?

❍ Does the essay include appropriate forms of indirect speech?

❍ Has vocabulary from the unit been used?

ALTERNATIVE WRITING TOPICS

Choose one of the topics. Write an essay using the vocabulary and grammar from the unit.

1. Do you think home schooling is a good idea? Why or why not?

2. What do you think is the most important factor in a student's schooling success? Is it parents, teachers, curriculum, class size, technology? Something else? A combination?

RESEARCH TOPICS, see page 263.

UNIT
8 Eat to Live or Live to Eat?

1 FOCUS ON THE TOPIC

A PREDICT

Look at the photographs and the unit title. Then discuss the questions with a partner.

1. What do the photographs show? What are the people doing? How do you think they feel?

2. How are the two photos similar? How are they different?

3. What is the difference between the two expressions in the unit title: *eat to live* and *live to eat*?

1 *What is the most memorable meal you have ever had? Interview three classmates. Ask about their most memorable meal. Complete the chart with your notes.*

	YOU	CLASSMATE 1	CLASSMATE 2	CLASSMATE 3
What was the meal?				
Where did you eat it?				
Who was at the meal?				
Why was it so memorable?				

2 *Share your information with the class. What were the common reasons the meals were memorable. Is it the food, the place, or the people?*

C **BACKGROUND AND VOCABULARY**

Read the restaurant review on the next page. Look at the boldfaced words. Two of the definitions define the words as they are used in the review. Circle the two best definitions for each word.

1. a. in name only
   b. in a small way
   c. usually

2. a. extraordinary
   b. traditional
   c. expected

3. a. correct
   b. natural
   c. suitable

4. a. partially
   b. completely
   c. really

5. a. demand
   b. strongly request
   c. suggest

6. a. avoided
   b. needed
   c. required

7. a. permanently connected
   b. partly corrected
   c. strongly related

8. a. obvious
   b. clear
   c. usual

9. a. make clear
   b. specialize
   c. indicate

10. a. ordered
    b. refused
    c. turned down

11. a. defiance
    b. respect
    c. compliance

12. a. sharing
    b. choosing
    c. communicating

Bamboo Garden is a delightful new restaurant located in the newly renovated Mill Building on Main Street. Unlike other Asian restaurants that often seem overly American and only **(1) nominally** Asian, *Bamboo Garden* offers its clientele a truly Asian experience. We visited *Bamboo Garden* last Saturday and before our meal even began, we realized that the food as well as the entire experience was going to be authentically Asian. For example, as is **(2) customary** in many Asian countries, service at the table began with cleaning our hands with a warmed lemon scented hand towel. We were then greeted with a **(3) proper** bow from the chef, Ming Li. As we were **(4) literally** overwhelmed by the number of dishes on the menu, Ming Li would later graciously **(5) insist** that we let him choose our dinner. We happily accepted his offer as choosing our own meal would have **(6) necessitated** our having at least another hour just to read the menu! Before leaving our table, Ming explained to us that in most Asian cultures food is **(7) inextricably linked** with tradition and history. By this he meant that foods must be prepared in certain ways, and that specific foods are eaten on special holidays. From talking to him, it was **(8) evident** that cooking and all of its ramifications were extremely important to him.

Our meal began with a tofu and vegetable soup. Unfortunately, we did not **(9) specify** that we did not want it too spicy, but it was delicious nonetheless. We then had our main dishes of stir-fry chicken with vegetables and beef with curry sauce. The portions were enormous and the taste was incredible. By the time we finished the main course, we had eaten so much food that we almost **(10) declined** dessert, which was homemade sweet ginger ice cream. However, out of **(11) deference** to Ming Li, we agreed to try it. We were not disappointed!

Before we left, we were sure to thank Ming for **(12) imparting** his wisdom to us; it really made the whole experience memorable.

Ⓐ READING ONE: The Chinese Kitchen

Eileen Yin-Fei Lo is a chef, cooking teacher and cookbook writer. In Reading One, she celebrates the cooking traditions of her native China as she remembers her childhood days growing up in her family's kitchen.

Read the first paragraph. Write three questions that you think the reading will answer. Then read the rest of the story.

1. _____

2. _____

3. _____

THE CHINESE KITCHEN

BY EILEEN YIN-FEI LO
(from *The Chinese Kitchen*)

1   Food is not only life-giving but also a source of familial or societal leanings.[1] Our food is **inextricably linked** with manners, with form, with tradition, with history. I grew up with these beliefs. I remember my father, Lo Pak Wan, my first cooking teacher, telling me that we must eat our food first with our eyes, then with our minds, then with our noses, and finally with our mouths. He believed this. He taught this to my brother and me.

2   He would say, only partly joking, that fine vegetables should be chosen with as much care as one would a son-in-law. He would show me the correct way to prepare rice, telling me that if our rice was old then perhaps more water than **customary** might be needed to give our congee[2] its fine and silky finish. "Keep an open mind," he would say. "Cook the way it has been written, but keep an open mind. If you keep walking only in a straight line, you will go into a wall. You must learn to make a turn if necessary. Do not be narrow." Or he would tell me, *"Tau mei haw yan tiu, mo mei haw yan tiu,"* an aphorism[3] that translates as "if you don't have a tail, you cannot imitate the monkey; if you do have a tail, then do not imitate the monkey." By this he was telling me to follow the classical manner but not to be a simple, mindless imitator.

---

[1] **leanings:** tendencies to prefer or agree with certain beliefs
[2] **congee:** a thick rice porridge
[3] **aphorism:** a short expression that says something true

3   My mother, Lo Chan Miu Hau, encouraged me to cook as well. I recall her saying to me, "If you are wealthy and know how to cook, then servants cannot take advantage of you. If you are poor and know how to cook, you will be able to create wonderful meals with few resources." Cooking and its ramifications were that important to her, as well as to my father, when I was young and growing up in Sun Tak, a suburb of Canton, now Guangzhou.

4   They and my Ah Paw, my mother's mother, insisted that I be involved in our family table. Ah Paw, despite her household of servants and despite the presence of a family cook, made certain whenever I visited her, which was every opportunity I had, every school holiday, that I was in her kitchen.

5   My Ah Paw knew instinctively, without ever having had to personally put a spatula into a wok,[4] how things ought to be cooked, what foods wedded[5] in combination, and what clashed. I am tempted to suggest that she was a brilliant, instinctive kitchen chemist. I will say it. Brilliant she was indeed, her knowledge about foods was encyclopedic, and she was never wrong about cooking, then or now, in my memory. I spent much of the Lunar New Year at her house. I liked her home, I liked her kitchen, and she spoiled me. Except when it came to **imparting** cookery lessons.

6   When we ate raw fish, *yue sahng*, she taught, one had to prepare the fish in the **proper** manner. You hit the fish at the front of its head to stun it, then, when it was still **nominally** alive, you scaled it, gutted and cleaned it, then sliced it for eating. This special dish, which we ate on important birthdays, and on the eves of family weddings, had to be prepared this way, only this way, Ah Paw said.

7   When we steamed a fish, she taught me to softly lay the fish atop a bed of rice at the precise moment that the rice was in the final state of its absorption of water. It would then be perfectly prepared.

8   Once I steamed a fish, quite well, I thought, and proudly carried it to her at the family table. She sniffed. I had forgotten to pour boiled peanut oil over it just before serving. "Take it back to the kitchen and add the oil," she ordered. My grandmother's kitchen always had a crock of boiled peanut oil near the stove. To pour it over fish was to give the fish fragrance and to dispel[6] any unpleasant odors. It does, even if the oil is not warm.

Chinese kitchen gods

---

[4] **wok:** a large, round Chinese cooking pan
[5] **wedded:** went well with
[6] **dispel:** to chase away

(continued on next page)

9   She would eat no vegetables that were older than two hours out of the ground, which **necessitated** repeated trips to the markets by her servants, a lesson of the importance of freshness that was not lost on me.

10   She cautioned me to eat every kernel[7] of rice in my bowl, for if I did not, she warned, the man I married would have a pockmarked[8] face, one mark for each uneaten rice kernel. I did as she cautioned, and I must have eaten well, for my husband's face is clear.

11   Do not shout in the kitchen, Ah Paw would **insist**. Do not use improper words in the kitchen. Do not show shortness of temper in the kitchen by, for example, banging chopsticks[9] on a wok. All of these would reflect badly on us as a family, she would say, when done in front of Jo Kwan, the Kitchen God, whose image hung on the wall over the oven. For just before the Lunar New Year the image of Jo Kwan, his lips smeared with honey, was always burned so that he would go up to heaven and report only nice things about our family.

12   Ah Paw would consult her Tung Sing, an astrological book, for propitious[10] days on which to begin preparing the special dumplings we made and ate during the New Year festival. She would **specify** to the second time to make the dough, heat the oven, add the oil, in what we called *"hoi yau wok,"* or, **literally** translated, "begin the oil in the wok." So admired was she for her knowledge that young married couples, not even of our family, would consult with her. A memory I have is of pumping the pedal of the iron and stone grinding mill in our town square, at her orders, to get the flour that we would use for our dumplings.

13   She was an observant Buddhist who **declined** to eat either fish or meat on the first and the fifteenth of each month and for the first fifteen days of the New Year, and our family ate similarly out of **deference** to her. She was happy that my mother always encouraged me to cook, happy that my father brought kitchen discipline to me as well. She nodded with pleasure, in support of my father, I remember—not in sympathy with me—when I complained how boring it was when my father gave me the task of snapping off the ends of individual mung bean sprouts. "If you wish to learn how to make spring rolls[11] well, learn the beginning of the spring roll. It must be done," Ah Paw said.

14   We had no grinders.[12] We chopped meats and other seafood with the cleaver[13] on a chopping board. "Clean it," Ah Paw would say when I was finished. "If you do not, the food you chop next will not stick together. It will

---

[7] **kernel (of rice):** piece of rice
[8] **pockmarked:** covered with small holes or marks
[9] **chopsticks:** a pair of thin sticks used for eating food, especially by people in Asia
[10] **propitious:** good, likely to bring favorable results
[11] **spring roll:** cooked vegetables wrapped in a special thin dough
[12] **grinder:** machine that cuts and chops up food
[13] **cleaver:** knife with a large square blade

fall apart. There will be no texture. If it falls apart, I will know that you did not listen."

15   All of this she conferred on me without ever setting foot in the kitchen of her house. As a further example of her vision I should note in passing that my Ah Paw, a most independent woman, as is **evident**, refused to have bound the feet of my mother, her daughter, much the practice of high born women. This, despite the fact that her own feet had been bound since babyhood and were no more than four inches long. This extraordinary woman, never more than seventy-five pounds, who could not totter more than one hundred feet and was usually carried by servants, brought my mother and then me into modern times in her own way. I wanted nothing more than to be with her, and I would listen, wide-eyed and receptive, to her talk about food and its meanings . . .

◖ READ FOR MAIN IDEAS

1   Eileen Yin-Fei Lo talks about the three people who influenced her cooking most. Complete the sentences with information describing why each person was important to her.

    a. Her father was important because _____

    _____

    _____

    b. Her mother was important because _____

    _____

    _____

    c. Her grandmother was important because _____

    _____

    _____

2   What influenced Eileen Yin-Fei Lo's family's cooking practices and techniques?

_____

_____

_____

1 *Write **T** (true) or **F** (false) for each statement. Write the number of the paragraph that supports your answer. If the statement is false, change it to make it true.*

Paragraph

_____ 1. The author's mother thought being able to cook was important for all people, rich and poor. _____

_____ 2. Ah Paw was an experienced cook. _____

_____ 3. In Ah Paw's house, any food could be prepared and eaten at any time of the year. _____

_____ 4. It was well known that Ah Paw was very knowledgeable about cooking. _____

_____ 5. Ah Paw was very demanding concerning the quality of food she ate. _____

_____ 6. At Ah Paw's house, the servants helped with the preparation of the food. _____

_____ 7. The author's father believed in the importance of choosing vegetables carefully. _____

2 *The author talks about how her family links food with cooking processes, traditions, superstitions, and religious beliefs. Complete the chart with an example of each. Write the number of the paragraph where you found your example.*

COOKING PROCESS	TRADITION	SUPERSTITION	RELIGIOUS BELIEF
Paragraph _____	Paragraph _____	Paragraph _____	Paragraph _____

◖ MAKE INFERENCES

Answer the questions about the quotations from Reading One.

1. "I remember my father, Lo Pak Wan, my first cooking teacher, telling me that we must eat our food first with our eyes, then with our minds, then with our noses, and finally with our mouths." (paragraph 1)

   Why do you think he chose that specific order for eating? _____

   _____

   _____

2. "He would say, only partly joking, that fine vegetables should be chosen with as much care as one would a son-in-law." (paragraph 2)

   Why does he compare choosing vegetables to choosing a son-in-law? _____

   _____

   _____

3. "Cook the way it has been written, but keep an open mind. If you keep walking only in a straight line, you will go into a wall. You must learn to make a turn if necessary. Do not be narrow." (paragraph 2)

   What implications does this belief have for cooking? _____

   _____

   _____

4. "I liked her kitchen and she spoiled me. Except when it came to imparting cookery lessons." (paragraph 5)

   Why do you think cooking was the only area where Aw Paw did not spoil

   Eileen? _____

   _____

   _____

5. "She cautioned me to eat every kernel of rice in my bowl, for if I did not, she warned, the man I married would have a pockmarked face, one mark for each uneaten rice kernel. I did as she cautioned, and I must have eaten well, for my husband's face is clear." (paragraph 10)

   Do you think Eileen believed Aw Paw's ideas about uneaten rice? _____

   _____

   _____

Discuss the questions with a partner. Share your answers with the class.

1. Eileen Yin-Fei Lo states, "Our food is inextricably linked with manners, with form, with tradition, with history." Do you believe that the same is true in your culture?

2. Eileen Yin-Fei Lo adds that, "Cooking and its ramifications were that important to her (my grandmother), as well as to my father." How important is cooking in your family and what are its ramifications?

3. Do you continue to eat and/or prepare traditional foods? Is it easy to keep these practices in the modern world? Why or why not?

Ⓑ READING TWO: "Slow Food" Movement Aims at Restoring the Joy of Eating

Now that the twenty-first century has begun, it is clear that the pace of life is ever increasing. Nevertheless, some people are consciously slowing down where food is concerned. They are embracing the idea of the importance of good food and meaningful companionship at the table. People are also taking more interest in how food is grown, how it is prepared, and even how and with whom it is eaten. There is also a renewed interest in cultural food traditions. All of these issues are part of an international food movement known as the "Slow Food" movement.

Discuss the questions with a partner. Then read the article about Slow Food.

1. The term "fast food" refers to food that is prepared quickly in order to save time. McDonald's, Burger King, Pizza Hut, and KFC are examples of fast food. What other examples of fast food can you think of? Do you like fast food? Which is your favorite and why?

2. What do you think "Slow Food" means?

"Slow Food" Movement Aims at Restoring the Joy of Eating

By Cathy Heiner (from *USA Today*)

1   "The Slow Food movement is committed to the preservation and restoration of a traditional convivial joy, the joy of the table," says Jonathan White, a member of the Slow Food organization and owner of Egg Farm Dairy in Peekskill, N.Y. "And that's not just about food and wine; it's also about kinship and companionship, which you just don't get going to a drive-through[1] and eating in traffic."

2   Whopper[2] lovers, don't have a meltdown.[3] Slow Food may use a snail as its logo, but it's not anti-fast food. "We're not against anything," White says. "Our agenda is to educate people who don't know about the pleasures of the table and, through education, to help traditional food artisans—bakers, cheesemakers, farmers growing heirloom vegetables[4]—to survive by sustaining demand for their product."

3   Members of Slow Food meet for long, leisurely meals. They talk food, wine, culture, and philosophy. They organize wine tastings and cooking classes. But most of all, they work to eradicate the "nuke[5] it and eat it" American lifestyle.

4   "Slow Food is not only about literally eating slowly, but also about savoring and appreciating the pleasures of good food and drink. Slow Food is "a way of life," says its Web site (www.slowfood.com).

5   The movement got cooking in the late 1980s when a fast-food burger joint[6] was about to open on Rome's beloved Piazza Spagna. A young Italian organization called Arcigola, dedicated to rediscovering and advocating authentic Italian traditions, protested. From the fray,[7] Slow Food was born.

6   "It was just a game at first," says founder Carlo Petrini, "a chance to remind people that food is a perishable[8] art, as pleasurable in its way as a sculpture by Michelangelo."

7   Today, Slow Food is 20,000 strong in Italy, where the joy of the table is a matter of national pride. And there are Slow Food organizations in more than 15 countries, from Switzerland to Singapore.

8   Although the movement is new to these shores, adherents say they believe Americans will take to it like pigs to truffles.[9] "Every year Americans are going to more restaurants, asking and learning more about food," says Paul Bartolotta, Slow Foodist and owner of Chicago's Spiaggia restaurant.

---

[1] **drive-through:** a fast-food restaurant that can be used without getting out of your car
[2] **Whopper:** a type of hamburger from Burger King
[3] **meltdown:** an emotional breakdown
[4] **heirloom vegetables:** vegetables (or fruit) with a superior flavor or an unusual color
[5] **nuke:** to cook or heat food in a microwave oven
[6] **joint:** a slang word for place—usually a restaurant, club, or bar
[7] **fray:** a fight or argument
[8] **perishable:** unpreserved and therefore can become bad or decay quickly
[9] **like pigs to truffles:** an expression meaning enthusiastically

(continued on next page)

9   He says the USA is ripe for Slow Food. "Ten years ago, there were hardly any (farmers) markets, we were fast-food-driven, and there was less interest in food and wine. It has dramatically changed. Now there are organic supermarkets. There's a cultural awareness of what we're eating and why."

10   Slow Food could even tame America's obsession with dieting, White says. "If you only feed the body, you get fat. It's important not to deny the spiritual aspects of eating, to milk[10] the most joy out of the bodily function of eating."

11   And time at the table is time well spent, says Bartolotta. "The Slow Food movement's message is, 'Let's eat well and enjoy it.' No matter how crazy and hectic our lives are, the pleasure of the table is a fundamental right."

How to Slow Down

12   Can harried soccer moms[11] and overworked dads become Slow Foodists? How fast-food fanatics can add joy to their tables:

13   • **Turn off the TV.** "Cooking with your kids is a great family activity," says Jonathan White, a Slow Foodist from Peekskill, N.Y. "The preparation of food is one of the oldest human cultural traditions, and it's always been a parent-to-child thing."

14   • **Throw away the microwave.** "It's a myth when people say they don't have time to cook," says David Auerbach, leader of a chapter in Raleigh, N.C. "There's lots of good cookbooks that tell you how to make a meal in 30 minutes or less."

15   • **Shop at farmers markets.** "Get to know the growers," says Barbara Bowman, co-director of the Sonoma, Calif., chapter. The freshness of your food is guaranteed.

16   • **Perpetuate your family's traditions.** "Food, jokes, proverbs, toasts. Slow Food is not just about feasting; it's also about preserving traditions," Bowman says.

17   • **Patronize[12] restaurants that specialize in local, regional cuisine.** "When traveling, eat what and where the locals eat," Bowman says.

To join, write to
***Slow Food**, c/o Egg Farm Dairy,*
2 John Walsh Blvd., Peekskill, N.Y. 10566

---

[10] **to milk:** to get all the advantages you can from a situation
[11] **soccer moms:** a term meaning mothers who spend a lot of time driving their children to and from activities.
[12] **patronize:** to regularly use a particular store, restaurant, company, etc.

Copyright 1998, Gannett Co., Inc. Reprinted with permission

Answer the questions. Then share your answers with a partner.

1. What are some of the beliefs of the Slow Food movement?

2. How is "local" important in this movement?

C INTEGRATE READINGS ONE AND TWO

STEP 1: Organize

Eileen Yin-Fei Lo grew up before the Slow Food movement started. Yet, there are many similarities between her food experiences and the Slow Food movement's beliefs. Complete the chart with examples of how Yin-Fei Lo's experiences relate to the Slow Food movement.

SLOW FOOD BELIEFS	EILEEN YIN-FEI LO'S FOOD TRADITIONS
1. **Cooking**: "Cooking with your kids is a great family activity. The preparation of food is one of the oldest human cultural traditions, and it's always been a parent-to-child thing."	Her father was her first cooking teacher. Her mother and grandmother also taught her about cooking. She spent many hours in her grandmother's kitchen.
2. **Eating**: "If you only feed the body, you get fat. It's important not to deny the spiritual aspects of eating, to milk the most joy out of the bodily function of eating."	
3. **Food shopping:** "Get to know the (local) growers." The freshness of your food is guaranteed.	
4. **Family traditions:** Perpetuate your family's traditions. "Food, jokes, proverbs, toasts. Slow Food is not just about feasting; it's also about preserving traditions."	

STEP 2: Synthesize

Imagine that Eileen Yin-Fei Lo has opened up a Slow Food restaurant. You visit her restaurant and talk to her about what inspired her and how she integrates her upbringing into her restaurant. On a separate piece of paper, write a restaurant review. Be sure to incorporate her beliefs and traditions.

③ FOCUS ON WRITING

A VOCABULARY

◖ REVIEW

Complete the sentences using the words in the boxes on the next page.

declined	inextricably linked	insisted	necessitated	specified

1. The recipe for the cookies _____ that I had to use exactly half a cup of sugar.

2. At dinner, my mother offered me another piece of meat, but I _____ because I had eaten enough.

3. Finding all the ingredients for the recipe _____ trips to more than one market.

4. When I suggested that we buy fast food for the kids, my wife got mad. She _____ that we give them the same food we were going to eat.

5. Most chefs would agree that the taste of a meal is _____ to the freshness of the ingredients.

authentic	customary	pleasurable	proper

6. In many restaurants, it is _____ to tip the waiter or waitress.

7. Some people believe it is hard to find _____ Japanese cuisine outside of Japan.

8. Eating a home-cooked meal with your family and friends can be a very _____ experience.

9. If you want to make good rice, you need to use the _____ amount of water: not too much or too little.

leisurely	literally	nominally

10. Although the name of the restaurant is "Acapulco," the food was only _____ Mexican. I doubt that someone from Mexico would have been able to identify any of the dishes.

11. One of the beliefs of the Slow Food movement is that a _____ meal will make the experience of eating more enjoyable.

12. We had eaten so much that we _____ couldn't eat another bite.

deference	evident	imparting

13. Out of _____ to our guest's customs, we chose not to serve alcohol with the meal.

14. I don't think I'll ever be able to thank my cooking teacher enough for _____ his knowledge on me.

15. It is _____ that the time spent in her grandmother's kitchen greatly influenced Yin-Fei Lo's cooking practices as an adult.

◖EXPAND

Work in a small group. Read the sentences. Circle the best explanation for each underlined phrasal verb.

1. I grew up with the belief that food is inextricably linked with tradition.
   a. got taller   **b.** was born   **c.** was raised

2. Yin-Fei Lo's grandmother insisted she learn to cook because if you are wealthy and know how to cook, then servants cannot take advantage of you.
   a. help   **b.** pay   **c.** exploit

3. I liked her home, I liked her kitchen, and I also liked that she usually spoiled me. However, when it came to imparting cookery lessons, she was a hard teacher.
   a. involved   **b.** arrived   **c.** awoke

4. Once I steamed a fish, quite well, I thought, but I had forgotten to pour boiled oil over it just before serving. "Take it back to the kitchen and add the oil," my grandmother ordered.
   a. cook   **b.** return   **c.** remember

5. All of this she conferred on me without ever setting foot in the kitchen of her house.
   a. leaving   **b.** dressing   **c.** entering

6. Slow Foodists tell people to turn off their TV because they believe it is more pleasurable to eat without the sound of the TV in the background.
   a. dislike   **b.** exit   **c.** stop use of

7. They also say to throw away your microwave; you can't cook food properly with a microwave.
   a. discard   **b.** improve   **c.** arrange

8. Although the Slow Food movement is new here, its followers believe we will take to it enthusiastically.
   a. control   **b.** like   **c.** bring

◖ CREATE

Read the information and complete the activity.

Imagine a large international restaurant chain wants to build a fast food restaurant in a community that does not have any fast-food restaurants. Think about the ramifications for the community. How will it affect small restaurant owners, employment opportunities, and quality of life? Will it improve the community or make it worse?

Form two groups. Group A is in favor of building a fast-food restaurant and discusses reasons why the restaurant is a good idea. Group A then decides on the six most important reasons and everyone in the group writes the same six reasons on their papers. Leave space under each reason so that a student from the other group can write a response.

Group B is against building a fast-food restaurant and discusses reasons why the restaurant is a bad idea. Group B then decides on the six most important reasons and everyone in the group writes the same six reasons on their papers. Leave space under each reason so that a student from the other group can write a response.

Then, work in pairs. Each pair has one student from Group A and one from Group B. Exchange papers with your partner and respond to each other's reasons.

In your reasons and responses, use six or more words from the Review and Expand sections. The words below may be especially useful, but you can use any vocabulary words from the unit.

authentic	declined	leisurely	pleasurable	take to
customary	evident	necessitated	take advantage of	throw away

B GRAMMAR: Phrasal Verbs

1 *Examine the sentences and answer the questions with a partner.*

   a. Slow Foodists say you should throw away your microwave.

   b. They also say you should turn off your television.

   c. Cooks constantly come up with new ideas of how to cook fish.

   1. What is the verb in each sentence?

   2. What is the difference between *throw* and *throw away*?

   3. What is the difference between *turn* and *turn off*?

   4. What is the difference between *come* and *come up with*?

PHRASAL VERBS

1. A **phrasal verb** consists of a verb and a particle (an adverb or preposition). The combination often has a meaning that is different from the meaning of the separate parts. Phrasal verbs are often used in everyday communication.

2. Phrasal verbs (also called two-part or two-word verbs) combine a verb with a **particle**.

Verb	+	Particle	=	Meaning
take	+	back	=	return
look	+	over	=	examine
give	+	up	=	quit

3. Some phrasal verbs (also called three-part or three-word verbs) combine with a **preposition**.

Phrasal Verb	+	Preposition	=	Meaning
come up	+	with	=	imagine or invent
think back	+	on	=	remember

4. Some phrasal verbs are **transitive**. They take a direct object. Many (two-word) transitive phrasal verbs are **separable**. This means the verb and the particle can be separated by the direct object.

    She **looked over** the recipe.
       [verb] [particle] [object]

    She **looked** the recipe **over**.
       [verb]   [object]   [particle]

5. However, when the direct object is a pronoun it must go between the verb and the particle.

    She **picked** it **up**.
       [verb] [object] [particle]

    NOT

    She **picked** up **it**.
       [verb] [particle] [object]

6. Some phrasal verbs are **intransitive**. They do not take a direct object. Intransitive phrasal verbs are always **inseparable**. This means that the verb and particle are never separated.

    I liked that restaurant. I want to **go back** next week.
              [verb] [particle]

7. The words in a phrasal verb are usually common, but their meaning changes when the words are used together. Therefore, it can be difficult to guess the meaning of the verb from its individual parts.

    call off   = cancel

    drop out of = quit

(continued on next page)

8. Some phrasal verbs have more than one meaning.

She **took off** her apron.	=	She **removed** her apron.
She **took off** for the market at 7:00 A.M.	=	She **departed** for the market.
She **took** the day **off** from the restaurant.	=	She **didn't** work in the restaurant that day.

9. Some verbs are combined with different particles or prepositions. Each combination creates a phrasal verb with a different meaning.

She **turned down** the heat in the oven.	=	She **lowered** the heat in the oven.
She **turned on** the stove.	=	She **started** the stove.
She **turned over** the fish in the pan.	=	She **flipped** the fish in the pan.
A fast-food restaurant **turned up** on the Piazza Spagna in the 1980s.	=	A fast-food restaurant **appeared**.

2 Work in a small group. Complete the sentences with the word or phrase that has the same meaning as the underlined phrasal verb.

become popular	entered	invent	~~was raised~~

1. Eileen Yin-Fei Lo <u>grew up </u>in a family that has many food traditions.
   _____was raised_____

2. Many experienced cooks are able to <u>come up with</u> a meal after seeing what they have in their refrigerators. _____

3. Although Ah Paw never <u>set foot in</u> the kitchen, she knew instinctively which spices a certain dish necessitated. _____

4. The idea of cooking with natural organic ingredients is starting to <u>catch on</u> all over the world. _____

clean	discard	like	remove from

5. When the soup is done, <u>take</u> it <u>off</u> the stove. _____

6. After you finish cooking, you should always <u>pick up</u>, so you will be ready to cook again. _____

7. Don't <u>throw away</u> oil when you finish cooking. Use it again later.

   _____

8. Although, at first, Americans were only nominally interested in ethnic restaurants, now they are starting to <u>take to</u> them. _____

eliminate	examine	exploit	remember

9. Ah Paw often imparted her wisdom on Eileen Yin-Fei Lo. For example, she told her that it was important to know how to cook so if she were rich, servants couldn't <u>take advantage of</u> her. _____

10. Slow Food advocates work to <u>do away with</u> the "nuke it and eat it" American lifestyle. _____

11. The smell of food coming from the kitchen caused Marco to <u>think back on</u> the dishes his mother used to cook when he was a child. _____

12. My mother insists that before I start cooking, I should <u>look over</u> the recipe to make sure I understand it and have all the ingredients. _____

appear	flip	lower	start

13. Don't forget to <u>turn over</u> the fish before it burns. _____
14. If you don't <u>turn</u> the heat <u>down</u>, the meat will burn. _____
15. I'm going to <u>turn on</u> the computer to look for recipes. _____
16. Although a few years ago they weren't so popular, fast-food restaurants are beginning to <u>turn up</u> all over the world. Slow Food advocates worry about what the ramifications of this trend will be. _____

3 Complete the paragraph with phrasal verbs from Exercise 2 on pages 192–193 and the grammar box on pages 191–192 in place of the verbs in parentheses. Be sure to use the correct verb tense.

Many years ago, when we were first married, my wife and I had very little money. I often worried that we couldn't afford to celebrate birthdays and holidays. On the day of her birthday, I woke up and realized that I still didn't have a present. I thought about what I had given her previous years, but this didn't help me to _____ an idea for that year. Suddenly, I had an idea—I would
1. (imagine)
prepare a leisurely meal for her. I knew she would _____ the idea
2. (like)
because she was always tired after work, and the last thing she would want to do on her birthday was cook. As soon as I _____ in the kitchen, I put on an
3. (entered)
apron. Then I was ready to start. I wanted to make an authentic Spanish feast, so I

_____ some cookbooks. I decided to start with a *tortilla Española*
4. (examine)
(potato omelet). First, I peeled two medium potatoes. Next, I _____
5. (started)
the stove and heated some oil in a pan. When the oil was sufficiently hot, I added the potatoes and _____ the heat. I then added a sliced onion and salt.
6. (lowered)
While this was cooking, I beat six eggs in a bowl. When the potato and onion mixture was ready, I added it to the bowl with the eggs and mixed it all together. I then added the egg mixture to the heated pan and started cooking the omelet. After a few minutes, I had to _____ it _____. When it was
7. (flip)
finished cooking, I transferred it to a platter and it was ready to serve. The only problem was that I felt so tired from making the tortilla that I couldn't make anything else except a salad. When I finished, I _____ the kitchen and
8. (cleaned)
_____ the trash. I then _____ my apron and sat down
9. (discarded) **10. (removed)**
to wait for the "birthday girl." She arrived about five minutes later. Although the meal ended up being quite simple, we both really enjoyed it. In fact, my wife says it was one of her best birthday "presents" and we often _____ it and smile.
11. (remember)

In this unit, you read two stories about food. Eileen Yin-Fei Lo wrote about her memories growing up in her family's kitchen while the Slow Food reading was about the importance of enjoying "the table," meaning both food and friends. What is your most memorable food experience? Is there a meal that stands out in your memory more than any other?

You are going to **write a narrative essay describing a memorable meal.***

◀ PREPARE TO WRITE: Notetaking

In **notetaking**, you write notes about the topic of your essay or paragraph before you begin to write.

Think about your most memorable meal. Take notes in the organizer. Then share your notes with a classmate. Discuss your ideas and add to your notes.

Month/Year/Season of the meal:

Location of the meal (include city and country, home, restaurant, or other):

Reason for the meal (special holiday, birthday, or no specific reason):

People the meal was shared with:

(continued on next page)

---

*For Alternative Writing Topics, see page 200. These topics can be used in place of the writing topic for this unit or as homework. The alternative topics relate to the theme of the unit, but may not target the same grammar or rhetorical structures taught in the unit.

Description of the meal (include look, taste, touch, smell):

Information about preparation (how the meal was prepared/served):

Interesting events that happened at the meal:

Why the meal was memorable:

◖ WRITE: A Narrative Essay

A **narrative essay** uses events, memories, and personal experiences to tell a story. The story is one that deeply influenced the writer; a story that the writer would like to share with others. A narrative must be well-organized and interesting in order to keep the reader engaged. Here are some important points:

1. **Have a clear topic and thesis**. Think about the event (the topic) and why this is a story worth telling (the thesis). The thesis answers the question: Why do you want to share this story? What new insight or awareness did you gain from the event?

2. **Support your thesis throughout your writing**. Use examples and details to support and enhance your thesis. Make sure they directly relate to the thesis.

3. **Use a chronological sequence**. Use transition words to show the sequence of events. For example use *first, next, then, before, after, later, finally, that day, today, tomorrow, at night*.

4. **Describe how one event relates to another in time**. Use time referents; for example, *while, when, meanwhile, at the same time, at that moment, as soon as, not a moment later*.

1 *Read the narrative essay and answer the questions.*

A Most Memorable Meal

When I am asked to think back on my most memorable meal, it is very easy to recall. The meal was neither the fanciest nor most expensive meal I have ever eaten, but it was the most satisfying for many other reasons. It was in Paris, on a cold gray December day, on the Left Bank. I must have been in my early twenties, traveling with my friends. We were always broke and, as a result, we ate a lot of hot dogs and food sold on the street. Even so, we thought we lived like kings. One day we thought we shouldn't worry about money and actually eat in a sit-down restaurant. Of course, having very little money, we had to be careful where we ate: a nominally-priced restaurant that still had the incredibly delicious food for which Paris is famous. These criteria necessitated our spending the day looking over the menus of every restaurant on the Left Bank before committing to the perfect one. This act in itself was memorable. After much searching, we finally found it. We knew it was perfect before we even set foot in it. It was a lovely authentic Algerian restaurant with white tablecloths and napkins, real silverware, and flowers on every table. But most important: It served all the couscous[1] you could eat! We were very very hungry, so we knew we had to take advantage of this opportunity.

We returned that night, freshly showered and dressed for our night out. As soon as we sat down, delicious French bread was served with tall glasses of icy cold water with lemon. Moments after we ordered, the waiter appeared with appetizers explaining that the cook sent them out to us because we looked so desperately hungry. We laughed in agreement. At the very moment we finished our appetizers, the main course arrived. It was extraordinary! An enormous silver bowl of steaming couscous[1] and savory chicken was set in the middle of the table with a large silver spoon. We served ourselves and ate. And ate. As soon as we finished, the waiter removed the bowl . . . and before we could speak, replaced it with another! We declined desert even though our waiter insisted we have some. After that meal, we did not just think we were kings. We knew it! We stumbled back to our hotel, deliriously happy, with full stomachs and wonderful memories.

1. What is the topic and thesis of the narrative?

_____

_____

---

[1] **couscous**: semolina wheat pasta

2. What are some examples and details the writer used to support the thesis?

   a. _____

   b. _____

   c. _____

3. Briefly describe the chronology of the narration.

   Beginning: _____

   Middle: _____

   End: _____

4. What transitional words and referents does the writer use to describe the sequence of events?

   _____

   _____

5. Why do you think the writer wanted to share this story?

   _____

   _____

   _____

   _____

2 *Now write the first draft of your narrative essay. Use the information from Prepare to Write. State your topic and thesis. Add details and examples to describe how things looked, smelled, tasted, and sounded. Use transition words to show time sequences and how events are related. Be sure to use vocabulary and grammar from the unit.*

◀ **REVISE: Varying Sentence Length**

Use **sentences of varying length** to help to make your narrative more interesting to read. One short sentence after another can make your writing feel choppy. However, all long sentences can make your writing hard to read. Varying sentence length and style can also help you to add emphasis.

1 *Read the passage. Notice the variety in sentence length. Circle the shortest sentence. How many words is it? Underline the longest sentence. How many words is it?*

> It was a first lunch that changed the course of history. Julia Child remembers it well: sole poached in white wine and draped in a cream sauce, with oysters on the side, nestled in their half shells.
>
> It was 1948 in Paris. Paul and Julia Child, an American couple, had come by boat for a stint[1] in the Foreign Service, and their first lunch became the impetus[2] for Mrs. Child's culinary coup[3] of the American diet. "I couldn't get over it," recalls Mrs. Child, nearly 50 years after the event. "I'd never had such food in my life." She found the French stuff heady and it filled her with delight and wonder. What began simply as love at first bite turned into a lifelong affair with French cooking and French food.
>
> *Source:* Adapted from "Julia Child—A Butcher, A Baker, A Mover and Shaker." By Kira Albin. 1997. *www.grandtimes.com*

2 *Read the paragraph. Some of these sentences are very short. Combine them to make them longer and more effective. Share your answer with a partner.*

My wife and I ate at the new restaurant. It was on Center Street. Some friends were with us. We ordered a Japanese dish made with tofu. The dish tasted delicious. It wasn't expensive. Unfortunately, we all got sick. We decided we would never go there again.

3 *Read the paragraph. The sentences are too long. Rewrite them to make them shorter and more effective. Share your answer with a partner.*

After an exhausting day of sightseeing, we were looking forward to our meal, but when the tour bus stopped in front of a pizza parlor instead of a nice restaurant, we all felt very disappointed and asked the tour leader if we could go to another restaurant with more ambiance and more importantly, authentic food. The tour leader agreed, but said he would have to ask his boss if it was all right and also that if we really wanted to go to a restaurant that had food customary for the region, we would have to drive for at least another hour and stop for gas because the bus had very little gas left.

_____

_____

_____

_____

_____

---

[1] **stint:** a short period of time

[2] **impetus:** cause; influence that makes something happen quickly

[3] **coup:** unexpected success

4 *Look at your first draft. Find the shortest sentence and the longest. Do your sentences vary in length? Or are they all the same length? Can you see any pattern in your writing? Can you combine or break up sentences so that they vary?*

◀ **EDIT: Writing the Final Draft**

Write your final draft. Carefully edit it for grammatical problems and mechanical errors, such as spelling, capitalization, and punctuation. Make sure you used some of the grammar and vocabulary from the unit. Use the checklist to help you write your final draft. Then neatly write or type your essay.

✓ **FINAL DRAFT CHECKLIST**

○ Does the narrative have a clear topic and thesis?
○ Does the essay have effective details and support?
○ Does the essay use effective transition words to show a clear sequence of events?
○ Is there a variety of sentence lengths?
○ Does the author effectively explain why the meal was important?
○ Are there phrasal verbs?
○ Has vocabulary from the unit been used?

ALTERNATIVE WRITING TOPICS

Choose one of the topics. Write an essay using the vocabulary and grammar from the unit.

1. The Slow Food movement suggests that you go to restaurants that specialize in local, regional cuisine. They state, "When traveling, eat what and where the locals eat." Do you follow this advice? What interesting food-related experience(s) have you had while traveling?

2. Think about the expression "you are what you eat" and apply it to yourself. Choose one of your favorite foods or food traditions and discuss how it reflects who you are.

RESEARCH TOPICS, see page 264.

The Grass Is Always Greener...

Jamaica Kincaid
Born: Antigua,[1] 1949
Occupation: Writer
Immigrated to the U.S. in 1966

Arnold Schwarzenegger
Born: Graz, Austria, 1947
Occupation: Actor/
Governor of California
Immigrated to the U.S. in 1968

Gloria Estefan
Born: Havana, Cuba, 1957
Occupation: Singer
Immigrated to the U.S. in 1959

1 FOCUS ON THE TOPIC

A PREDICT

Look at the photographs and the unit title. Then discuss the questions with a partner.

1. What do the people have in common?

2. How do you think their life would have been different if they had not immigrated?

3. The unit title is part of a famous saying, "The grass is always greener on the other side of the fence.[2]" Do you think the saying is about other things besides grass and fences? What do you think the unit will be about?

---

[1] **Antigua**: an island in the Caribbean

[2] **fence**: a structure made of wood, metal, etc. that surrounds a piece of land

B SHARE INFORMATION

Work in a small group. Brainstorm reasons why people immigrate. Complete the chart with economic, political, and personal reasons. Discuss your list with the class. If you wish, share some personal experiences.

ECONOMIC REASONS	POLITICAL REASONS	PERSONAL REASONS

C BACKGROUND AND VOCABULARY

1 *Read the story about Gustavo. Try to understand the boldfaced words from the context.*

For Gustavo, like countless people around the world, **discontent** with life in his own country and the hope for a better life in a new place inspired him to think about immigration. In his **fantasy**, he saw himself successfully integrated into the new society with a good job, a new car, and a big house. Gustavo certainly had feelings of **fright** when thinking about the challenges he would face, but he was **impatient** to start his new life. The first few weeks in the new country were happy ones for Gustavo. He was staying with his brother and he was excited and determined. Many things about the new culture were different from what he was used to; nothing was **predictable**. Even hand **gestures** had different meanings. He once motioned for someone to come over to him and the person thought he was waving and so waved back and walked away. He never knew what to expect next. He had **sensations** of confusion and sometimes felt defeated, yet he saw all of this as positive. These feelings began to change, however, when he started to look for a job. After looking for weeks, he finally came to the **realization** that he might not be able to get a job that was similar to the job he'd had in his own country. Eventually he did find a job although it was not the type of job he had envisioned in his fantasy of his new life. **Formerly**, he had been a respected businessman; now he was working as a gardener. He would have to work long and hard to be able to afford even a small apartment. He then began to realize that things he had **taken for granted** in the past—his home, transportation, language, and food—were proving to be difficulties now. It was at this point that he started to **long** for his old life. Nevertheless, he still felt in his **soul** that he had made the right decision to come to this new country. He felt that if he worked hard, he and his family would be successful and in the long run their lives would be better.

2 *Find the boldfaced words in the story above. Circle the best synonym or definition for the word.*

1.	**discontent**	=	unhappiness	or	interruption
2.	**fantasy**	=	attraction	or	imagination
3.	**fright**	=	conflict	or	fear
4.	**impatient**	=	anxious	or	scared
5.	**predictable**	=	expected	or	related
6.	**gestures**	=	shakes	or	movements
7.	**sensations**	=	feelings	or	ideas
8.	**realization**	=	understanding	or	accomplishment
9.	**took for granted**	=	missed	or	undervalued
10.	**long**	=	wish	or	enlarge
11.	**formerly**	=	definitely	or	before
12.	**soul**	=	heart	or	ghost

② FOCUS ON READING

A READING ONE: Poor Visitor

Read the first paragraph of Poor Visitor. *Write answers to the questions. Share your answers with a partner. Then read the rest of the story.*

1. Which words tell you about Lucy's emotions on her first day in New York?

_____

_____

2. What do you think will happen? What do you think the author will describe in the rest of the story?

_____

_____

POOR VISITOR

BY JAMAICA KINCAID
(from *Lucy*)

1   It was my first day. I had come the night before, a gray-black and cold night before—as it was to be in the middle of January, though I didn't know that at the time—and I could not see anything clearly on the way in from the airport, even though there were lights everywhere. As we drove along, someone would single out[1] to me a famous building, an important street, a park, a bridge, that when built was thought to be a spectacle.[2] In a daydream I used to have, all these places were points of happiness to me; all these places were lifeboats to my small drowning **soul**, for I would imagine myself entering and leaving them, and just that—entering and leaving over and over again—would see me through a bad feeling I did not have a name for. I only knew it felt a little like sadness but heavier than that. Now that I saw these places, they looked ordinary, dirty, worn down by so many people entering and leaving them in real life, and it occurred to me that I could not be the only person in the world for whom they were a fixture of **fantasy**. It was not my first bout with the disappointment of reality and it would not be my last. The undergarments that I wore were all new, bought for my journey, and as I sat in the car, twisting this way and that to get a good view of the sights before me, I was reminded of how uncomfortable the new can make you feel.

---

[1] **single out:** to point out, choose from among a group
[2] **spectacle:** something remarkable or impressive

2   I got in an elevator, something I had never done before, and then I was in an apartment and seated at a table eating food just taken from a refrigerator. In the place I had just come from, I always lived in a house, and my house did not have a refrigerator in it. Everything I was experiencing—the ride in the elevator, being in an apartment, eating day-old food that had been stored in a refrigerator—was such a good idea that I could imagine I would grow used to it and like it very much, but at first it was all so new that I had to smile with my mouth turned down at the corners. I slept soundly that night, but it wasn't because I was happy and comfortable—quite the opposite; it was because I didn't want to take in anything else.

3   That morning, the morning of my first day, the morning that followed my first night, was a sunny morning. It was not the sort of bright-yellow sun making everything curl at the edges, almost in **fright**, that I was used to, but a pale-yellow sun, as if the sun had grown weak from trying too hard to shine;

but still it was sunny, and that was nice and made me miss my home less. And so, seeing the sun, I got up and put on a dress, a gay[3] dress made out of madras cloth—the same sort of dress that I would wear if I were at home and setting out for a day in the country. It was all wrong. The sun was shining but the air was cold. It was the middle of January, after all. But I did not know that the sun could shine and the air remain cold; no one had ever told me. What a feeling that was! How can I explain? Something I had always known—the way I knew my skin was the color brown of a nut rubbed repeatedly with a soft cloth, or the way I knew my own name—something I **took** completely **for granted**, "the sun is shining, the air is warm," was not so. I was no longer in a tropical zone, and this **realization** now entered my life like a flow of water dividing **formerly** dry and solid ground, creating two banks, one of which was my past—so familiar and **predictable** that even my unhappiness then made me happy now just to think of it—the other my future, a gray blank, an overcast seascape on which rain was falling and no boats were in sight. I was no longer in a tropical zone and I felt cold inside and out, the first time such a **sensation** had come over me.

4   In books I had read—from time to time, when the plot called for it—someone would suffer from homesickness. A person would leave a not so very nice situation and go somewhere else, somewhere a lot better, and then **long** to go back where it was not very nice. How **impatient** I would become with such a person, for I would feel that I was in a not so nice situation myself, and

---

[3] **gay:** happy; cheerful

(continued on next page)

The Grass Is Always Greener . . .   **205**

how I wanted to go somewhere else. But now I, too, felt that I wanted to be back where I came from. I understood it, I knew where I stood there. If I had had to draw a picture of my future then, it would have been a large gray patch surrounded by black, blacker, blackest.

5   What a surprise this was to me, that I longed to be back in the place that I came from, that I longed to sleep in a bed I had outgrown, that I longed to be with the people whose smallest, most natural **gesture** would call up in me such a rage that I longed to see them all dead at my feet. Oh, I had imagined that with my one swift act—leaving home and coming to this new place—I could leave behind me, as if it were an old garment[4] never to be worn again, my sad thoughts, my sad feelings, and my **discontent** with life in general as it presented itself to me. In the past, the thought of being in my present situation had been a comfort, but now I did not even have this to look forward to, and so I lay down on my bed and dreamt I was eating a bowl of pink mullet[5] and green figs cooked in coconut milk, and it had been cooked by my grandmother, which was why the taste of it pleased me so, for she was the person I liked best in the world and those were the things I liked best to eat also.

—————————————

[4] **garment:** a piece of clothing
[5] **pink mullet:** a type of fish

◖ READ FOR MAIN IDEAS

*Write **T** (true) or **F** (false) for each statement. Write the number of the paragraph that supports your answer. If the statement is false, change it to make it true.*

Paragraph

_____ **1.** Lucy feels very comfortable in her new country.   _____

_____ **2.** Lucy finds everything very much the same as she expected
          and very similar to her own country.   _____

_____ **3.** Lucy is unsure of her future.   _____

_____ **4.** Lucy was a happy young girl in her home country.   _____

_____ **5.** Lucy is surprised that she is homesick.   _____

_____ **6.** Lucy's dreams became reality in the new country.   _____

Imagine that Lucy wrote a letter to her grandmother describing her new life in the United States. The letter has eight factual errors. Read it and underline the errors. Write the corrections above the errors. Discuss the letter with a partner. Explain the incorrect information by referring to the story.

Dear Grandmother,

I just wanted to tell you about my trip. The weather was warm and sunny, and I loved traveling by boat. Driving through the city, I saw many of the famous sights that I had dreamt about before my trip. They were beautiful.

The apartment building where I am staying has an elevator. As you know, I had never seen one before, much less been in one! It's great not to have to walk up the stairs. The apartment is furnished and it has a brand new refrigerator, just like the one we have at home.

After a good night's sleep, I awoke to another bright, sunny day. I put on a pretty summer dress. It was just the right thing. Despite the warm weather, I felt a feeling of homesickness coming over me. It's hard to explain why this would happen, but it did. Perhaps it has to do with the insecurity I feel about my future.

If you had told me before I left that I would miss my life back home, I wouldn't have believed you. Nevertheless, that is what has happened. Don't worry about me; I'll be fine. I'll write again as soon as I have more to tell you.

Love,

Lucy

P.S. I enjoyed eating the pink mullet and green figs that you cooked for me to eat on my trip. It made me feel less homesick.

◖ MAKE INFERENCES

Read the excerpts from Reading One. Then answer the questions.

1. "In a daydream I used to have, all these places were points of happiness to me; all these places were lifeboats to my small drowning soul." (paragraph 1)

   Why were the places "points of happiness" even though Lucy had never been to them?
   a. Because Lucy always thought about happy things.
   b. Because her life in her country was very difficult and she needed something to look forward to.
   c. Because although her life was good, she still liked to think bout the future.

2. "I was reminded of how uncomfortable the new can make you feel." (paragraph 1)

   What does Lucy mean by this?
   a. New things, even if they are good, can be difficult to get used to.
   b. New underwear is often scratchy and uncomfortable.
   c. Moving to a new country can be scary.

3. "But at first it was all so new that I had to smile with my mouth turned down at the corners." (paragraph 2)

   What do you think "smile with my mouth turned down" means and why does Lucy smile that way?
   a. Because she didn't like to eat food that had been stored in a refrigerator.
   b. Because she is not really sure if new is always good.
   c. Because she didn't want to appear to others to be too happy.

4. "If I had had to draw a picture of my future then, it would have been a large gray patch surrounded by black, blacker, blackest." (paragraph 4)

   How does Lucy feel about her future?
   a. She is unsure, but thinks her future will be good.
   b. She thinks her future is going to be better than if she had stayed in her old country.
   c. She is unsure about her future, and also very worried.

5. "What a surprise this was to me, that I longed to be back in the place that I came from, that I longed to sleep in a bed I had outgrown, that I longed to be with the people whose smallest, most natural gesture would call up in me such a rage that I longed to see them all dead at my feet." (paragraph 5)

   Why do you think Lucy longed for these things?
   a. Because her new bed is even worse than her old one.
   b. Because although she didn't like them at the time, she at least knew what to expect.
   c. Because she felt bad for wanting to see those people dead and wanted to apologize to them.

6. "Oh, I had imagined that with my one swift act—leaving home and coming to this new place—I could leave behind me, as if it were an old garment never to be worn again, my sad thoughts, my sad feelings, and my discontent with life in general as it presented itself to me." (paragraph 5)

What does Lucy realize about herself and her feelings?

   a. She realizes that you can't leave your problems behind just by moving.
   b. She realizes that sometimes moving can help you overcome your problems.
   c. She realizes that her life in her country wasn't so bad after all.

◖ EXPRESS OPINIONS

Discuss the sentences from Poor Visitor *with a partner. Have you experienced these feelings? When? What happened? Share your answers with the class.*

1. "Now that I saw these places, they looked dirty, worn down. . . . It was not my first bout with the disappointment of reality."

2. "I was reminded of how uncomfortable the new can make you feel."

3. "I slept soundly that night, but it wasn't because I was happy and comfortable—quite the opposite; it was because I didn't want to take in anything else."

4. "Something I had always known . . . something I took completely for granted . . . was not so."

5. "But now I, too, felt that I wanted to be back where I came from. I understood it, I knew where I stood there."

B READING TWO: Nostalgia

This poem was written by Puerto Rican poet Virgilio Dávila, who describes his nostalgia for his homeland. Nostalgia is the sometimes slightly sad feeling you get when you long for something good from your past.

1 *Read the first stanza (group of lines) of the poem and answer the questions. Then read the rest of the poem.*

1. What do you think "this country" is?

2. How does the author compare this country and his homeland?

Nostalgia

By Virgilio Dávila (1869–1943)

1 "Mama, Borinquen[1] calls me,
this country is not mine,
Borinquen is pure flame
and here I am dying of the cold."

2 In search of a better future
I left the native home,
and established my store
in the middle of New York.
What I see around me
is a sad panorama,[2]
and my spirit calls out,
wounded by much nostalgia,
for the return to the home nest,
Mama, Borinquen calls me!

3 Where will I find here
like in my criollo[3] land
a dish of chicken and rice,
a cup of good coffee?
Where, oh where will I see
radiant in their attire
the girls, rich in vigor,
whose glances bedazzle?[4]
Here eyes do not bedazzle,
this country is not mine!

4 If I listen to a song here
of those I learned at home,
or a danza[5] by Tavarez,
Campos, or Dueño Colon,
my sensitive heart
is more enflamed with patriotic love,
and a herald[6] that faithful proclaims
this holy feeling
the wail "Borinquen is pure flame!"
comes to my ears.

5 In my land, what beauty!
In the hardest winter
not a tree is seen bare,
not a vale[7] without green.
The flower rules the garden,
the river meanders talkative,
the bird in the shadowy wood
sings his arbitrary[8] song,
and here . . . The snow is a shroud,[9]
here I am dying of the cold.

---

[1] **Borinquen:** the name the people of Puerto Rico use when referring to their homeland; the Borinquen Indians, or Boriqueños, were the original inhabitants of Puerto Rico
[2] **panorama:** a view over a wide area of land
[3] **criollo:** Spanish-American
[4] **bedazzle:** to impress, surprise
[5] **danza:** a type of dance music from the nineteenth century
[6] **herald:** messenger
[7] **vale:** a wide, low valley
[8] **arbitrary:** decided or arranged without a reason or plan; random
[9] **shroud:** a cloth that is wrapped around a dead person's body before it is buried

2 Write four things Virgilio Dávila misses about his homeland. Then share your answers with the class.

_____   _____

_____   _____

C INTEGRATE READINGS ONE AND TWO

STEP 1: Organize

1 There are several similar themes or topics described in both readings. Complete the chart with three more themes and an example of each from the readings. Discuss your answers with a partner.

THEME OR TOPIC	READING ONE Jamaica Kincaid	READING TWO Virgilio Dávila
1. weather		
2.		
3.		
4.		

STEP 2: Synthesize

On a separate piece of paper, use the information in Step 1 to write a paragraph explaining how Dávila and the character Lucy view these themes. In what ways are their views similar? In what ways are they different?

3 FOCUS ON WRITING

A VOCABULARY

REVIEW

1 *Complete the chart with the vocabulary words from the box. Decide if the word is associated with the authors' home country, new country, or both.*

bedazzle	formerly	predictable	soul
discontent	fright	radiant	to long
established	impatient	realization	took for granted
fantasy	nostalgia	sensation	vigor

HOME COUNTRY	NEW COUNTRY	BOTH COUNTRIES

2 *Work with a partner and compare your answers. Explain why you put the words where you did. Discuss what the words in each column have in common. Why did the authors choose these words to describe their feelings?*

EXPAND

An **analogy** is a comparison between two words that seem similar or are related in some way. Sometimes the words are related because they are synonyms or antonyms, and sometimes there is another relationship. For example, in item 1, *happiness* is a type of *emotion*; in the same way, *rain* is a type of *weather*.

Work with a partner. Discuss the relationship between the words. Circle the word that best completes each analogy.

1. emotion : happiness = weather : _____
   a. signal   b. rain   c. fantasy

2. fright : fear = movements : _____
   a. souls   b. fantasies   c. gestures

3. impatient : anxious = set : _____
   a. unhappiness   b. established   c. patient

4. overvalued : took for granted = realization : _____
   a. misunderstanding   b. vigor   c. feeling

5. beauty : bedazzles = nostalgia : _____
   a. rules   b. frightens   c. saddens

6. idea : concept = feeling : _____
   a. understanding   b. discomfort   c. sensation

7. fantasy : reality = unexpected : _____
   a. predictable   b. surprising   c. true

8. building : city = flower : _____
   a. garden   b. rose   c. radiant

9. radiant : shining = unhappiness : _____
   a. soul   b. discontent   c. nostalgia

10. long : desire = heart : _____
    a. soul   b. vigor   c. sensation

11. dress : garment = rice: _____
    a. white   b. eat   c. food

12. vigorous : energetic = arbitrary : _____
    a. homesick   b. random   c. predictable

◖ CREATE

Imagine you are either Lucy's grandmother in Antigua or a relative of Virgilio Dávila's in Puerto Rico. On a separate piece of paper, write a letter to respond to Lucy's or Virgilio's feelings. Use 10–12 words and phrases from the Review and Expand sections.

1 *Examine the sentences and answer the questions with a partner.*

a. By the time Lucy arrived in New York, she **had** already **imagined** what New York would look like.

b. Lucy **had** just **put** on her summer dress when she realized it was cold outside.

c. Before Lucy moved to New York, she **had longed** to go there.

1. In sentence *a*, did Lucy arrive in New York first, or did she imagine what New York looked like first?

2. In sentence *b*, did Lucy realize it was cold outside before she put on her summer dress?

3. In sentence *c*, which happened first—Lucy's move to New York or her longing to go there?

4. What helped you decide the order of events in these sentences?

PAST PERFECT	
1. The **past perfect** form of a verb is used to show that an event happened (and concluded) before another event in the past, or before a specific time in the past.	
2. The **past perfect** is formed with *had* + **past participle**.	Lucy **had** never **been** in an elevator before.
3. The past perfect with *by* + **a certain time in the past** is used to show that something happened before a specific time in the past.	**By the next morning**, Lucy **had become** very homesick.
4. When talking about two events that happened in the past, use the past perfect for the event that happened first. The simple past is often used for the second event.	After Lucy **had eaten** the figs, she **thought** about her grandmother.
5. Time words such as *after* and *as soon as* are used to introduce the first event (past perfect).	**As soon as** she **had put on** her summer dress, she felt a strange sensation. *(First she put on her dress. Then she had a strange sensation.)*
6. *Before* and *by the time* are used to introduce the second event (simple past).	Lucy **had lived** with her grandmother **before** she moved to New York. *(First she lived with her grandmother. Then she moved to New York.)*

7. **When** can be used to introduce either the first or the second event. Notice the difference.	Lucy **had put on** her dress **when** she realized the weather was cold. *(First she put on her dress. Then she realized the weather was cold.)* Lucy **put on** her coat **when** she realized the weather was cold. *(First she realized the weather was cold. Then she put on her coat.)*
8. *Already, never,* and *ever* are often used with the past perfect to emphasize the event that happened first.	Lucy **had never eaten** food from a refrigerator before then. No one **had ever told** Lucy that the sun could shine and the air remain cold.
GRAMMAR TIP: When a sentence begins with a dependent clause (the clause beginning with a time word), use a comma to separate it from the main clause. When a sentence begins with the main clause, do not use a comma.	

2 *Each of the sentences talks about two events which happened in the past. The individual events are below each sentence. In what order did the events happen? Write **1** for the first (earlier) event and **2** for the second (later) event.*

1. By the time Lucy arrived in New York, she had already imagined what New York would look like.

   __2__ Lucy arrived in New York.

   __1__ Lucy imagined what New York looked like.

2. Before Dávila established his store in New York, he had lived in Puerto Rico.

   _____ Dávila established his store in New York.

   _____ Dávila lived in Puerto Rico.

3. The immigrants had already seen the Statue of Liberty when Ellis Island came into view.

   _____ The immigrants saw the Statue of Liberty.

   _____ Ellis Island came into view.

4. Dávila had never felt so alone before he moved to New York.

   _____ Dávila moved to New York.

   _____ Dávila never felt so alone.

5. After Lucy had eaten pink mullet and green figs, she put on a gay summer dress.

   _____ Lucy ate pink mullet and green figs.

   _____ Lucy put on a gay summer dress.

6. The immigrants had never felt such homesickness before they moved to the new country.

_____ The immigrants never felt such homesickness.

_____ The immigrants moved to a new country.

7. By the time Dávila established his store in New York, he had grown very nostalgic for his homeland.

_____ Dávila was nostalgic for his homeland.

_____ Dávila established his store in New York.

3 *Complete the sentences about Jamaica Kincaid's life. Use the past perfect or the simple past. Use the event in the time line that is closest to the event in the sentence.*

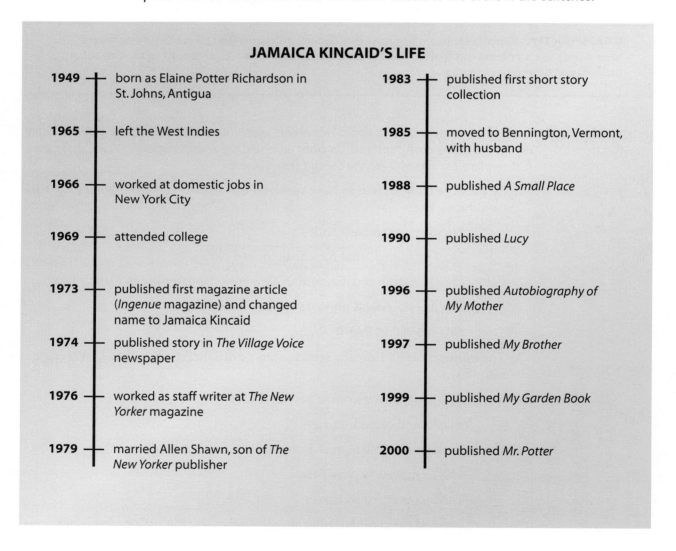

JAMAICA KINCAID'S LIFE

1949 — born as Elaine Potter Richardson in St. Johns, Antigua	**1983** — published first short story collection
1965 — left the West Indies	**1985** — moved to Bennington, Vermont, with husband
1966 — worked at domestic jobs in New York City	**1988** — published *A Small Place*
1969 — attended college	**1990** — published *Lucy*
1973 — published first magazine article (*Ingenue* magazine) and changed name to Jamaica Kincaid	**1996** — published *Autobiography of My Mother*
1974 — published story in *The Village Voice* newspaper	**1997** — published *My Brother*
1976 — worked as staff writer at *The New Yorker* magazine	**1999** — published *My Garden Book*
1979 — married Allen Shawn, son of *The New Yorker* publisher	**2000** — published *Mr. Potter*

1. After Elaine Potter Richardson had changed her name to Jamaica Kincaid, <u>she</u> <u>published a story in the Village Voice.</u>

2. By the time she published *Autobiography of My Mother*, _____

   _____

3. Jamaica Kincaid had moved to Bennington, Vermont, before _____

   _____

4. As soon as _____

   she found a domestic job in New York.

5. By 1977, _____

   _____

6. She had already worked as a staff writer at *The New Yorker* magazine when

   _____

7. After _____ ,

   she worked as a staff writer at *The New Yorker* magazine.

C WRITING

In this unit, you read about how two people feel about their immigration experience, including their feelings of excitement about new possibilities and of nostalgia for the things they left behind. Have you had similar feelings after making a change?

You are going to **write a comparison and contrast essay describing your experiences before and after an important change in your life.***

---

*For Alternative Writing Topics, see page 226. These topics can be used in place of the writing topic for this unit or as homework. The alternative topics relate to the theme of the unit, but may not target the same grammar or rhetorical structures taught in the unit.

PREPARE TO WRITE: Charting

Charting is another prewriting activity that helps you organize information before you write. It is especially useful when you are comparing and contrasting, because you can easily make sure that you included similar information for both things that you are going to write about.

1 *Think of an event that changed your life significantly (for example, starting a new school, moving to a new country, getting married, having a child, getting a new pet, a new job). Discuss it with a partner.*

2 *Look at the chart. The writer has described her life before and after she moved from Peru to the United States.*

POINTS TO COMPARE/CONTRAST	LIVING IN PERU	LIVING IN THE UNITED STATES
Housing	Lived in a house	Live in an apartment
Family	Lived with parents and brother	Same
Food	Ate Peruvian food Ate more home-cooked food	Same Eat more take-out food
Weather	No extreme cold	Cold and snow
Transportation	Drove to school	Take subway to school
Friends	Peruvian Big group of friends	All nationalities Small group of friends
Hobbies	Listened to music Went to the movies	Same
Language	Spoke only Spanish	Speak Spanish and English
School	Religious Spoke only Spanish	Nonreligious Speak only English

3 *Brainstorm a list of things that were affected by the event that changed your life. Make a chart like the one above. Complete it with details about how your life was before and after the change.*

WRITE: A Comparison and Contrast Essay

A **comparison and contrast essay** explains the similarities and differences between two topics (ideas, people, or things).

Here are some important points:

1. **Have an introduction.** Include relevant background information about the two topics being compared and contrasted.

2. **Include a thesis statement.** Make sure it indicates the purpose for comparing and contrasting.

3. **Support your thesis throughout the essay.** Make sure your examples and details relate directly to the thesis.

4. **Include all points of comparison and contrast.** All points need to be discussed for each topic.

5. **Add specific details and examples.** Make sure they illustrate the similarities and differences.

6. **Have a conclusion.** Summarize the main ideas of the essay and include any final thoughts.

There are two common ways to organize a comparison and contrast essay. With **point-by-point organization**, you write about the similarities and differences of different aspects of each of the two topics you are comparing. With **block organization**, you first write a paragraph only about all aspects of the first topic and then another paragraph only about all aspects of the second topic. Note that in the block method, you usually compare the same aspects of each topic, but in separate paragraphs. It is also possible to put all similarities in one paragraph and all differences in another. This is another type of block organization.

1 *Look at the outlines showing point-by-point organization and block organization. Are the differences between them clear? Discuss with a partner.*

POINT-BY-POINT ORGANIZATION

I. Weather
- **A.** Similar temperature all year long vs. extreme heat and cold
- **B.** No extreme cold vs. cold and snow

II. Friends
- **A.** Large group of friends vs. small group
- **B.** All Peruvian vs. different nationalities

III. School
- **A.** Religious vs. nonreligious school
- **B.** Spanish vs. English

BLOCK ORGANIZATION

I. Peru
- **A.** Family—Live with parents and brother in a house
- **B.** Food—Eat Peruvian food, usually eat at home
- **C.** School—Religious, speak only Spanish
- **D.** Friends—All Peruvian, many friends
- **E.** Weather—Similar temperature all year around

II. United States
- **A.** Family—Live with parents and brother in an apartment
- **B.** Food—Eat Peruvian food, but also eat take-out American food
- **C.** School—Nonreligious, speak English and Spanish
- **D.** Friends—Friends of different nationalities, small group of friends
- **E.** Weather—Extreme temperature changes

2 *Look at the essay excerpts. How are they organized? How do you know? Circle point-by-point or block. Discuss your answers with a partner.*

a. In Lima, my school was very small. There were only about 75 students and we all knew each other well. The teachers knew every student by name. In New York, my school is gigantic. There are over 400 students. The immense halls are filled with unfamiliar faces. In Lima, we only spoke Spanish at school. Here we mostly speak English, but sometimes Spanish. At my old school, the students had to wear uniforms. Uniforms are not required in New York and students wear all different kinds of clothes. I like school in New York, but sometimes I miss the intimacy of my old school.

At home in Lima the weather is the same all year around. It is always about 70° Fahrenheit (21° Celsius). The temperature only fluctuates if you go up in the mountains where it is cooler. We really only have two seasons and the temperature in both is the same. The only difference is that in the winter months it rains a lot. In New York, there are four seasons and the weather changes from season to season. It is very hot in the summer; often the temperature reaches 90° F (32° C). In the spring and fall, there is lots of rain and it is cooler. The winter has a lot of snow and ice with freezing temperatures. It has been very hard for me to adapt to the changes in climate. **(Point-by-Point / Block)**

b. In Lima, my house was filled with comforting smells of home. Every day when I returned from school, the house was filled with the aromas of my favorite dishes flavored with onion, garlic, cumin, and chili peppers. My house always held the sweet scent of my grandmother's perfume, which she left behind when she walked through a room. Ever since I was a small child, smelling her fragrance has made me feel safe and loved.

Our life is different in New York. In New York, our apartment is on the second floor and the only smells in it are those of the Italian restaurant on the ground floor. You can still smell garlic and onions, but instead of cumin and chili peppers, you smell tomato sauce and cooking pasta. Grandma is not with us in London. I miss her sweet smell.
(Point-by-Point / Block)

c. The winter weather in Lima is mild. It is usually cloudy and the air is humid, but the temperature doesn't go below 0° Fahrenheit (−18 Celsius). In New York, the winters are very cold. It snows several times each year, and the temperature is often near zero. Even on sunny days, the air can be freezing cold.

There are basically three languages that you hear in Lima- Spanish, Quechua, and Aymara. Spanish is predominant, but immigrants from the Andean mountain regions often speak Quechua or Aymara. In New York, English is the language that you hear most often, but Spanish is very common especially in certain parts of the city. Because New York has a large immigrant population, languages from all over the world can also be heard. **(Point-by-Point / Block)**

3 *Look at your chart from Prepare to Write. Make outlines using both types of organization. Then share your outlines with a partner. In what ways are the two types of organization different? Which outline was easier to read and which was easier to write? Discuss which of your outlines you think works best and why.*

4 *Now write the first draft of your comparison and contrast essay. Use the outline you have chosen and the information from Prepare to Write to plan your essay. Include relevant background about yourself and the change that took place in your life. Include a thesis statement that indicates how much your life has changed. Be sure to add specific details and examples to illustrate the similarities and differences in your life. In your conclusion, summarize the main ideas in the essay and include any final thoughts about your experience. Be sure to use vocabulary and grammar from the unit.*

◀ **REVISE: Using Subordinators and Transitions**

Certain words act as signals to introduce points of comparison or contrast.

1 *Examine the paragraph and answer the questions with a partner.*

> Lucy faces many changes upon her arrival in New York City. First she is struck with the change in climate. Antigua is warm and the sun is brilliant **while** New York in January is very cold and the sun is lifeless. Her living conditions are different, too. In New York she lives in an apartment building. **In contrast**, she lived in a house in her native country. In addition, she now eats food that has just been taken from the refrigerator **whereas** she always ate her grandmother's freshly cooked meals in her homeland. Other aspects of her life remain the same. Lucy faces many different problems and issues in New York **in the same way** she did in Antigua. She has learned that she cannot leave her troubles behind like clothes she has outgrown.

1. Look at the boldfaced words. Which words introduce ideas that are similar? Which words introduce ideas that are different?

2. Four topics are compared and contrasted in this paragraph. What are they?

COMPARISONS AND CONTRASTS

Comparisons point out ideas that are similar. **Contrasts** point out ideas that are different.

Subordinators

Subordinators are used to compare or contrast the ideas in two clauses. They join the independent clause to the dependent clause being compared or contrasted. Examples of subordinators include *while, whereas, just as, as.* These words introduce dependent clauses, not complete thoughts. The independent clause usually describes the point that is being emphasized or is more important.

Her native climate is warm and the sun is brilliant **while** New York in January is very cold and the sun is lifeless.

More emphasis: The weather in her native country is warm.
Less emphasis: The weather in New York is cold.

Whereas the sun in New York is lifeless, the sun in her native country is brilliant.

Less emphasis: The sun in New York is lifeless.
More emphasis: The sun in her native country is brilliant.

Comparison subordinators include:	Contrast subordinators include:
just as	whereas
as	while

Transitions

Transitions show the connection between two independent clauses (two sentences).

Comparison transitions include:	Contrast transitions include:
similarly	in contrast
in the same way	on the other hand
likewise	however

- Two independent clauses can be combined in one sentence by using a semicolon (;) and a comma (,):

  In New York she lives in an apartment building; **however**, she lived in a house in her native country.

- The two independent clauses can also be written as separate sentences:

  In New York she lives in an apartment building. **However**, she lived in a house in her native country.

- Two independent clauses can also be combined as a simple sentence using the phrase *in the same way*.

  Lucy came to New York in search of a better future *in the same way* Dávila did.

2 *Combine the pairs of sentences to make comparisons and contrasts.*

1. likewise
- Lucy feels homesick.
- Dávila feels nostalgic.

  Lucy feels homesick; likewise, Dávila feels nostalgic.

2. in the same way
- Dávila dislikes harsh winter with its bare trees.
- Lucy dislikes the pale winter sun.

_____

3. similarly
- Lucy misses her grandmother's home cooking.
- Dávila misses his country's native food.

_____

4. on the other hand
- Dávila opened his own store in New York.
- Lucy worked for a family as a nanny.

_____

5. in contrast
- Lucy is a young woman.
- Dávila is an older man.

_____

6. while
- "Poor Visitor" was written in the last half of the twentieth century.
- "Nostalgia" was written in the first half of the twentieth century.

_____

3 _Read the paragraphs. Decide whether the writer is comparing or contrasting. Add transitions or subordinators of comparison or contrast to each paragraph to make the writer's meaning clear. Notice which type of organization requires more transitions and subordinators._

1.   In Lima, my school was very small. There were only about 75 students and we all knew each other well. The teachers knew every student by name. In New York, my school is gigantic. There are over 400 students. The immense halls are filled with unfamiliar faces. In Lima, we only spoke Spanish at school. Here we mostly speak English, but sometimes Spanish. At my old school, the students had to wear uniforms. Uniforms are not required in New York and students wear all different kinds of clothes. I like school in New York, but sometimes I miss the intimacy of my old school.

    At home in Lima the weather is the same all year around. It is always about 70° Fahrenheit (21° Celsius). The temperature only fluctuates if you go up in the mountains where it is cooler. We really only have two seasons and the temperature in both is the same. The only difference is that in the winter months it rains a lot. In New York, there are four seasons and the weather changes from season to season. It is very hot in the summer; often the temperature reaches 90° F (32° C). In the spring and fall, there is lots of rain and it is cooler. The winter has a lot of snow and ice with freezing temperatures. It has been very hard for me to adapt to the changes in climate.

2.   In Lima, my house was filled with comforting smells of home. Every day when I returned from school, the house was filled with the aromas of my favorite dishes flavored with onion, garlic, cumin, and chili peppers. My house always held the sweet scent of my grandmother's perfume, which she left behind when she walked through a room. Ever since I was a small child, smelling her fragrance has made me feel safe and loved.

Our life is different in London. In London, our apartment is on the second floor and the only smells in it are those of the Italian restaurant on the ground floor. You can still smell garlic and onions, but instead of cumin and chili peppers, you smell tomato sauce and cooking pasta. Grandma is not with us in London. I miss her sweet smell.

3.   The winter weather in Lima is mild. It is usually cloudy and the air is humid, but the temperature doesn't go below 0° Fahrenheit (−18 Celsius). In New York, the winters are extremely cold. It snows several times each year, and the temperature is often near zero. Even on the sunniest days, the air can be freezing cold.

There are basically three languages that you hear in Lima—Spanish, Quechua, and Aymara. Spanish is predominant, but immigrants from the Andean mountain regions often speak Quechua or Aymara. In New York, English is the language that you hear most often, but Spanish is very common especially in certain parts of the city. Because New York has a large immigrant population, languages from all over the world can also be heard.

4 *Look at your first draft. Add compare and contrast transitions and/or subordinators as needed.*

◖EDIT: Writing the Final Draft

Write your final draft. Carefully edit it for grammatical problems and mechanical errors, such as spelling, capitalization, and punctuation. Make sure you used some of the vocabulary and grammar and from the unit. Use the checklist to help you write your final draft. Then neatly write or type your essay.

○ Does the essay have an introduction which includes relevant background information about yourself and the change that took place in your life?

○ Does the essay have a thesis statement that indicates how much your life has changed?

○ Does your essay clearly follow a point-by-point or block organization?

○ Does the essay use effective subordinators and transitions to show comparison and contrast?

○ Does the essay include specific details and examples to illustrate the similarities and differences in your life?

○ Does the essay have a conclusion summarizing the main ideas of the essay?

○ Does the essay use the past perfect?

○ Has vocabulary from the unit been used?

ALTERNATIVE WRITING TOPICS

Choose one of the topics. Write an essay using the vocabulary and grammar from the unit.

1. Have you ever left your home country to live in another country? What were your feelings about your home country when you first arrived in the new country? What feelings did you have after being away for a while? Did you experience nostalgia? If so, what did you do to overcome it?

2. Read the quotation.

"Living in another language means growing another self, and it takes time for that other self to become familiar."

—Alistair Reed
translator and author

Discuss the meaning of this quotation and how it applies to you and your experiences. Has studying English changed your life? If so, how? What is different about you now, since studying English? Are the changes positive or negative?

RESEARCH TOPICS, see page 264.

UNIT 10 Take It or Leave It

1 FOCUS ON THE TOPIC

A PREDICT

Look at the cartoon and the unit title. Then discuss the questions with a partner.

1. How do you think the character in the cartoon feels about technology?

2. Are these feelings similar to or different from your own feelings? Explain your answer.

3. What do you think the unit title means? What would be the consequences of your taking—or leaving—technology?

Think about how easy it would be for you to live without the technology listed below. Check (✓) four items in each column. Add anything you feel is missing from the list. Compare your opinions in a small group.

TECHNOLOGY	FOUR THINGS I COULDN'T LIVE WITHOUT FOR ONE WEEK	FOUR THINGS I MIGHT BE ABLE TO LIVE WITHOUT FOR ONE WEEK	FOUR THINGS I COULD LIVE WITHOUT FOR ONE WEEK
electricity			
washing machine/ dryer			
cell phone			
automatic dishwasher			
microwave oven			
CD player			
air conditioning			
television			
desktop computer			
DVD player			
laptop computer			
car			

Bill Gates is the co-founder and chairman of Microsoft© Corporation and one of the wealthiest people in the world. In 2006, he began to move away from some of his responsibilities at Microsoft to focus on global health and education work at his multi-billion dollar charity, the Bill and Melinda Gates Foundation.

Gates has built a state-of-the-art home near Seattle, Washington. His home incorporates a variety of "smart home" technologies. A smart home is a home that has mechanical or electronic conveniences, many controlled by computers, that help make life easier and often save energy.

Reading One is an excerpt from a book by Bill Gates about the house he was planning at the time he wrote the book. Imagine that a reporter from the magazine Architectural Gazette interviewed Bill Gates before the house was completed. Read the interview. Try to understand the boldfaced words from the context.

ARCHITECTURAL GAZETTE: First of all, let me thank you for granting us this interview. I realize you are a very busy man and appreciate your taking the time to talk to me. I'm here because I understand you are planning to build your dream house.

BILL GATES: Yes, I've been thinking about it for quite a while. I've done a lot of research about houses in general and thought a lot about what I need to **accommodate** my lifestyle.

AG: So, what have you decided?

BG: First of all, I'm interested in **craftsmanship**. The house has to be beautifully constructed by skilled workers and artisans using the finest materials.

AG: How big is it going to be?

BG: Most people might assume that I would build a big **ostentatious** house, but for me what's more important is how the house functions, not the size. It won't be a small house, but it will be low and **unobtrusive**; you might not even realize it's there. My goal is not to impress people with its size, but rather to provide my family with a comfortable home enhanced by technology.

AG: Can you be more specific?

BG: The living area for my family will not actually be so big, and there will be **cozy** little spaces for reading, listening to music, or watching TV. Of course, the latest technology will also play a big role in the house.

AG: So, are you talking about a "smart home"?

BG: Yes, that's exactly what I am talking about.

AG: So, I guess many parts of the house will be run by computers, but what else will the house have that makes it a smart home?

BG: Well, guests will have **access** to many different types of technology, but I don't want to tell you too much now. I'd rather you wait until I can give you a tour of the house. However, I will say that there will be technology in many of the rooms, but, again, you won't feel like you are **confronted** by it. You won't even notice it.

AG: How are you going to do that?

BG: There are many **options** for how to do it. One that I currently favor is to **conceal** much of the technology behind artwork or in specially constructed areas in the rooms. That way, you won't see it.

AG: I know you are concerned about the environment. Can't you tell our readers a little about exactly what kind of eco-friendly smart home technology your house will have?

BG: Sure, there are many environmentally friendly aspects to the house. For example, when a room is **unoccupied**, the house will be able to sense it and turn off any unnecessary electrical devices that are on such as a television, lights, or a stereo.

AG: That's great! What else can you tell us about your house?

BG: Well, I **anticipate** this home will be a model for how homes in the future can become better . . . and smarter.

Find the boldfaced words in the reading passage. Circle the best synonym or definition for the word.

1. **accommodate**	assist	make comfortable	feed
2. **craftsmanship**	skill and artistry	boat	technology
3. **ostentatious**	smart	quiet	showy
4. **unobtrusive**	loud	modest	modern
5. **cozy**	quiet	comfortable and intimate	crowded
6. **access**	interest	success	admittance
7. **confronted**	upset	confused	faced with
8. **options**	parts	decisions	choices
9. **conceal**	reveal	hide	use
10. **unoccupied**	warm	lighted	empty
11. **anticipate**	expect	ignore	agree with

②FOCUS ON READING

A READING ONE: Inside the House

Reading One describes Bill Gates's dream house. What kind of a dream house would you want? Where would it be located? What five types of technology would you want in it? Do you think Bill Gates has them in his house? Answer the questions. Share your answer with a partner.

_____

_____

_____

_____

_____

_____

_____

_____

INSIDE THE HOUSE

By Bill Gates
(from *The Road Ahead*)

Bill Gates's home

1   I began thinking about building a new house in the late 1980s. I wanted **craftsmanship** but nothing **ostentatious**. I wanted a house that would **accommodate** sophisticated, changing technology, but in an **unobtrusive** way that made it clear that technology was the servant, not the master.

(continued on next page)

Take It or Leave It   **231**

2   I found some property on the shore of Lake Washington within an easy commuting distance of Microsoft. Living space will be about average for a large house. The family living room will be about fourteen by twenty-eight feet, including an area for watching television or listening to music. And there will be **cozy** spaces for one or two people, although there will also be a reception hall to entertain one hundred comfortably for dinner.

3   First thing, as you come in, you'll be presented with an electronic pin to clip on your clothes. This pin will tell the home who and where you are, and the house will use this information to try to meet and even **anticipate** your needs—all as unobtrusively as possible. Someday, instead of needing the pin, it might be possible to have a camera system with visual-recognition capabilities,[1] but that's beyond current technology. When it's dark outside, the pin will cause a moving zone of light to accompany you through the house. **Unoccupied** rooms will be unlit. As you walk down a hallway, you might not notice the lights ahead of you gradually coming up to full brightness and the lights behind you fading. Music will move with you, too. It will seem to be everywhere, although, in fact, other people in the house will be hearing entirely different music or nothing at all. A movie or the news or a phone call will be able to follow you around the house, too. If you get a phone call, only the handset nearest you will ring.

4   You won't be **confronted** by the technology, but it will be readily and easily available. Hand-held remote controls and discreetly visible consoles[2] in each room will put you in charge of your immediate environment and of the house's entertainment system. You'll use the controls to tell the monitors[3] in a room to become visible and what to display. You'll be able to choose from among thousands of pictures, recordings, movies, and television programs, and you'll have all sorts of **options** available for selecting information.

5   If you're planning to visit Hong Kong soon, you might ask the screen in your room to show you pictures of the city. It will seem to you as if the photographs are displayed everywhere, although actually the images will materialize on the walls of rooms just before you walk in and vanish after you leave. If you and I are enjoying different things and one of us walks into a room where the other is sitting, the house might continue the audio and visual imagery for the person who was in the room first, or it might change to programming both of us like.

6   I will be the first home user for one of the most unusual electronic features in my house. The product is a database[4] of more than a million still images, including photographs and reproductions of paintings. If you are a guest, you'll be able to call up portraits of presidents, pictures of sunsets, airplanes, skiing in the Andes, a rare French stamp, the Beatles in 1965, or reproductions of High Renaissance paintings, on screens throughout the house.

---

[1] **camera with visual-recognition capabilities:** a camera connected to a computer that can identify individual faces
[2] **console:** a cabinet or a case that holds a computer or television
[3] **monitor:** a computer or television screen
[4] **database:** a large collection of information stored in a computer

7   I believe quality images will be in great demand on the information highway.[5] This vision that the public will find image-browsing worthwhile is obviously unproven. I think the right interface will make it appealing to a lot of people.

8   A decade from now, **access** to the millions of images and all the other entertainment opportunities I've described will be available in many homes and will certainly be more impressive than those I'll have when I move into my house. My house will just be getting some of the services a little sooner.

9   One of the many fears expressed about the information highway is that it will reduce the time people spend socializing. Some worry that homes will become such cozy entertainment providers that we'll never leave them, and that, safe in our private sanctuaries,[6] we'll become isolated. I don't think that's going to happen. As behaviorists[7] keep reminding us, we're social animals. We will have the option of staying home more because the highway will create so many new options for home-based entertainment, for communication—both personal and professional—and for employment. Although the mix of activities will change, I think people will decide to spend almost as much time out of their homes.

10   The highway will not only make it easier to keep up with distant friends, it will also enable us to find new companions. Friendships formed across the network will lead naturally to getting together in person. This alone will make life more interesting. Suppose you want to reach someone to play bridge with. The information highway will let you find card players with the right skill level and availability in your neighborhood, or in other cities or nations.

11   I enjoy experimenting, and I know some of my concepts for the house will work out better than others. Maybe I'll decide to **conceal** the monitors behind conventional wall art or throw the electronic pins into the trash. Or maybe I'll grow accustomed to the systems in the house, or even fond of them, and wonder how I got along without them. That's my hope.

---

[5] **information highway:** a term used from the mid-1980s through the mid-1990s to describe the Internet
[6] **sanctuary:** a safe and peaceful place
[7] **behaviorist:** a scientist who studies the way people act

◖ READ FOR MAIN IDEAS

Reading One has three main ideas. What does the reading say about each idea? Circle the sentence that best summarizes the idea.

1. Description of the house
    a. Even though the house is larger than an average house, Bill Gates does not want it to feel cold or unfriendly.
    b. Bill Gates's main concern is that the house is big enough to accommodate a large group of people.

2. Description of the technology in the house
    a. The technology is designed to be impressive and complex.
    b. The technology is designed to be easy to use and energy-efficient.

3. Analysis of the technology
    a. Technology is a necessary part of everyone's life.
    b. Technology has both positive and negative aspects, but basically has a positive impact on most people.

◖ READ FOR DETAILS

An **outline** is a visual guide that shows the main ideas, supporting ideas, examples, and further explanations in a text. Outlines are useful when taking notes from a text or when organizing information to write an essay. Some outlines are specific and show all the details; others are general.

Complete the detailed outline with information from Reading One, including main ideas, supporting ideas, examples, and further explanations. Look at Reading One if you need help. Compare completed outlines with a partner.

(main idea) **I. Introduction: Thinking about home in the late 1980s**

(supporting idea)   **A.** Style preferences

    (example)   **1.** _____

        2. not ostentatious

  B. Must accommodate sophisticated and changing technology

    1. not obtrusive

    2. functions as servant, not master

II. Selecting the perfect property

  A. Location

    1. _____

    2. easy commuting distance

  B. Living space—average size

    1. living room

(further explanation)   **a.** size = _____

      b. area for _____ or _____

    2. other cozy spaces for one or two people

    3. _____

      a. accommodates 100

III. **Controlling the home environment with** _____

    A. Tells the home _____ and _____

    B. House uses pin information to meet your needs

        1. _____ follows you

        2. _____ follows you

        3. _____ follows you

        4. _____ follows you

IV. **Other readily and easily available technology**

    A. Hand-held remotes and consoles in each room

        1. controls tell monitors

            a. _____

            b. _____

    B. Visual displays

        1. large choice

            a. thousands of pictures

            b. _____

            c. _____

            d. television programs

            e. many options for selecting information

        2. house can control visual displays

            a. materialize when you _____ and vanish when you _____

            b. house can change programming depending on _____

V. **State-of-the-art database**

    A. First homeowner to have it

    B. Database has more than _____

        1. includes photographs

        2. includes _____

    C. Guests can call up anything they like

        1. _____

        2. pictures of sunsets

        3. skiing in the Andes, etc

VI. Future availability of quality images

    A. On the information highway

    B. In homes

VII. Fears about _____

    A. Reduces the time people spend socializing

        1. homes will become too cozy and self-contained

        2. people will become _____

    B. Not in agreement

        1. people are social animals

        2. highway only provides more entertainment and _____ options

            a. _____

            b. _____

            c. _____

        3. people will decide to spend as much time out of their homes

VIII. Benefits of the information highway

    A. Makes it easier to

        1. maintain _____

        2. find _____

    B. Makes life more interesting

        1. people will meet in person

        2. meet people with common interests

IX. Conclusion: Experimenting and the future

    A. Bill Gates enjoys experimenting and may decide to

        1. _____

        2. _____

    B. Hopes

        1. may like everything

        2. wonders how _____

These statements about *Bill Gates* can be inferred from the reading. After each statement, note the sentence(s) and the paragraph number(s) that support the inferences. Some statements are supported by more than one sentence or more than one paragraph.

Paragraph

1. Bill Gates wants to be a good host. _____

   Supporting sentence(s) _____

   _____

2. Bill Gates is concerned about the environment and saving energy. _____

   Supporting sentence(s) _____

   _____

3. Bill Gates is an art lover. _____

   Supporting sentence(s) _____

   _____

4. Bill Gates probably has children. _____

   Supporting sentence(s) _____

   _____

5. Bill Gates is a person who is willing to change his mind. _____

   Supporting sentence(s) _____

   _____

6. Bill Gates probably enjoys boating. _____

   Supporting sentence(s) _____

   _____

7. Bill Gates doesn't want technology to overwhelm the décor of his house. _____

   Supporting sentence(s) _____

   _____

8. Bill Gates agrees with behaviorists who say that man is a social animal. _____

   Supporting sentence(s) _____

   _____

Discuss the questions in a small group. Share your ideas with the class.

1. According to Reading One, "one of the many fears (critics have) expressed about the information highway is that it will reduce the time people spend socializing." What do you think? Has the Internet affected the time you spend socializing? Do you believe it is isolating or has it created " . . . many new options for home-based entertainment, for communication—both personal and professional—and for employment"?

2. What is your reaction to Bill Gates's home? Do you find it appealing? Why or why not? Would you incorporate any of his ideas into your "dream house"? If so, which ones?

B ▸ READING TWO: Thoreau's Home

Henry David Thoreau was an American author, philosopher, and naturalist whose ideas inspired generations of readers to think for themselves and appreciate the ways of nature and humankind. In 1845, he moved to the woods outside of Concord, Massachusetts. He chose to live a life that reflected his philosophy: Live life in the simplest of ways. He did not believe luxuries or comforts were necessary; in fact, he felt they actually stopped human progress.

1 *Discuss the question with a partner.*

In what ways might technology stop or interfere with human progress?

THOREAU'S HOME

by Henry David Thoreau (edited, from *Walden*)

1   Near the end of March 1845, I borrowed an axe and went down to the woods by Walden Pond[1] nearest to where I intended to build my house, and began to cut down some tall arrowy white pines, still in their youth, for timber.[2] . . . It was a pleasant hillside where I worked, covered with pine woods, through which I looked out on the pond, and a small open field in the woods where pines and

Replica of Thoreau's cabin

[1] **Walden Pond:** a pond (small area of fresh water) in Concord, Massachusetts
[2] **timber:** trees that are cut down and used for building or making things

hickories were springing up.[3] The ice on the pond was not yet dissolved, though there were some open spaces, and it was all dark colored and saturated with water. . . .

2   So I went on for some days cutting and hewing timber, and also studs and rafters,[4] all with my narrow axe, not having many communicable or scholar-like thoughts, singing to myself,

> *Men say they know many things;*   *And a thousand appliances;*
> *But lo! they have taken wings—*   *The wind that blows*
> *The arts and sciences,*   *Is all anybody knows.*

3   My days in the woods were not very long ones; yet I usually carried my dinner of bread and butter, and read the newspaper in which it was wrapped, at noon, sitting amid the green pine boughs which I had cut off, and to my bread was imparted some of their fragrance, for my hands were covered with a thick coat of pitch[5] . . .

4   Before winter I built a chimney, and shingled the sides of my house, which were impervious to[6] rain. . . .

5   I have thus a tight shingled and plastered house, ten feet wide by fifteen feet long, and eight-feet posts, with a garret[7] and a closet, a large window on each side, two trap doors, one door at each end, and a brick fireplace opposite. The exact cost of my house, paying the usual price for such materials as I used, but not counting the work, all of which was done by myself, was as follows; and I give the details because very few are able to tell exactly what their houses cost, and fewer still, if any, the separate cost of the various materials which compose them:

Boards	$8.03½	Mostly shanty boards
Refuse shingles for roof and sides	4.00	
Laths	1.25	
Two second-hand windows with glass	2.43	
One thousand old bricks	4.00	
Two casks of lime	2.40	That was high.
Hair (to strengthen plaster)	0.31	More than I needed.
Mantle-tree iron	0.15	
Nails	3.90	
Hinges and screws	0.14	
Latch	0.10	
Chalk	0.01	
Transportation	1.40	I carried a good part on my back.
In all	$28.12½	

[3] **springing up:** suddenly start growing
[4] **studs and rafters:** beams and pieces of wood that form the structure of a building
[5] **pitch:** sap (watery liquid) from a pine tree
[6] **impervious to:** not allowing anything to pass through
[7] **garret:** a small room at the top of a house

2 *Discuss the questions in a small group.*

1. What does "The wind that blows / Is all anybody knows" mean? How does this relate to what you know about Thoreau?

2. What do you think appealed to Thoreau about the location that he chose for his house?

3. How did he keep the price of the house so low?

4. How did Thoreau feel about building his own home?

C INTEGRATE READINGS ONE AND TWO

◀ **STEP 1: Organize**

Both Readings One and Two discuss unique houses and the philosophies of their builders/owners. Complete the chart with information from the readings. Some additional information not found in the readings has been filled in.

	READING ONE	READING TWO
1. **Year built**		
2. **Size of house**		
3. **Cost of house**	Estimated as between $53 and $97 million	
4. **Location**		
5. **Accommodations for friends**		Thoreau noted that he had three chairs in his cabin: "One for solitude, two for friendship, three for society."
6. **Luxuries/technology in the house**		Books Hinges, screws, hoe, axe
7. **Philosophy of luxuries/technology**		

Work with a partner. Imagine that one of you is Bill Gates and the other is Henry David Thoreau. On a separate piece of paper, write five questions that you would like to ask each other. Use the information from Step 1. Exchange your questions with your partner, and write answers.

3 FOCUS ON WRITING

A VOCABULARY

REVIEW

*Look at the boldfaced words. Write **S** if they are synonyms and **A** if they are antonyms.*

_____ 1. Thoreau didn't want an **ostentatious** home. He was interested in a **modest,** yet functional, house.

_____ 2. There are many **options** to consider when heating a house. Some of the **choices** are oil, gas, solar, and passive solar.

_____ 3. Unfortunately, the carpenters who worked on my house lacked **skill**; its level of **craftsmanship** is very low.

_____ 4. Perhaps Thoreau lived such a simple life because he didn't want to **confront** the problems brought on by the technology of his time. By living in his simple house he could **avoid** them.

_____ 5. Bill Gates sees **various** ways that the Internet can actually help people to be more sociable. But some people have very **different** ideas about how the Internet will affect personal communication.

_____ 6. Bill Gates does not **intend** for technology to be the master in his house; he **plans** to be the master and for technology to be the servant.

_____ 7. Bill Gates's philosophy of technology is that it should be **unobtrusive**. His neighbor seems to have a different philosophy; he has a large **conspicuous** satellite dish in his front yard.

_____ 8. Thoreau's house **accommodated** his needs. It **provided** him with everything that he wanted.

_____ 9. Smart technology turns on the lights in the room if it is **not empty** and turns them off when it is **unoccupied**.

_____ 10. In his interview in *Architectural Gazette,* Bill Gates stated he planned to **conceal** the monitors behind artwork in his house, but he didn't **reveal** much more about the rest of the technology he planned to use.

1 Complete the chart with the forms of the words from the readings. Not all of the words have all four forms. If you need help, use a dictionary.

NOUN	VERB	ADJECTIVE	ADVERB
anticipation	anticipate	anticipated	X
	access		X
craftsmanship		X	X
		opposite opposing	X
	accommodate		
	X	ostentatious	
X	X	cozy	
option			X
X	X	unobtrusive	
	conceal		X
	confronted		
		(un)occupied	X
	intend		
		communicable	X
		various	variously

2 *Now complete the sentences with the correct forms of the words.*

intend	unobtrusive

1. The monitors in Bill Gates's home will be ___unobtrusive___ ; they will be concealed behind paintings

2. It is not Bill Gates' _____ to impress people with the size of his house.

3. Thoreau _____ chose to live far way from other people because he valued a life of solitude.

4. The pin will allow the house to anticipate and meet a guest's needs—all as _____ as possible.

5. I'm sure that if Thoreau offended any of his friends with his writings, it was not _____.

communicable	opposite	option

6. Thoreau and Bill Gates seem to have _____ ideas about the need for technology.

7. Personal computers, modems, e-mail, and fax machines have increased the speed of _____ dramatically.

8. Because of the large database in Bill Gates' house, guests will have many _____ regarding what type of art to view on the monitors.

9. One of the advantages of the Internet is that it allows people to _____ with co-workers without actually traveling to the office.

10. Bill Gates _____ the idea that the information highway (Internet) will reduce the amount of time people spend socializing.

11. Although Bill Gates will encourage guests to wear the pins, they won't have to; their use will be _____.

access	anticipate	various

12. A smart home will _____ which pictures to put on the walls of the rooms just before you walk in.

13. Some of Thoreau's friends felt that he was not _____ because he lived out in the woods and kept to himself.

14. Thoreau used a _____ of materials to build his home.

15. The _____ of more than a million still images is one of the most unusual electronic features of Bill Gates's home.

16. Bill Gates is excited that he will have the ability to _____ the artwork on the wall of his house with the push of a button.

◖ CREATE

Imagine you are a reporter interviewing the people below. How would they respond to the questions? Write answers using six to ten of the words from the Review and Expand sections.

1. REPORTER: How would you describe your house to someone who has never seen it?

   BILL GATES: _____

   _____

   _____

2. REPORTER: How would you describe your house to someone who has never seen it?

   HENRY DAVID THOREAU: _____

   _____

   _____

3. REPORTER: What is your philosophy about the role of technology in life?

   BILL GATES: _____

   _____

   _____

4. REPORTER: What is your philosophy about the role of technology in life?

   HENRY DAVID THOREAU: _____

   _____

   _____

GRAMMAR: Future Progressive

1 *Examine the paragraph and answer the questions with a partner.*

As technology advances, our lives **will be changing** day by day. In the future, more and more people **will be building** smart homes like Bill Gates's. People of all ages **are going to be using** technology more and more in their everyday lives. It is possible we **will be using** technology to enable us to have driverless cars, free and clean energy, and maybe even live forever. Our children certainly **won't be living** as we live; they will have many more electronic conveniences, but also some inconveniences. For example, today if we have a complaint or suggestion about a product or service, we are sometimes still able to speak to a "live" person. In the future, our children may not have this option. They probably **won't be complaining** to a person, but only to a machine. Although technological advances are designed to improve the quality of life, you **will be talking** about the "good old days" when life was simpler, just as your parents did before you. Technology may change our lifestyle but not our human nature.

1. Is the paragraph describing past, present, or future events?

2. Is the focus of the boldfaced words in the paragraph on the events themselves or the fact that the events are ongoing?

FUTURE PROGRESSIVE	
1. The **future progressive** is used to talk about actions that will be in progress at a specific time in the future. It is also used to emphasize the ongoing nature of the action.	
2. The future progressive is formed with *will (not)* + *be* + base form + *-ing* OR *be (not) going to* + *be* + base form + *-ing*	Tomorrow afternoon, **I will be studying in the library.** I **won't be talking** on my cell phone at that time. **I'm going to be using** the computer all day. **I'm not going to be using** my laptop computer in class.
3. As with all progressive tenses, the future progressive is not usually used with non-action (stative) verbs.	Bill Gates **will be** in New York at 6:00 P.M. tomorrow. INCORRECT: Bill Gates will be being in New York at 6:00 P.M. tomorrow.

(continued on next page)

4. If there is a **time clause** in the sentence, use the simple present or the present progressive, not the future.	He**'ll be flying** to Spain while the other executives **conclude** the conference. While the other executives **are concluding** the conference, he**'ll be flying** to Spain.

GRAMMAR TIP: When a sentence begins with a dependent clause (the clause beginning with a time word), use a comma to separate it from the main clause. When a sentence begins with the main clause, do not use a comma.

2 *Complete the paragraph. Use the future progressive where it is possible. Remember to use the simple present for the time clauses and for non-action (stative) verbs.*

Matt Olsen is a very busy man. Every day he has a full schedule. Tomorrow, for example, before he even eats breakfast, he ___'ll be communicating___ with
                                          1. (communicate)
associates in France via email. At 9:00 A.M. he _____ with
                                                    2. (meet)
Microsoft development engineers. At 9:45 he _____ out a
                                              3. (try)
new version of Windows Vista. From 10:30 to 11:00 he _____
                                                        4. (check)
his email. After he _____ to his wife on the phone, he
                      5. (talk)
_____ lunch with his plant manager. After lunch, he and
   6. (eat)
his staff _____ the visual-recognition capabilities of the
            7. (test)
new smart camera. Don't try calling him after 3:00 P.M., however, because he

_____ some time exercising in his personal gym. At 4:45 he
   8. (spend)
_____ back in his office. Before he _____
   9. (be)   **10. (eat)**
dinner, he _____ to his Japanese business associates for about
             11. (talk)
thirty minutes. For dinner, he _____ a fresh salad, salmon
                                 12. (have)
steaks, and couscous. Remember not to call him after 10:00 P.M. because he

_____. He certainly _____ for your call.
   13. (sleep)   **14. (not wait)**

3 Sam Woodson, a high school history teacher, has been reading Henry David Thoreau's writing. He has decided to take a year off from his job to recreate some of Thoreau's trips and projects. Look at his tentative calendar for next year.

TENTATIVE PLANS FOR NEXT YEAR			
JANUARY	**FEBRUARY**	**MARCH**	**APRIL**
Go on winter camping trip in western Massachusetts	Visit Walt Whitman's home in New York	Build full-size model of cabin at Walden Pond	Walk the beaches of Cape Cod and write about experiences
MAY	**JUNE**	**JULY**	**AUGUST**
(Continue to) build full-size model of cabin at Walden Pond	Live in model of Walden pond cabin	Travel by boat on the Concord River	Study transcendentalist philosophy
SEPTEMBER	**OCTOBER**	**NOVEMBER**	**DECEMBER**
Take railroad from Concord, Massachusetts, to Bangor, Maine	Live in the backwoods of Maine	Travel by boat on the Merrimack River	Write about experiences following the footsteps of H. D. Thoreau

Sam had to make some changes in his schedule. The calendar shows his revised plans.

REVISED PLANS FOR NEXT YEAR			
JANUARY	**FEBRUARY**	**MARCH**	**APRIL**
Visit Walt Whitman's home in New York	Go on winter camping trip in western Massachusetts	Build full-size model of cabin at Walden Pond	(Continue to) build full-size model of cabin at Walden Pond
MAY	**JUNE**	**JULY**	**AUGUST**
Live in model of Walden pond cabin	Walk the beaches of Cape Cod and write about experiences	Travel by boat on the Concord River	Take railroad from Concord, Massachusetts, to Bangor, Maine
SEPTEMBER	**OCTOBER**	**NOVEMBER**	**DECEMBER**
Live in the backwoods of Maine	Travel by boat on the Merrimack River	Study transcendentalist philosophy	Write about experiences following the footsteps of H. D. Thoreau

Complete the sentences using the information in both calendars. Be careful—the information given below reflects his tentative plans. Many of these plans have changed. Check the revised calendar and complete the sentences. Use the future progressive and remember to use the simple present in the time clauses.

1. In January, Sam ___won't be going on a winter camping trip in western___
   (go / winter camping trip)

   ___Massachusetts. He will be visiting Walt Whitman's home in New York.___

2. In February, Sam _____
   (visit / Walt Whitman's home in New York)

   _____

3. In March, Sam _____
   (build / model of cabin)

   _____

4. In April, Sam _____
   (walk / beaches of Cape Cod)

   _____

5. In May, Sam _____
   (build / model of cabin)

   _____

6. In June, Sam _____
   (live / model of Walden Pond cabin)

   _____

7. In July, Sam _____
   (travel / boat on Concord River)

   _____

8. In August, Sam _____
   (study / transcendentalist philosophy)

   _____

9. In September, Sam _____
   (take / railroad from Concord, Massachusetts)

   _____

10. In October, Sam _____
    (live / backwoods of Maine)

    _____

11. In November, Sam _____
    (travel / boat on Merrimack River)

    _____

12. In December, Sam _____
    (write / experiences)

    _____

In this unit, you read two very different perspectives on living with technology.

You are going to *write a cause and effect essay focusing on the effects that a technology used today has had on society.**

PREPARE TO WRITE: Using a Flowchart

A **flowchart** is a prewriting organizer that shows how a series of actions, events, or parts of a system are related to each other. Look at the flowchart showing the effects of the Internet. Which effects are positive? Which are negative? Note how some of the effects cause another effect and in some cases a further effect, much like a chain.

1 *In your opinion, are these effects positive, negative, or both? Mark them as (+), (−), or (+ −). Then discuss with a partner. Did you agree with your partner?*

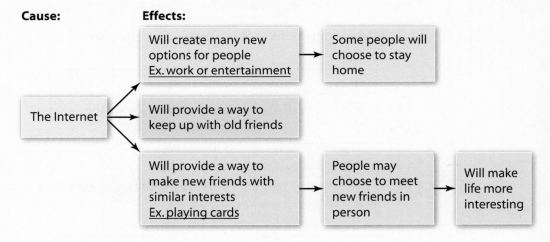

Cause:

Effects:

| The Internet | Will create many new options for people Ex. work or entertainment | → | Some people will choose to stay home |
| Will provide a way to keep up with old friends |
| Will provide a way to make new friends with similar interests Ex. playing cards | → | People may choose to meet new friends in person | → | Will make life more interesting |

2 *Create a flowchart of the effects of a technology you would like to discuss in your essay. Mark the effects as positive or negative, or both.*

WRITE: A Cause and Effect Essay

A **cause and effect essay** discusses the causes (reasons) for something, the effects (results), or both causes and effects. Your essay will focus primarily on the effects a particular technology has had on society, not the causes leading up to its creation.

---

*For Alternative Writing Topics, see page 258. These topics can be used in place of the writing topic for this unit or as homework. The alternative topics relate to the theme of the unit, but may not target the same grammar or rhetorical structures taught in the unit.

1 *Read the excerpt from Reading One. Then answer the questions with a partner.*

> One of the many fears expressed about the information highway {Internet} is that it will reduce the time people spend socializing. Some worry that homes will become such cozy entertainment providers that we'll never leave them, and that, safe in our private sanctuaries, we'll become isolated. I don't think that's going to happen. As behaviorists keep reminding us, we're social animals. We will have the option of staying home more because the highway will create so many new options for home-based entertainment, for communication—both personal and professional—and for employment. Although the mix of activities will change, I think people will decide to spend almost as much time out of their homes.
>
> The highway will not only make it easier to keep up with distant friends, it will also enable us to find new companions. Friendships formed across the network will lead naturally to getting together in person. This alone will make life more interesting. Suppose you want to reach someone to play bridge with. The information highway will let you find card players with the right skill level and availability in your neighborhood, or in other cities or nations.

1. What negative effects of the Internet are mentioned? How are they related?

   _____

   _____

2. What positive effects are mentioned? How are they related?

   _____

   _____

3. Is Gates more interested in discussing causes or effects? Is he more interested in the positive or negative aspects?

   _____

   _____

There are many ways to organize causes and effects and show how they are related. A cause may have only one effect, multiple effects, or cause a chain of effects.

A **simple** cause and effect:

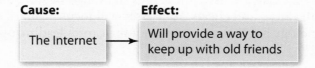

Cause:

The Internet → **Effect:** Will provide a way to keep up with old friends

One cause with **multiple effects**:

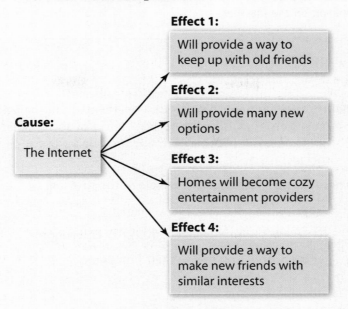

A cause leads to an effect, which in turn can become a cause for a new effect. This is called a **causal chain**.

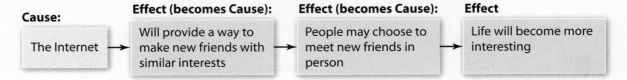

If your essay has a causal chain, describe all steps of the chain so the reader can fully understand how the causes and effects relate. In other words, you cannot jump directly from the initial cause to the final effect.

Example

a. ~~Because of the Internet, life has become more interesting.~~

b. The Internet provides a way to make new friends with similar interests. People may eventually choose to meet these new friends in person. This will make people's lives more interesting.

2 *Answer the questions with a partner.*

1. Look at the flowchart from Prepare to Write. What are some examples of multiple effects of the Internet?

2. What is an example of a causal chain?

3. Look at your flowchart from Prepare to Write. Look for examples of multiple effects and causal chains. Look at your partner's flowchart. Can you find examples of multiple effects and causal chains?

3 *Use an outline to organize your cause and effect essay. Look at the outline for Bill Gates's opinion on the Internet.*

I. **Introduction**

    A. Background: Internet is a common household tool.

    B. Thesis Statement: There is disagreement about the Internet's effects on society, including the negative effect of social isolation. However, in fact, the Internet may actually provide a way for people to increase social contact.

II. **There are possible negative effects of the Internet**

    A. People will spend less time socializing

        1. people's homes will become "cozy entertainment providers"

            a. people won't leave their homes

                1. people will become isolated

III. **Social isolation will not happen**

    A. Behaviorists insist we are social animals

        1. people have the need to interact with people face to face

    B. The Internet will actually create many new personal and professional options

        1. we will have the *option* to stay home; this should not be confused with social isolation

IV. **Other positive social effects of the Internet**

    A. Communication with old friends and maintaining friendships will be easier

    B. Internet will help us find new friends

        1. we can meet new friends in person if we choose

            a. this option will make life more interesting

V. **Conclusion**

    A. People will experience both positive and negative effects but the overall result will be a more interesting future with more options.

4 *Complete the cause and effect outline using the information below.*

| used cheap second hand materials | used the money to buy oil for his lamps | was able to read at night | Thoreau didn't have a lot of money for the house |
| had lots of vegetables to eat | leave his family's home in Concord, Massachusetts | fished and hunted for food | |

I. Henry David Thoreau wanted to live a simple life, free from dependence on the modern technology of his time, relying on nature and himself.

    A. Henry David Thoreau wanted solitude

        1. decided to _____

        2. decided to build a home in the woods

    B. _____

        1. built home with his own labor

        2. _____

    C. Thoreau needed to live cheaply

        1. _____

        2. planted vegetables to eat and took good care of them

            a. the vegetables thrived

                1. _____

                2. he made money by selling excess vegetables

                    a. _____

                        1. _____

5 *Make an outline about the effects a technology has had on society. Think about how you will organize and order the causes and effects from your flowchart. Make sure to include background information, a thesis, and a conclusion. Your conclusion could be a prediction, a solution, or a summary of key points. Share your outline with a partner and suggest changes if necessary.*

6 *Now write the first draft of your cause and effect essay. Use the information in Prepare to Write, your flowchart, and your outline to plan your essay. Be sure to use grammar and vocabulary from the unit.*

◀ **REVISE: Signal Words: Subordinators, Prepositional Phrases, and Transitions**

Certain words act as signals in sentences to show cause and effect relationships. Sentences in cause and effect essays have two clauses. The **cause clause** explains why something happened. The **effect clause** explains the result of what happened.

Cause: Because more and more people communicate via email and text messaging,

Effect: people have fewer opportunities to have personal interactions.

SUBORDINATORS, PREPOSITIONAL PHRASES, AND TRANSITIONS

Subordinators, prepositional phrases, and transitions show the relationship between the two clauses.

Introducing the Cause	Introducing the Effect
Subordinators	**Transitions**
	as a result
since	consequently
because	so
as	for this reason
	therefore
	thus
	as a consequence
Prepositional Phrases	
due to (the fact that)	
due to + (noun)	
as a consequence of + (noun)	
as a result of + (noun)	
because of (the fact that)	
because of + (noun)	

Stating Causes with Subordinators and Prepositional Phrases

- The **cause clause** is introduced by *because, since, as.* When the cause is at the beginning of the sentence, use a comma (,).

  Because more and more people communicate via email and text messaging, people have fewer opportunities to have face-to-face and voice-to-voice interactions.

- When the cause is at the end of the sentence, do not use a comma.

  People have fewer opportunities to have face-to-face and voice-to-voice interactions **because more and more people communicate via email and text messaging.**

Stating Effects with Transitions

- The **effect** is introduced by words such as *consequently, as a result, for this reason, therefore,* and *thus*. Cause and effect can be combined into one sentence by using a semicolon (;) and a comma (,).

  More and more people communicate via email and text messaging; **consequently, people have fewer opportunities to have face-to-face and voice-to-voice interactions.**

- They can also be two separate sentences.

  More and more people communicate via email and text messaging. **As a result, people have fewer opportunities to have personal interactions.**

- Be careful. A sentence with *so* only uses a comma.

  More and more people communicate via email and text messaging, **so people have fewer opportunities to have personal interactions.**

1 *Complete the paragraph based on the outline in Exercise 4, page 253 with appropriate subordinators and transitions.*

Henry David Thoreau wanted a life of solitude free from a dependence on technology. _____, he decided to leave the comfort of his family's home. He decided to build a cabin in the woods near Walden Pond. Thoreau didn't have a lot of money; _____, he built the cabin by himself with little help from other people. In addition, he used cheap and second hand materials _____ of his lack of money. Even when the home was completed, Thoreau needed to continue to live frugally. _____, he fished and hunted for some of his food. He also planted vegetables. His vegetable garden flourished _____ he took good care of it, constantly weeding and watering. _____ the many vegetables he was able to grow, he not only had enough for himself, but also was able to sell those that he didn't need for himself. _____, he actually made money on his garden. He was even able to buy lamp oil and other necessities _____ his harvest had been so big. _____, he was able to read at night, which made him very happy.

2 *Write **C** (cause) or **E** (effect) for each set of sentences. Then combine the sentences two ways.*

1. __C__ Technology has allowed more people to telecommute," or work from home.

   __E__ Telecommuters spend less money on gas and help to control gas emissions.

   (as a result) __Technology has allowed more people to__ "telecommute," or work from home; as a result, telecommuters spend less money on gas and help to control gas emissions.

   (Because) __Because home computers, Internet, and email have__ allowed more people to "telecommute," or work from home, telecommuters spend less money on gas and help to control gas emissions.

2. _____ It is easy to stay in contact with people even when they are not at home.

_____ Many people have cell phones.

(Since) _____

_____

(therefore) _____

_____

3. _____ Many families are in closer contact than in the past.

_____ E-mail allows us to have daily contact with people around the world.

(consequently) _____

_____

(Due to) _____

_____

4. _____ There is a higher frequency of early detection of many types of cancer.

_____ Technology has given us many new advances in medicine.

(as a result) _____

_____

(thus) _____

_____

5. _____ Smart home technology turns off electricity when it is not being used.

_____ Homeowners save money and help to cut down on the use of fossil fuels.

(because) _____

_____

(so) _____

_____

6. _____ The use of libraries for traditional research has declined.

_____ Many students use the Internet for research.

(for this reason) _____

_____

(Because of the fact that) _____

_____

7. _____ Playing video games has become a very popular hobby with young people.

_____ Young people are becoming more socially isolated and less physically active.

(since) _____

_____

(as a consequence) _____

_____

3 *Look at your first draft. Add cause and effect signal words as needed.*

◗ **EDIT: Writing the Final Draft**

Write your final draft. Carefully edit it for grammatical problems and mechanical errors such as spelling, capitalization, and punctuation. Make sure you use some of the vocabulary and grammar from the unit. Use the checklist to help you write your final draft. Then neatly write or type your essay.

✓ FINAL DRAFT CHECKLIST

- ○ Does the essay have a clear topic and controlling idea?
- ○ Does the essay follow your outline?
- ○ Does the essay have effective support and details or examples?
- ○ Does the essay have appropriate cause and effect sentences?
- ○ Does the essay have an effective or thought provoking conclusion?
- ○ Does the essay include any future progressive statements?
- ○ Has vocabulary from the unit been used?

ALTERNATIVE WRITING TOPICS

Choose one of the topics. Make an outline. Then, write an essay using the vocabulary expressions and grammar from the unit.

1. Thoreau wrote, "Our life is frittered away by detail. An honest man has hardly need to count more than his ten fingers, or in extreme cases he may add his ten toes, and lump the rest. Simplicity, simplicity, simplicity!" Thoreau felt that we need only a simple life without modern comforts and technology to appreciate the world around us. Do you agree or disagree?

2. Imagine you have to eliminate five technological devices from your life. What would they be? What, if anything, would you replace them with? How would your life be different as a result?

RESEARCH TOPICS, see page 266.

RESEARCH TOPICS

UNIT 1: Untruth and Consequences

Step 1: Report on news functions. Select a newspaper or weekly news magazine.

Step 2: Read your selection, examining it for the news functions mentioned in Background and Vocabulary on pages 2–3. Complete the chart with examples of each function from your selection.

FUNCTION	EXAMPLES
Gives instant coverage of important events	
Provides facts	
Makes money for the newspaper or magazine	
Sensationalizes events	

Step 3: Present your findings to the class.

UNIT 2: Dreams Never Die

Step 1: Report on a person overcoming an obstacle. Many famous people have overcome great obstacles, including emotional, physical, and political obstacles. Research a person you admire or choose a person from the list on the next page.

Step 2: Write a short biography, including answers to these questions.
- What is (was) the person famous for?
- What did this person achieve?
- What obstacles did this person have to overcome? How did he or she overcome them?
- What personal characteristics helped this person overcome his or her obstacles?
- What has researching this person taught you about life and overcoming obstacles?

Artists / Performers

Christopher Reeve
Mary Cassat
Charlie Chaplin
Marc Chagall
Vincent van Gogh
Michelangelo
Stevie Wonder

Sport Figures

Lance Armstrong
Jackie Robinson
Magic Johnson
James Blake

Writers / Scientists

Steven Hawking
Sigmund Freud
Charles Darwin
Thomas Edison
Hans Christian Andersen

Politicians / Leaders

The Dalai Lama
Mahatma Ghandi
Golda Meir
Nelson Rockefeller

Step 3: Present your biography to the class.

UNIT 3: Dying for Their Beliefs

Step 1: Report on a medical treatment. Take a survey of your classmates. Complete the chart. What do you and your classmates do to help cure the ailments? List the treatments under *conventional* or *nonconventional*.

AILMENT	CONVENTIONAL	NONCONVENTIONAL
Cold		
Cough		
Headache		
Backache		
Stomachache (nausea)		

Step 2: Share your findings with the class. Then discuss these questions.

- Which treatments are most commonly used by your classmates?
- Which treatments do you personally use most often?
- Are there any treatments your classmates use that you would like to try?
- Do you and your classmates have the same ideas about conventional and nonconventional treatment? If not, discuss the differences.

Step 3: Work in groups. Which treatment would you like to know more about? Brainstorm places to get information. Research the treatment. Share your research with your group. Then write a report including answers to these questions.

- What is the name of the treatment?
- What does it cure?
- Where does it originate from (for example, a plant, man-made products)?
- Where can you get it (for example, a drugstore, a health food store)?
- Is it commonly used in your country or where you live now? Do you need a doctor's approval to get it?
- How do you take it (for example, a pill, a drink, a compress, a massage)?
- How does it make you feel (for example, tired, dizzy, happy)?

Step 4: Present your report to the class.

UNIT 4: Animal Intelligence: Instinct or Intellect?

Step 1: Report on an "intelligent" animal. Throughout history, many people have attributed intelligence to specific animals. Research an animal from the list.

Step 2: Write a summary of the information that you find, including answers to some of the *Wh-* questions—*who?, what?, when?, where?, why?,* and *how?* Conclude your summary by explaining whether or not you think the animal is really exhibiting intelligence and why.

Koko the gorilla	Twiggy the squirrel
Bimbo the killer whale	Jonathan and Chantek the orangutans
Betty the crow	Lulu the pig
Ruby the elephant	Washoe the chimpanzee
Akeakemai the dolphin	Siri the elephant
Michael the gorilla	Orky and Corky the killer whales
Alex the parrot	

Step 3: Present your report to the class.

UNIT 5: Longevity: Too Much of a Good Thing?

Step 1: There are a few areas of the world where people have longer life spans than average. Select one of these areas to research.

Step 2: Write key words or search words that would best describe your search.

_____

_____

_____

_____

Step 3: Write two questions that you would use to guide your research or that you would like answered.

Where _____ ?

Why _____ ?

Step 4: Go to the library or use the Internet and conduct your research. Use the information from Steps 2 and 3. Make sure you note the sources, including websites where you found your information.

Step 5: Present your research to the class.

UNIT 6: Give and Learn

Step 1: Report on a community center or project. As a class, brainstorm a list of community centers or community work being done in your area, or list types of community centers you have heard about. Discuss the types of services these centers offer: serving food, offering shelter, meeting medical or educational needs, helping repair homes, cleaning up the neighborhood, or others.

Step 2: Work in a small group. Research one of the community centers or projects. Individually, or in groups, go to a center or project headquarters and gather information to complete the chart. If there is not a center or project near you, go to the library or use the Internet to find information about activities in another area.

Step 3: Combine your information and write a report Use the chart to organize your ideas.

Name of center or project	
History: When was it started? Who started it? Why?	
Type of people helped	
Type of people who work there: Are there volunteers? How many? Who are they?	
Funding: How are activities paid for? Where does the funding come from?	

Step 4: Present your report to the class.

Step 1: Report on homeschooling. Work in a small group. Go to the library or use the Internet to do your research (key words *homeschooling organizations, homeschool*).

Step 2: Prepare a list of questions you would like to find answers to as you research homeschooling. Divide your questions among your group, and conduct your research.

Step 3: Share your research with your group. Combine your information and write a report using this outline.

Part I: Introduction
- A brief introduction to your topic (homeschooling)
- An explanation of what information you were looking for (your original questions)
- An explanation of where and how you found your information

Part II: Results
- The information you collected and the answers to your questions

Part III: Conclusions
- Final conclusions and opinions you have about homeschooling

---

Step 4: Present your report to the class.

UNIT 8: Eat to Live or Live to Eat?

Step 1: Report on a special cultural food. Think about a particular food or drink that symbolizes your country or culture. What is its origin and history?

Step 2: Research the food or drink and write a report. Use the chart to help you organize your ideas.

Name	
Ingredients	
Preparation	
When it is eaten	
What other dishes or drinks accompany it	
History and origin	
Changes to it that have taken place over time	

Step 3: Present your report to the class.

UNIT 9: The Grass Is Always Greener...

Step 1: Report on a U.S. immigrant. Work in a small group. Look at the list of famous U.S. immigrants on the next page. Brainstorm a list of other famous or not so famous immigrants (relatives, friends, classmates). Write as much information as you know about them—for example, occupation, home country , country of immigration, and reasons for immigrating.

Step 2: Choose an immigrant from your list or from the list below. If you choose someone you know, arrange a personal interview. If you choose someone famous, go to the library or use the Internet.

Step 3: Write a report including answers to these questions.
- Who is the person?
- Where was the person born?
- Where did the person immigrate to?

- How old was the person when he or she immigrated?
- Why did this person immigrate?
- How long has the person been living in the new country?
- What other personal information did you find?

SOME FAMOUS U.S. IMMIGRANTS

Politicians

Madeleine Albright, former U.S. Secretary of State (Czech Republic)
Henry Kissinger, former U.S. Secretary of State (Germany)
Elaine Chao, U.S. Secretary of Labor (Taiwan)

Authors

Jamaica Kincaid (Antigua)
Isabel Allende (Chile)
Frank McCourt (Ireland)
Deepak Chopra (India)

Musicians

Carlos Santana, rock guitarist (Mexico)
Plácido Domingo, opera singer (Spain)
Yo Yo Ma, cellist (France)
Midori, classical violinist (Japan)
Elton John, singer/composer (England)

Actors

Andy Garcia (Cuba)
Audrey Hepburn (Belgium)
Penelope Cruz (Spain)

Athletes

Maria Sharapova, tennis player (Russia)
Sammy Sosa, baseball player (Dominican Republic)
Wayne Gretzky, retired hockey player (Canada)
Nadia Comaneci, gymnast (Romania)
Hideki Matsui, baseball player (Japan)

Other People

George Soros, philanthropist (Hungary)
Albert Einstein, physicist (Germany)
Oscar de la Renta, fashion designer (Dominican Republic)
Ang Lee, movie director (Taiwan)
I. M. Pei, architect (Taiwan)

Step 4: Present your report to the class.

Step 1: Report on the role technology has in your life. Think about what types of technology you have now that did not exist when you were younger. How has technology changed the quality of your life? Make a chart like the one below and complete it with your information. Share your chart with a partner.

THINGS I USED IN THE PAST	REPLACEMENTS	EFFECTS ON MY LIFE
Books, library	Internet	I'm able to get information faster and more easily. It also saves a lot of time. On the other hand, I stay at home more and never go to the library or bookstore.

Step 2: Interview an older person about the changes he or she has seen in technology during his or her lifetime. Use your chart as a guide. Write a report including answers to these questions. Add three or more of your own questions.

- What is the most significant technological advance in your lifetime? Why do you think so?
- What technological advance has affected you most personally? How has it changed your life?
- _____
- _____
- _____

Step 3: Present your report to the class.

GRAMMAR BOOK REFERENCES

NorthStar: Reading and Writing Level 4, Third Edition	*Focus on Grammar Level 4,* Third Edition	*Azar's Understanding and Using English Grammar,* Third Edition
Unit 1 Passive Voice	**Unit 18** The Passive: Overview	**Chapter 11** The Passive: 11-1, 11-2
Unit 2 Gerunds and Infinitives	**Unit 9** Gerunds and Infinitives: Review and Expansion	**Chapter 14** Gerunds and Infinitives, Part 1 **Chapter 15** Gerunds and Infinitives, Part 2
Unit 3 Past Unreal Conditionals	**Unit 24** Past Unreal Conditionals	**Chapter 20** Conditional Sentences and Wishes: 20-1, 20-4
Unit 4 Identifying Adjective Clauses	**Unit 13** Adjective Clauses with Subject Relative Pronouns **Unit 14** Adjective Clauses with Object Relative Pronouns or *When* and *Where*	**Chapter 13** Adjective Clauses
Unit 5 Contrasting the Simple Past, Present Perfect, and Present Perfect Continuous	**Unit 3** Simple Past, Present Perfect, and Present Perfect Progressive	**Chapter 1** Overview of Verb Tenses: 1-1, 1-3, 1-4, 1-5 **Chapter 2** Present and Past, Simple and Progressive: 2-9 **Chapter 3** Perfect and Perfect Progressive Tenses: 3-1, 3-2

(continued on next page)

NorthStar: Reading and Writing Level 4, Third Edition	Focus on Grammar Level 4, Third Edition	Azar's Understanding and Using English Grammar, Third Edition
Unit 6 Concessions	*Not applicable* See *Focus on Grammar 5, Third Edition, Unit 18: Adverb Clauses*	**Chapter 19** Connectives that Express Cause and Effect, Contrast, and Condition: 19-6
Unit 7 Direct and Indirect Speech	**Unit 25** Direct and Indirect Speech	**Chapter 12** Noun Clauses: 12-6, 12-7
Unit 8 Phrasal Verbs	**Unit 11** Phrasal Verbs: Review **Unit 12** Phrasal Verbs: Separable and Inseparable	**Appendix** Unit E: Preposition Combinations See also Appendix 1: Phrasal Verbs in Azar's *Fundamentals of English Grammar, Third Edition*
Unit 9 Past Perfect	**Unit 4** Past Perfect and Past Perfect Progressive	**Chapter 3** Perfect and Perfect Progressive Tenses: 3-3
Unit 10 Future Progressive	**Unit 5** Future and Future Progressive	**Chapter 4** Future Time: 4-5

CREDITS

Page 231 "Plugged in at Home" from "Inside The House" (Newsweek 11/27/95) from *The Road Ahead* by Bill Gates. Copyright © 1995, 1996 by William H. Gates III. Used with permission of Viking Penguin, a division of Penguin Group (USA) Inc; **Page 238** "Thoreau's Home" by Henry D. Thoreau, from Walden. Text is reprinted from a first edition of *Walden, or Life in the Woods 1854,* published by Ticknor and Fields, Boston.

Photo Credits: Page 1 Tim Graham/Getty Images; **Page 8** S. Martin-Atlanta Journal/Corbis Sygma; **Page 25** Bettmann/Corbis; **Page 26 (a)** Copyright Anne Frank-Fonds, Basle/Switzerland, **(b)** Laurent Rebours/AP Images, **(c)** Bettmann/Corbis, **(d)** Underwood & Underwood/Corbis; **Page 28** Katy Winn/Corbis; **Page 34** Fitzroy Barrett/Retna Ltd.; **Page 47 (left)** Don Farrall/Getty Images, **(right)** Michael Newman/PhotoEdit; **Page 55** Compliments of Wisconsin Center for Film and Theater Research; **Page 67** Larry Lettera/Wagner International Photos, Inc.; **Page 72** Mary Evans Picture Library/The Image Works; **Page 77** Kelley McCall/AP Images; **Page 91** Mark Parisi/Atlantic Feature Syndicate; **Page 95** Laura Ronchi/Getty Images; **Page 101** The New Yorker Collection 1996 Peter Steiner from cartoonbank.com. All rights reserved; **Page 115 (left)** Matthew Cavanaugh/epa/Corbis, **(middle left)** Steve Granitz/Getty Images, **(middle right)** Lynn Goldsmith/Corbis, **(right)** Chris Bacon/AP Images; **Page 121** from *It's Our World Too!* by Phillip Hoose. Copryright © 1993 by Phillip Hoose. Photo reprinted with permission from Little, Brown and Company; **Page 145** Calvin and Hobbes © 1988 Watterson. Dist. by Universal Press Syndicate. Reprinted with permission. All rights reserved; **Page 148** Russell Illig/Getty Images; **Page 150** Polka Dot Images/Jupiterimages; **Page 175 (top)** Annette Coolidge/PhotoEdit, **(bottom)** Ariel Skelley/Corbis; **Page 179** Special Collections, Yale Divinity School Library; **Page 185** Slowfood.com; **Page 201 (left)** Sigrid Estrada/Estrada Studio, **(middle)** Chad Buchanan/Getty Images, **(right)** Mitchell Gerber/Corbis; **Page 227** © Bill Layne; **Page 231** Reuters/Corbis; **Page 238** Lee Snider/Photo Images/Corbis.

Illustration Credits: Aphik Diseño, **Page 184**; Paul Hampson, **Pages 202, 219**; Derek Mueller, **Pages 94, 205**; Dusan Petricic, **Pages 65, 75, 76**; Gary Torrisi, **Page 112.**

Notes

Notes

Notes

Notes